Dedicated to

This book is dedicated to the former occupants who continue to inhabit the Whaley House, especially... Thomas, Anna, Violet, Yankee Jim and Dolly!

Death does not diminish their desire or need to remain or return here, and the preservation of their physical environment is essentially a tribute to the contribution they made to their community while living. The Whaley family was an active, integral part of the history of Old Town, San Diego in life and in the afterlife they are still participating members of the local community of spirits... as our friend and gifted psychic Peter James reminded us, "As in life, so in death!"

To June Reading, who passed away in January 1998 at age 79. She was the director of the Historical Shrine Foundation and an avid local historian. Reading dedicated her life to preserving the history of the Whaley House, and she embodies the spirit of this house. Even in death, June continues to guard this precious historic resource with the same loving affection and attentiveness that she provided in life. This book is a lasting tribute to her dedication to preservation... God bless you, June!

Finally, to SOHO the current manager and caretaker of this historic landmark for the County of San Diego... The torch was passed to SOHO in November of 2000, and they have managed not only to continue the work begun by June Reading, but have aspired to further preserve, protect and enhance the quality and integrity of the Whaley House. They have added their imprint to its storied legacy and no doubt, brought a smile to Thomas and Anna who watch over their house from beyond the thin veil that separates our two worlds.

The Haunted Whaley House II

A History and Paranormal Guide to America's Most Haunted House
Old Town San Diego, California

Published by:

G-HOST Publishing

8701 Lava Place, West Hills, California 91304-2126
Telephone/Fax: 818-340-6676, E-mail: robanne@ix.netcom.com

All books are available through **G-Host Publishing**,
www.prairieghosts.com; www.Amazon.com or www.sdparanormal.com

The Haunted Queen Mary ($13.95); **Haunted Catalina** ($12.95); **Haunted Alcatraz** ($13.95); **Spirits of the Leonis Adobe** ($13.95); **Southern Fried Spirits** ($16.95); **Spirits of the Alamo** ($16.95); **Dinner and Spirits** ($24.95); **A Texas Guide to Haunted Restaurants, Taverns & Inns** ($18.95); **California Hauntspitality: A Ghostly Guide to Haunted Inns, Restaurants and Taverns** ($18.95); and **Louisiana Hauntspitality: A Ghostly Guide to Haunted Inns, Restaurants and Taverns** ($15.95)

If you purchased this book without a cover, you should be aware that the book is probably stolen property. It was reported as "unsold and destroyed" to the publisher, and neither the authors nor the publisher has received any payment for this "stripped book."

The stories appearing in this book are based on factual accounts of people who have visited or worked in the Whaley House. The historical information was initially provided by June Reading and updated by Save Our Heritage Organization (SOHO).

The authors would love to hear from readers about their paranormal experiences at the Whaley House. The more interesting of these may be included in future printings. Please write of e-mail your stories.

The authors take no responsibility for the veracity of each story except that we believe the storytellers. We have attempted to detail the encounter described in this book as accurately as possible. Although the publishers have made every effort to ensure that the information was correct at the time the book went to press, they do not assume and hereby disclaim any liability to any party for any loss, damage, or injury caused by information contained in this book. Furthermore, the publishers disclaim any liability resulting from the use of this book.

All rights are reserved. No part of this book may be reproduced or transmitted in any form by any means, electronic or mechanical, including photocopying, recording, or by any informational storage or retrieval system in English or in any other language (except by a reviewer who may quote brief passages in a review to be printed in a magazine or newspaper) without permission in writing from the publisher.

Copyright © 2004 **G-HOST Publishing**, ITF: By Robert Wlodarski and Anne Wlodarski
G-HOST Publishing, Second Edition
Library of Congress Catalog Card Number: 2003019538
ISBN: 0-9649088-7-5 Softcover

All photographs are provided courtesy of Sandé Lollis of Save Our Heritage Organization (SOHO), the San Diego Historical Society Photograph Collection, the authors, and other individuals noted below the photograph. The drawing of Violet Whaley was provided by SOHO docent, Robin M. Sweeton. The drawings of two spirits sighted in the house on June 21, 2003 were provided by gifted psychic Colin Birch, who was visiting from England at the time of his encounters. The spirit photographs were provided courtesy of SOHO from their extensive ghost photo files based on submission from visitors, as well as individual submissions by visitors directly to the authors.

The set-up format for this edition was provided by Parva M. Zadeh of M&M Printing
Printed in the United States by M & M Quality Printing, Woodland Hills, California

"I have referred to the Whaley House of San Diego as "America's Most Haunted House" in every one of my ghost books from Where the Ghosts Are to Great American Ghost Stories because it has three elements that raise it far above other sites of possible ghostly presences: historical verification, a great dramatic story, and ample witnesses for the still-ongoing phenomena at the house.

Thus, visiting the Whaley House is far more than sightseeing—it is an encounter with adventure depending only on the visitor's innate psychic abilities and, perhaps, on the time of the visit when the spirit of the unhappy Thomas Whaley or one of the other two presences I found in my investigations are particularly restless and take advantage of the visit to manifest. Then, too, the Readings treated the house like a favorite child truly caring for it in every sense. One might even think the ghosts would not want to leave so warm and friendly an environment!

Perhaps, I shall revisit the Whaley House again with one of my talented psychics though the work of the late Sybil Leek, so many years ago remains superbly unique and evidential to a high degree. Were it not for an excited Regis Philbin (then doing a television show in San Diego) who shone his flashlight at what appeared to us as the beginning of a materialization, we might even have met Mr. Whaley himself, not flesh, but ectoplasm!

Professor Hans Holzer, Ph.D. (February 27, 1997)

Disclaimer

The stories appearing in this book are based on factual accounts of people who have worked or visited the Whaley House since it became a heritage structure open to the public. Those individuals, who have chosen to remain anonymous, have been respectfully accommodated. When and where possible we have given credit where credit is due.

The authors take no responsibility for the veracity of each story except for the fact that we believe the storytellers. Although over 32 years of researching and interviewing have provided us some ability to judge when someone is telling the truth or not, only they really know the real truth, and we can only trust our instincts and hope for the best when relaying the information to you in an honest fashion.

We have researched each paranormal encounter described in this book as much as humanly possible, and have tried to portray the hauntings as accurately as possible. Although we have made every effort to ensure that the information was correct at the time the book went to press, we do not assume and hereby disclaim any liability to any party for any loss, damage, or injury caused by information contained in this book. Furthermore, the publishers disclaim any liability resulting from the use of this book.

We ask that you please check with the owners, managers or caretakers of any place you plan to investigate, before beginning your otherworldly journey. Always obtain permission to enter, as well as obtain a release to photograph, tape, or otherwise intrude on the normal activities of an establishment. Never enter a place illegally, and never put you or others in harms way while conducting your research. Always use common sense in approaching the paranormal and use precaution while inside any building, old or new. Attempting to secure floor plans before entering doesn't hurt.

We apologize if there is inaccurate information presented herein, and will attempt to rectify future additions if we are contacted by mail, fax, or e-mail, and provided with the correct information If you do find mistakes in this publication, please consider that they are there for a reason. In an effort to publish something for everyone, we realize that some people are always looking for mistakes, and we would like to please those individuals.

The authors would love to hear from our readers about their paranormal experiences at the Whaley House and/or welcome any photographic documentation you may have regarding the spirits of the house.

Address all inquiries, or story submissions or photographs for future editions to: **G-host Publishing**, 8701 Lava Place, West Hills, California 91304-2126; by telephone or fax to: 818-340-6676; or by E-mail to: robanne@ix.netcom.com.

Hauntingly yours!

Table of Contents

About the Authors	viii
Foreword	x
Acknowledgements	xi
About SOHO	xv
On the Subject of Ghosts	xvi
Lillian Corinne Whaley - The Last Occupant	xxi
To Anna	xxiii
A Historical Perspective	1
A Textbook Case for Hauntings	38
Thomas Whaley House Museum, Old Town, San Diego	42
The Ghost of Yankee Jim Robinson	43
Sybil Leek and Hans Holzer Meet the Whaley House Spirits	46
Another Perspective of the 1965 Séance	55
The Phantoms of the Opera Group	61
Another Perspective of the Phantoms of the Opera Group	63
California's Most Haunted House	67
A Psychic View of the Whaley House	70
June A. Reading: "I'm sure there's a pattern to all of this"	74
After Hour Hauntspitality	80
My Whaley House Experience	90
Not welcome at the Whaley House	93
A Convocation of Souls	96
Haunted or not, this place is definitely alive	100
A Whale[y] of a Tale… or two	104
From the files of San Diego Paranormal	107
I wished I had a camera then!	107
A tune for Anna	108
The truth about cats and dogs	109
Halloween orbs	109
Girl at the top of the stairs	110
Halloween at the Whaley House	110
Sometimes, Lex is more	112
September Spirits: A Fall Investigation at the Whaley House	113
The Solstice Investigation	121
The Whaley House of Spirits	131
A Psychic Greets the Ghosts	135
A Docent's encounters with the unknown	143

Visitors and Employees Speak Their Peace	150
The Authors	151
Mrs. Kirbey of Canada	152
Trick or Treat	153
J.P. got his Money's Worth	154
The Late June Reading's spirited encounter	155
P.H. While visiting the Whaley House	155
William H. Richardson	156
Grace Borquin	156
Guest	157
One Docent's Perspective	157
Visitor from San Diego	158
Julie, Docent	158
Too much of a ghostly thing	159
M.G.	159
Jule Milton Keller	160
School daze, school haze	162
Anita Kirwin	163
E for Extraordinary	165
Oh, the tangled web[site] we weave of paranormal ponderings	165
Millicent Brabant	167
Lawrence Riveroll	168
Four from Texas	169
Charles, Docent	170
Suzanne Pere	170
Mrs. Allen	171
Kay Sterner	172
Canadian Visitor	175
Illinois Meets the Whaley Spirits	176
New Zealander Finds a Ghost	177
Epilogue	179
Haunted Whaley House References	180
Additional Paranormal Reading	182
What to do if you see a Ghost	192
The Ghost Hunters' Kit	193
How to Stalk Ghosts	195
Photograph Release Form	
Documenting Your Whaley House Encounter	
The Haunted Whaley House II Order Form	

About the Authors

Robert James Wlodarski

Born in Los Angeles, California, Wlodarski has a B.A.'s in history and anthropology and an M.A. in anthropology from California State University, Northridge. The President of the **H**istorical, **E**nvironmental, **A**rchaeological, **R**esearch, **T**eam (H.E.A.R.T.) since 1978, Wlodarski has administered over 1100 archaeological and historical projects for federal, state, county, city, and private sector agencies and companies, and has authored and co-authored over 20 articles for journals and magazines throughout California and the Southwest.

Mr. Wlodarski, the President of Mayan Moon Productions, has co-authored seven screenplays: *The Crawling Eye*, *Cities of Stone*, *The Cool Change*, *Illusion*, *No Innocents*, *Ghost Glass*, and *The Palace of Unknown Kings*, and has served as a Technical Archaeological Consultant for *Catalina, A Treasure from The Past* for Ironwood Productions. Additionally, Wlodarski co-founded G-Host Publishing, and has co-authored and published: A Guide to the Haunted Queen Mary: Ghostly Apparitions, Psychic Phenomena, and Paranormal Activity; Haunted Catalina: A History of the Island and Guide to Paranormal Activity; The Haunted Alamo: A History of the Mission and Guide to Paranormal Activity; The Haunted Whaley House: A History and Guide to the Most Haunted House in America; and, Haunted Alcatraz: A History of La Isla de los Alcatraces and Guide to Paranormal Activity; Spirits of the Alamo; The Haunted Queen Mary, Long Beach, California; Southern Fried Spirits: A Guide to Haunted Restaurants, Inns, and Taverns; Dinner and Spirits: A Guide to America's Most Haunted Restaurants, Taverns, and Inns; A Texas Hauntspitality: A Guide to the Most Haunted Restaurants, Taverns and Inns of the Lone Star State; California Hauntspitality: A Ghostly Guide to Haunted Inns, Restaurants, and Taverns; Spirits of the Leonis Adobe: History and Hauntings in Calabasas, California; and, Louisiana Hauntspitality: A Ghostly Guide to Haunted Inns, Restaurants, and Taverns.

Mr. Wlodarski has worked as a consultant with the History Channel/Greystone Productions on their **Haunted History** series; as a Consulting Producer with the Food Network on **Haunted Restaurants;** as a consultant with The Travel Channel/Indigo Productions on their **Most Haunted America** program; as a consultant with Authentic Entertainment/TLC on their **Haunted Hotels** series; and Mike Mathis Productions/The Travel Channel on the **Mysterious Journeys** program.

Anne Powell Wlodarski

Born in San Antonio, Texas, Ms. Wlodarski is a registered art therapist. She received her M.A. in behavioral science from University of Houston, and has published several articles including a chapter in California Art Therapy Trends. She has been an exhibiting artist and is the president and founder of HE**ART**WORLD Arts Center for Children, a non-profit organization for abused and disadvantaged youth. Ms. Wlodarski served as an education outreach coordinator, and gallery assistant for the City of Los Angeles's Artspace Gallery from 1989-1993 and has been featured in the media for her work with children and the arts. She was honored as a "Sunday Woman" by the Daily News, and was a J.C. Penney Golden Rule Award nominee. She is also a member of the Daughters of the Republic of Texas (DRT), and the Southern California Art Therapy Association (SCATA).

Ms. Wlodarski is Vice-President of Mayan Moon Productions, and has co-authored six screenplays: *The Crawling Eye*, *Cities of Stone*, *The Cool Change*, *Illusion*, *No Innocents*, and *Ghost Glass*. Ms. Wlodarski co-founded G-Host Publishing Company and has co-authored and published: A Guide to the Haunted Queen Mary: Ghostly Apparitions, Psychic Phenomena, and Paranormal Activity; Haunted Catalina: A History of the Island and Guide to Paranormal Activity; The Haunted Alamo: A History of the Mission and Guide to Paranormal Activity; The Haunted Whaley House: A History and Guide to the Most Haunted House in America; and, Haunted Alcatraz: A History of La Isla de los Alcatraces and Guide to Paranormal Activity; Spirits of the Alamo; The Haunted Queen Mary, Long Beach, California; Southern Fried Spirits: A Guide to Haunted Restaurants, Inns, and Taverns; Dinner and Spirits: A Guide to America's Most Haunted Restaurants, Taverns, and Inns; A Texas Hauntspitality: A Guide to the Most Haunted Restaurants, Taverns and Inns of the Lone Star State; California Hauntspitality: A Ghostly Guide to Haunted Inns, Restaurants, and Taverns; Spirits of the Leonis Adobe: History and Hauntings in Calabasas, California; and, Louisiana Hauntspitality: A Ghostly Guide to Haunted Inns, Restaurants, and Taverns.

Ms. Wlodarski has worked as a consultant with the History Channel/Greystone Productions on their **Haunted History** series; as a Consulting Producer with the Food Network on **Haunted Restaurants**; as a consultant with The Travel Channel/Indigo Productions on their **Most Haunted America** program; as a consultant with Authentic Entertainment/TLC on their **Haunted Hotels** series; and Mike Mathis Productions/The Travel Channel on the **Mysterious Journeys** program.

Forward

The Whaley House is officially haunted. So says the California State Government. It is one of two so designated by California (The other being the Winchester Mystery House in San Jose). However, this two-story brick house is much more than a simple haunted mansion. It is a true historic site standing in the Old Town of San Diego. This building has seen the history of the Golden West first hand and, if the stories are true, some of these impressions still linger on within those thick walls.

Many believe that the Thomas Whaley house is the most haunted place in the whole of the state but, after my own experiences I am ready to nominate this building as the most haunted house west of the Mississippi River. Numerous ghost hunters, psychics, reporters and historians have visited and investigated the house over the years. Most have collected some stories or had an experience or two to add to their collection of haunted sites and moved on.

This is not the case with Anne and Rob Wlodarski. Their book blends the ghostly tales with a crisp new look at the history of this legendary structure. I believe this work is the quintessential Whaley House Book, and as such is a "must read" for all that have heard of the ghosts that inhabit this place. It is both easy to read and clears away the myth from the real story of the building that was home, theater, and courthouse for so many years.

I know the house is haunted. I have seen, heard and smelled the supernatural events that happen here on a regular basis. This book not only reveals the scary tales but also the history behind them. I recommend this book and leave you with only this admonition: Don't read it at night before going to bed!

Richard Senate
Author of: **Ghosts of the Haunted Coast**, **Haunted Ventura**, **The Haunted Southland**, **Ghost Stalker's Guide to Haunted California**, **The Ghosts of the Olivas Adobe**, **Ghosts of the Ojai** ,**Ghosts of the Camino Real**, *and* **Hollywood's Ghosts**.

Acknowledgements

We began the initial research and writing of this book back in 1996. From the moment we contacted June Reading (now deceased) at the Whaley House, everything proceeded with barely a glitch. From gathering the stories of Whaley House hauntings, to obtaining historical information and photographs, help was always only a phone call away; and for this, we are truly grateful. As anyone who has written anything can attest, it is often a tedious and sometimes difficult process to conduct interviews, gather research data, synthesize the information, and "get it down" on paper—the Whaley House book was the exception.

This book is the result of two important events: 1) the prior book dealt with the house that was under the supervision of the Historic Shrine Foundation. Since then, Save Our Heritage Organization (SOHO) has become the current caretaker, and with the changing of the guard, so-to-speak, came major changes to the house. Since SOHO began its stewardship, the house has undergone a major facelift. The renovations include changes in the historical use of most rooms to reflect the 1860s-1880s and introducing new furnishings consistent with the historical period. Hence, the interior photographs from the original book were no longer applicable; and, 2) many more ghost stories materialized since the 1996 edition. Although the ghost stories have literally tripled over the years, this book still barely touches the tip of the paranormal iceberg regarding its haunted history. Therefore, we have: included a few stories from our first edition; added many new stories; updated the most recent haunted happenings; noted our own investigation results; and revised the history of the house. Finally, we have added new historical photographs and many new ghost photographs that were either donated to SOHO by visitors for display purposes or sent to us for eventual use in a new book by interested parties.

Without the help of numerous individuals, this book could not and would not have been updated. So our deepest and sincerest thanks are extended to the following people:

Foremost, our sincere thanks to Mrs. June Reading, who now resides beyond the veil who remain the "spirit" of the Whaley House. June helped us obtain some of the information contained herein. She firmly believed that a book on hauntings could successfully reach a large number of people both as an exposure to the paranormal and as a historical document. Essentially, this is a compendium of extant literature dealing with the reported hauntings of the Whaley House since it was opened to the public. Mrs. Reading also granted us permission to use previously unpublished "haunted" photos of the Whaley House from the Historical Shrine Foundation archives, as well as family photographs from the Whaley Family archives.

To Bruce and Alana Coons, the Board of Directors, and the friendly and courteous staff of SOHO for their tireless support and invaluable help during the completion of this revised edition. They continue to serve as caretakers for a landmark that has achieved legendary status as America's Most Haunted House. Now, children and adults can learn about the history of the Whaley Family and the house, and glimpse what life might have been like in southern California during the 1860s-1880s...as well as a spirit or two. We suggest that you look at SOHO's Website at: www.whaleyhouse.org for the latest information about the history and happenings at the Whaley House.

To the fine historical presentation by editors Sandy Sneider and Helen Angell, in the Volume XVII, November 1994, issue of the Hidden Valley Journal, regarding the Whaley Family Chronology which was updated in February of 2001. The Journal is published by the Escondido Genealogical Society, Inc.

To Margaret Heron James for her well-written and insightful account of "Tragedy at the Whaley House," describing the tragic circumstances surrounding the death of Violet Eloise Whaley who died in August 1885. James had saved the article since 1953 when her mother-in-law Mable Whaley James inherited the property from her aunt, Corinne Lillian Whaley. The account was published by the Escondido Genealogical Society, Inc.

To Mr. David Marshall, Architect, Milford Wayne Donaldson, FAIA - Phone: 619-239-7888 for allowing us to use his article, The Convocation of Souls at the Historic Whaley House (Save Our Heritage Organization Newsletter, June 2001) in our book. This story was based on a paranormal investigation performed by the authors during May 5-7, 2001, with a group of psychics and investigators from the Orange County Society for Psychic Research (OCSPR).

To Sande' Lollis (SOHO Graphics) the photographer at SOHO who provided us with many of the stunning photographs of the restored house that enhanced the text. She also helped in providing many of the ghost photos from SOHO archives. Her efforts and those of SOHO have gone a long way to making this revised edition, a memorable contribution to the local history of Old Town, San Diego.

To Kathy Flanigan who worked tirelessly to update the history of the Whaley House (sadly she has joined the spirit realm and will be sorely missed), Sande´ Lollis, George Plum, Robin Sweeton, and other members of the highly capable SOHO staff who provided their precious time, expertise, editing skills, insights, comments and suggestions, which greatly enhanced the quality of this edition.

To Robin Sweeton of SOHO for her wonderful drawing of Violet Whaley for this edition of the book, and for taking the time to list her encounters with the unknown.

To Jonathan P. Lamas for allowing us to use his haunting experiences in the Whaley House. Check out his Website: (www.findaghost.com) for other interesting articles and paranormal information.

To fellow paranormal investigator and friend, Chad Patterson for providing us with the story, "September Spirits: A Fall Investigation at the Whaley House." We have had the pleasure of working with Chad in the past at the Aztec Hotel in Monrovia, the Banning Residence Museum in Wilmington, and the George Gershwin/Rosemary Clooney House in Beverly House… with many more investigations to come. Chad is a diligent, gifted paranormal investigator and researcher from Corona, California. We suggest that you browse the California Society for Ghost Research Website at www.csgr.us for some extraordinary research information, or e-mail Chad at Sentrylight@cs.com

To Bonnie Vent, a Spirit Advocate and founder of the San Diego Paranormal Research Project, who sent us several interesting stories about her spirited encounters at the Whaley House. We recommend that you visit Vent's excellent Website at: www.sdparanormal.com. Here you can find updated information on local ghost investigations, buy books and find out more about haunted San Diego. We recommend her informative Website at: www.sdparanormal.com

A special thanks to our dear friend and gifted ghosthunter, Richard L. Senate, for permitting us to print two of his stories pertaining the Whaley House, one from his many interesting books on the paranormal, this one entitled, **The Haunted Southland** (1994second edition), published by Charon Press, Ventura, California; the other from his article in **Psychic World** in the Ventura County & Coast Reporter. Richard also graciously penned a foreword for our revised book, and we couldn't think of anyone better suited to do so, given the amount of investigative work, he's performed at this amazing house of spirits. His wonderful books: **Ghosts of the Haunted Coast** (1986) **Haunted Ventura** (1992), **Ghost Stalker's Guide to Haunted California** (1998), **Ghosts of the Ojai** (1998), **Ghosts of the Camino Real** (2003), **Ghosts of the Olivas Adobe** (n.d.), and latest, **Hollywood Ghosts: The Fabulous Phantoms of Filmdom**; are available through Del Sol Publications, P.O. Box 1112, Ventura, California 93002 (www.delsolpubliscations.com), and we encourage you to tap into his Website at www.ghost-stalker.com

Special thanks to our friend Dolly Boyd for providing us with her extraordinary experience at the Whaley House during her 1965 visit—a night she will never forget!

To Alex Sill, a young, enthusiastic paranormal investigator from West Hills, California, who represents the next generation of those seeking answers to mysteries of the afterlife. His love of the Whaley House is second to none, and he provided his wonderful story just for our book, as well as several photographs that appear herein. Thanks are also due, to his understanding and supportive parents, Lonnie and Nicci Sill, and his gifted sister, Natasha.

To Gary Beck, the former president of the Historical Shrine Foundation who provided stories and research materials for our first book; some of which we kept in this edition. He was instrumental in helping us gain access the Whaley House after hours, when the living could not interfere with our attempts to commune with the dead.

Thanks to Carol Myers, Photo Archivist of the San Diego Historical Society, for her help in sorting though the enormous amount of photographic archives pertaining to the Whaley House and Old Town and promptly processing our request for the duplication of photos to be used in this book.

To the International Paranormal Research Organization who were privileged to conduct over-night investigations and form a communication circle in the Whaley House. These gifted psychics and investigators definitely made contact on both occasions with several of the afterlife occupants. A special thanks to: Ginnie McGovern, Victoria Gross, Deann Burch, Robin Collier, Christi Flowers, Alma Carey, Peggy Stahler, Pat Bryan and Veral Pitsenbarger.

To gifted international psychic and dear friend, Alma Carey, for working with the author during an 18-hour drive/television shoot at the Whaley House for a Halloween television special. Alma's unique talent and gift of insight were on full display during the evening adding significantly to the haunted history of the house. We encourage you to contact Alma Carey at 818-972-2953 for psychic readings or special events, or check out her website at www.almacarey.com.

To renowned writer and psychic investigator Dr. Hans Holzer, for granting us permission to freely use his stunning 1965 Sybil Leek seance material in our book because of his fondness for the Whaley House, hoping that one day, the Whaley's find peace. His investigations into the Whaley House are well documented in his books, **Where the Ghosts Are: The Ultimate Guide to Haunted Houses** (1995), **True Ghost Stories** (1992), **America's Restless Ghosts (1992)**, and **Great American Ghost Stories** (1988). Holzer has authored of over 100 books during his 40 years dealing with the paranormal.

To those individuals who visited the Whaley House and sent us their stories and or photographs of unexplained phenomena, we are truly grateful. It's not usually the "big" stories that touch most people, but the accounts of everyday people whom in their own words, have made contact. It's the folklore-like quality and sincerity of these storytellers that often soften the hearts of skeptics to possibility of life after death. Keep those letters and photographs coming... please!

Finally, to the staff of the Best Western Hacienda Hotel Old Town San Diego who have always provided us with our lodging needs while conducting our Whaley House research. The rooms were always fantastic, and we can't imagine a better place to stay, with such a great view of Old Town, and the fact that you can't get much closer to the "Most Haunted House in America," without actually living in it. In addition, rumors have circulated for years that the hotel also has a phantom or two within its landscaped grounds. This is the only place we recommend staying while visiting Old Town and the Whaley House, where hospitality and hauntspitality go hand-in-hand. They are located at 4041 Harney Street, San Diego, California 92110 or by calling toll free at 1-800-888-1991.

To Parva M. Zadeh of M&M Printing, for her patience, help and expert skills during the set-up phase of this book; without her, this book would have not turned out so wonderfully, & Nikki Polisso for her help in designing the cover.

About S.O.H.O.

Since 1969, Save Our Heritage Organisation (SOHO), a 501 (c)3 non-profit organization, has led the community as a powerful catalyst for preservation by raising awareness and appreciation of the region's architectural and cultural heritage. All donations to SOHO support preservation of the historical links and landmarks that contribute to the community's special identity, depth and character.

SOHO manages the Whaley House Museum for the County of San Diego, and operates offices in the SOHO Museum Shop located on the Whaley House grounds at 2476 San Diego Avenue, San Diego, California 92110. Their Website is: www.whaleyhouse.org

If you would like to join SOHO, here are the basic membership levels.

___ $15 Student Membership- Annual
___ $30 Individual or Family Membership - Annual
___ $50 Professional Membership - Annual
___ $100 Executive Membership - Annual
___ $250 Benefactor Membership - Annual
___ $1000 Lifetime Membership
___ Please extend my membership for another year
___ Corporate Membership

Complete this form and send it with your check to:
Save Our Heritage Organization
2476 San Diego Avenue, San Diego CA 92110
Telephone: 619-297-9327 - Fax: 619-291-3576

Name _____

Address _____

City _____

State _____ Zip _____

Telephone _____ E-mail _____

Also, check if interested - I would like to help with:

__ Office __ Membership __ Tours __ Workshops __ Whaley House __ Other Events

Your Membership includes:
- Free admission to Whaley House Museum
- Subscription to the quarterly *Reflections* Newsletter
- 10% discount on Museum Shop items
- Advance notice and discounts to lectures, special events, and tours
- Invitations to special receptions and events
- Participation in volunteer programs

On the Subject of Ghosts?

We always like to respond to people who ask us what ghosts are, by saying, "Ghosts are us"; that is to say, they do everything we do, except without the shell or body. As our friend/paranormal investigator/author/psychic, Peter James likes to say about the personalities of spirits, "As if life so in death." Just because you die, doesn't mean your energy dies. Energy as we are told, never dies, it is transformed. Essentially, we are all energy separated only by the constructs of time and space. Ghosts or spirits may co-exist with us, perhaps in parallel universes which intersect the physical plane or dimension when the "cosmic clickers" somehow connect, or our frequencies are in tuned.

They seem invisible to us most of the time, and perhaps visa versa, yet our paths cross more frequently than most are willing to admit. Do they walk along side us, occupying the same space, yet exist at a different energy frequency? Although the phenomena of ghosts and hauntings may seem complex, most paranormal investigators will attest to the fact that interacting spirits are habitual, compulsive and often dysfunctional creatures who have feelings and emotions, and can do everything we can do under the apparent guise of invisibility. They may in fact continue to sleep, eat, work, play and fight side-by-side with us, though most people are completely unaware that this is taking place.

Sensitive people pick up on their presence, and can even converse with them, but interaction on a full time basis is rare. Imagine if you could see and feel the dead every minute of every day? Maybe we are given a paranormal filter when we enter this life, which allows us to conduct our business without the interference of the otherworldly. Maybe those locked away in the past for seeing things and hearing voices, lost their filter and were in fact, in direct contact with the dead and labeled crazy?

Call them what you will: Phantasm, wraith, phantom, spook, specter, supernatural being, manifestation, haunting, paranormal phenomena, haint, shadow, wisp, mist, apparition, poltergeist, spirit, but a rose by any other name... still spells a ghost. The fact is the living and deceased do make contact, and have been doing so for thousands of years. It is a cross-cultural phenomenon and transcends race, color, religion, philosophy, politics, etc. Do we see ghosts because we believe in them, or is it perhaps belief that makes seeing possible. Many a skeptic "wants" to believe and therefore see.

Ghosts can be encountered anywhere at any time by any person. They have been witnessed in taverns, pubs, bars, diners, restaurants, fast food outlets, markets, retail and outlet stores, hotels, hostels, inns, bed and breakfasts, cemeteries, burial grounds, mausoleums, crypts, graveyards, mortuaries, morgues, hospitals, sanitariums, asylums, battlefields, churches, missions, monasteries, nunneries, theaters, auditoriums, schools, dormitories, fraternity houses, sorority houses, prisons, jails, penitentiaries, houses, office buildings, condominiums, apartment and tenement buildings, bowling alleys, historic buildings, museums, caves, amusement parks, pyramids, archaeological sites, roads, bridges, trains, ships, lighthouses, automobiles and airplanes. In other words, wherever there was human contact, or a historical imprint, there is a likelihood for encountering ghosts.

According to renowned paranormal investigator and writer Troy Taylor in his book *The Ghost Hunter's Guidebook* (1999), 90% or more of the cases he's involved in have perfectly natural explanations behind the phenomena that is reported. However, he aptly concludes that it is the small percentage of "unexplained" phenomena that keeps all of us coming back for more. Taylor suggests that there are several different types of ghosts, and related paranormal activity. Two types of activity however, seem most prominent; the intelligent spirit and the residual haunting. The intelligent spirit is a lost personality that for some reason did not pass over to the other side at the moment of death. It shows intelligence and a consciousness and often interacts with people. Sometimes they manifest themselves as a rush of cold air, a chill or an overpowering presence. Their physical interactions can be a little more startling through sight, sounds, contact and even smells. Residual hauntings occur at a specific site, and represents an imprint left on the environment, marking an event or series of events that happened in the past. These events, often traumatic, are likened to a videotape playing repeatedly... a moment in time that is on instant and constant replay mode.

Furthermore, Taylor suggests that one part of the human perception uses our five senses while the brain processes the information. The brain only allows us to see what it thinks we can handle. Some individuals are simply on a different "wave-length", and act as "receivers" to an energy field that most of us cannot, or "will not" see. Taylor does not believe that ghosts are seen by people as they really are, which is why photographs sometimes show balls of light, orbs and strange mists which is more in character with how psychical energy is probably manifested. Taylor does believe that when people see ghosts wearing clothing they are actually witnessing residual impressions because they are not conscious spirits, merely imprints left behind. Conscious spirits will sometimes appear in clothing because people are sensitive enough to see the spirit as it once was. They see the spirit as it still visualizes itself.

According to L.B. Taylor in *The Ghosts of Virginia Volume III* (1994), stories of hauntings go back thousands of years. What are ghosts? Taylor suggests that the only real definitive and indisputable answer is, simply, no one knows; however, experts attempting to label and explain ghosts for centuries concluded that:

- Ghosts are the disembodied spirits or energy that manifests itself over a period of time, generally in one place.
- Ghosts are the souls of the dead.
- A ghost is the surviving emotional memory of someone who has died traumatically, and usually tragically, but is unaware of his or her death.
- A ghost is a person who has died and is stuck in a kind of limbo existence.
- Apparitions are the super-normal manifestations of people, animals, objects and spirits.
- Most apparitions are of living people or animals that are too distant to be perceived by normal senses.
- Apparitions of the dead are also called ghosts.

Some experts believe that a ghost is a manifestation or recordable occurrence of persistent personal energy, or is an indication that some kind of force or energy is being exercised after death which is in some way connected with a person previously known to have existed on the earth. A number of studies and investigations suggest that spirits appear:

- To communicate with the living in a time of crisis such as sickness or death.
- To provide a warning to the living of some impending tragedy or disaster.
- To comfort those who are grieving or lamenting as serious loss.
- To transmit or communicate to someone in particular valuable personal information.
- To complete a vocation, mission, or duty that was left incomplete while on earth.
- To right a wrong that was done to them, essentially seeking justice for a wrongdoing or transgression.
- To ask the living for help, guidance, or understanding. Sometimes, ghosts seek out individuals to help them complete a specific task such as find their missing body and give it a proper burial, or pinpoint the location of an object that must be given to someone in particular.

L.B. Taylor (1994) implies that a majority of ghostly manifestations involves sound and noises, unusual smells or odors, extreme cold, the movement or disappearance of objects, visual images, tactile sensations, and disembodied voices. While the most common perceived image of a ghost is a filmy apparition, in actuality, visual images are seen only in a small percentage of reported cases. Such figures are always clothed, and most often appear in period costume.

The term "haunt" comes from the same root as "home," and refers to the occupation of houses by the spirits of deceased people and animals who lived there. Other haunted sites seem to be places merely frequented or liked by the deceased, or places where violent death has occurred. Some haunts are continual; others are active only on certain dates that correspond to the deaths, or major events in the lives of the dead.

Are ghosts real? That question has remained unanswered through the ages. It is, ultimately, up to each individual to decide. A Gallop poll reported that 14 percent of Americans said they have had a ghostly experience, in Great Britain, and other parts of Europe, the percentage is much higher. Certainly, most reported supernatural happenings are usually explained by scientific or rational means. But not all! As psychic expert Hans Holzer once said, "There are theories, but no proof, as to why (hauntings) happen. But that the incidence of such happenings exceeds the laws of probability, and that their number establishes that there is some-thing to investigate, is beyond dispute."

Regardless of one's personal feelings, there is, unquestionably, an innate longing in human nature to "pierce the veil" which hides the future after death. Thus, the origin and nature of ghosts have popularly appealed to mankind at all times and in all places, and will doubtless continue to do so until the craving to know some-thing of the unseen world is satisfied.

According to Shadowlands, Ghosts and Hauntings (www.ttheshadowlands.net), "One of the greatest hindrances when investigating the paranormal is the popular disbelief ingrained into the general population by mainstream science. This stems mainly from the common tenant of science that a given phenomenon must be objectively measurable to be given credence. From this basic precept one can immediately witness the great hypocrisy of science, because this precept is rendered null if a given phenomenon is either mathematically possible, or the phenomenon is proposed by someone with a known scientific background.... Current science is dismissing many classical assumptions with the advent of Quantum Theory and Chaos science. Both state that reality is a subjective experience based on belief, a tenant of astrologers, alchemists, and priests for millennia. With these new precepts finding their way into traditional science, the study of the paranormal may be taken seriously within the next few decades, with the likely result that the prefixes para- and super- shall be removed and only the natural shall remain. When the first shift of these areas into modern science occurs, new equipment, methods, and ideas will be available for use in determining the nature of reality, and it is possible that the energies discovered could be harnessed for the good of all mankind. For now, though, the methods of researching the paranormal and supernatural remain stunted."

According to Dale Kaczmarek (1999), after being involved with many investigations both into private and public buildings, restaurants, churches, cemeteries, Indian burial grounds, historic locations, battlefields and murder sites, he has found that no area is totally free of ghostly activity. Most areas seem to begin to produce phenomena after a sudden, violent, emotional, tragic or traumatic death such as a murder, suicide, or tragic accident like a car or plane crash. The current theory is that because of the way that the people met their demise, an energy is released at that location and can be seen, felt, smelled or sensed in some way by people passing through the area. Other times a location where a person might have spent a great deal of their time such as a house, restaurant, church or tavern could become haunted by the deceased simply because the ghost might come back to "check in" once in a while to see loved ones or the structure itself.

So, what are ghosts, and why do they or their energy continue to intrude on our time and space reality? Well, it's a mystery!!! Transformed energy from a person that somehow remains tied to a specific location due to an event habitualized behavior; perhaps. The beauty of ultimate answer may simply be in believing that such a thing is possible, seeing something you can't explain, opening your mind and heart to the possibility of the existence of

We may not know why ghosts exist, but we know they do. This book is not intended to resolve philosophical or metaphysical issues regarding ghosts. Instead, it intends to provide the traveler searching for unusual getaway locations and the seekers of spirits by providing myriad places in California where ghosts or paranormal phenomena have been reported. Perhaps, at one of these destination spots, under the right circumstances, you might feel, hear, or see the other-worldly. Furthermore, you may even be the one to come home from an unusual holiday adventure with proof about the existence of ghosts that will stand the test of scientific scrutiny, and fill in yet another missing piece of the puzzle about the nature of ghosts. Until we meet again through our ghost books, and paranormal adventures; may the spirits be with you and Happy Haunting!

Lillian Corinne Whaley - The Last Occupant

This letter was penned by C. Lillian Whaley on November 26, 1882 in her pamphlet **California's Oldest Town**, edited by June Allen Reading.

I have been unexpectedly awakened from the comfortable sleep into which of late years I have fallen, to find that I am required to give my own history, in my old fashioned style. If it will interest you, however, I will relate the principal changes and chances that have befallen me and the cause of my present dilapidated appearance. The old tumble-down houses which are scattered over my face were once as neat, pretty and well kept as any of the more modern dwellings; and my quiet and comparatively deserted streets were then the scenes of more life and activity than even those of my sister town.

More than one hundred years ago, a party of Spaniards and Franciscan friars sailed into the beautiful bay of San Diego, and journeying up the land a short distance, they selected a snug and sheltered retreat where they founded the first Mission in California in 1769. It was not till many years after this however, that a town was built and the site selected was on one of the hills over looking the place on which I stand. The original town was as a matter of course not very large and it was built on the hill to protect it from the attack of the Indians, who together with bands of semi-barbarous Mexicans were the earliest inhabitants of the place. The inhabitants of the town were chiefly Spaniards and Mexicans, there being at that time no Americans in the place. Their manner of living was very simple, and the people being chiefly from Spain, brought Spanish customs and style of architecture with them. Their houses were made almost invariably of adobe or sun dried brick, the walls being sometimes six feet thick for better protection against the Indians. The roofs were made of stout rafters across which were laid cane or bamboo, crossed and twisted so as to make them impenetrable; and over this were laid the red tiles which from their shape were intended to carry off the water from the roof.

Though plain, their homes were not unattractive, the large comfortable rooms leading one into another, the rows of bamboo chairs, the cool ollas and earthen cups, the simple though neat furniture and above all the kindly and gracious welcome given to the stranger made them attractive and pleasant; for simple-minded though they were, they possessed the power of enjoying themselves n the highest degree, and no where could they be exceeded in hospitality. By degrees the old town on the hilltop was abandoned, the people preferring the more sheltered position of my present site; and the only remaining evidences of it are a few graves and ruins of houses. Here they lived in quiet seclusion, pursuing their various occupations and enjoying their simple pleasures, until the outbreak of the war between the United States and Mexico, which led to the erection of Fort Stockton on one of the highest hills overlooking the town.

After the war, the Americans and the simple pleasures of my peaceful people were soon brought into disfavor by the more practical Americans. Gradually they have retired to their ranchos, being unable to keep up with their more civilized intruders; and with their desertion, I have quietly and slowly fallen into decay. Fifty years ago, what is now known as New Town was an open plain without a single house upon it. I was then the only settlement in San Diego County and in my most thriving condition. There is no knowing what I shall be fifty years from now; but if the hopes of the oldest settlers and the present outlook be fulfilled, I may hope for the inevitable reaction, and perhaps see myself the chosen spot for the homes of those who love a quiet retreat.

There is nothing now within my walls to interest my former people; and by the calm that has settled on me, one would think it is Sunday all the time. At present I am honored by such names as "Old Sleepy Hollow," "Castle of Indolence," "Deserted Village" and many other such titles; but the place may stand forth yet and prove its right to the attention of those who look down upon it when a proper appreciation of its merits comes to be understood. The two old palm trees at the entrance to the town, stand like old and trusty sentinels, the only living witnesses of my growth and fall. Never again shall the same happy-hearted people walk my streets and share the primitive pleasures of the olden time. I stand today a dilapidated monument of the past. I am, indeed, deserted (Lillie C. Whaley Nov. 26, 1882)

As a footnote, Norman and Scott in **Historic Haunted America** (1995) state, "The colorful legacies provided by Yankee jim Robinson, Thomas Whaley, and others, together with at least one alleged murder, provide the Whaley House with a history of hauntings that began at least fifty years ago. The first to suggest the presence of ghosts was Corinne Lillian Whaley, Thomas and Anna's youngest daughter, who lived in the house until she died in 1953 at the age of eighty-nine. According to some accounts, she seldom ventured to the second floor. She wrote in her memoirs that a "force" of some sort didn't want her in the upstairs bedrooms. She said so many strange occurrences had taken place that she slept only fitfully and was always uncomfortable in her ancestral home. Lillian remained a gracious hostess, however, right up until her death, often inviting old friends over for visits. Christmas was her favorite time of the year. She would have the descendants of other pioneer families stop in for refreshments on Christmas Day. Even when she became too frail to put up a Christmas tree, she took out her charming assortment of antique ornaments and placed them in the lighted windows and on the fireplace mantel. What disturbed Lillian about the house also puzzled her visitors. Friends reported that as they sat chatting in the parlor, the distinct sounds of a man pacing in heavy boots were heard upstairs. Lillian tried to ignore the noises. Her friends often assumed another person was in the house. But as the afternoon or evening wore on no one else appeared. Lillian Whaley said it was Yankee Jim who walked in her house."

To Anna

The following poem was written by Thomas Whaley to Anna Eloise De Launay aboard the Sutton on his way to San Francisco on July 10, 1849 (in **Consignments to El Dorado, A Record of the Voyage of the Sutton by Thomas Whaley**, *edited by June Allen Reading (1972): Exposition Press, N.Y.*

I'am fond and true, though far away, from home's Sequestered Spot,
Where thy Sweet Kindness bade me stay, and choose a nearer lot;
Near the footstool of reception, Thy warm and glowing love,
That beats high at every motion, while in every meditation,
All was thoughtfully done.

Of thee I have an auburn curl, a daguerreotype too,
Treasures I'd not exchange for pearly, or slippery wealth 'tis true.
Hours I've beguiled from night till morn, with these, my chosen lot;
Light and free they've mellowed to storm, while on the ocean heavily borne,
I'd sigh—"Forget-me-Not."

Lo! dearest, midst, thy virgin thoughts, of tender youth and love,
The aim to wake in falt'ring hearts, a feeling far from hope;
As on the ocean's bellows lost near unto destruction
Memory, treacherous to the last, with it our mutual love, the past,
Seeks our Separation.

But a bright and more Serene Sky, dissolved the vision,
An hallowed back this sweetest tie, of life's dear provision.
The moonlight shades o'er the waters, were meet to this commune,
Lavished in their palely darkness, Our primeval love of tenderness
To muse my solitude.

The orange and banano clime, the grooves of cocoa-nut,
Do each their fruitful power combine, my thought more lenient,
To Sip from the fairest flowers, As does the honey bee,
The choicest juices of the bowers, To Stock its honey tree.

I would select one my true bride, the choicest of the bower,
Such as might prove my greatest pride, she should never lower:
Her grace and love would then inspire, A heart to it's recount;
Homage would kneel at Such o Shrine, And each aspiring soul would chime,
The Strains of good report.

Thus, at the hymeon altar, I'd seek to pay the vow,
How serious made, I'd yet master; and Most willing bow,
To the rule of an inclined heart, able, fondly to love,
Tho' neath the sting of a dull dart, espousing its dangerous art,

To force what's formed above. [sic]

A Historical Perspective

Haunts—whatever we call them, most towns and cities possess their own collection of strange happenings and ugly things that go bump in the night. Ghosts are woven into the fabric of our culture; they saturate our literature, religion, and communal consciousness...Human beliefs in ghosts and spirits are not some recent invention of the mind.

Richard Carrico, **San Diego's Spirits** (1991)

A present-day visit to the Whaley House represents a nostalgic trip back to the 1860s, a period of dusty streets, kerosene lamps, stage coaches, the horse and buggy, and frontier justice. It was a time when families from The East, came to tame The West, seek their fortune, and etch their name's in pioneer history. Prior to the 1850s, the cultural landscape contained the imprints of Native American, Spanish, Mission-period, Mexican and Anglo occupation. Old Town San Diego was a cultural melting pot as frontier America began its slow process toward industrialization.

According to archaeologists and scholars, the earliest inhabitants of the region occupied San Diego's coastal strip over 6,000 years ago. According to McKeever (1985:7-8), an influx of desert people reached the San Diego area at around 1000 B.C. Speaking a Hokan language similar to the desert Yuma and Mojave tribes, they assimilated with the local La Jollan peoples, and became known as the Kumeyaay. Marks of the Kumeyaay presence can still be seen today. Stone grinding bowls called metates that were used for grinding acorns are occasionally found hidden in the grass beneath oak trees. Chipped-stone tools have been found in the marshes at the southern tip of San Diego Bay. The Kumeyaay moved with the seasons settling into permanent villages by wintertime. Called "rancherias" by the Spanish, these villages were numerous; eight sites have been found around San Diego Bay alone.

In 1542, the Kumeyaay were introduced to the Spanish designs for "gold, God, and glory." The advent of European intrusion spelled the demise of the Kumeyaay people. On September 28, 1542, the Spanish under Portuguese born Juan Rodriguez Cabrillo landed in San Diego Bay. Wearing armor, carrying metal weapons, disembarking on huge wooden ships called the San Salvador and La Victoria, and flying the colors of imperial Spain, the invasion of Alta California began. It was short lived, however, because the Kumeyaay were unlike the Inca or Aztec people, possessing no great storehouse of gold or jewels. The disappointed Spanish left.

It was almost 60 years before Sebastian Vizcaino returned to San Diego, dropping anchor on November 10, 1602, in a place Cabrillo had named "San Miguel". Since it was the feast day of a recently proclaimed saint,

Vizcaino discarded Cabrillo's "San Miguel" and christened the area after the new saint—San Diego de Alcala. Both Cabrillo and Vizcaino were impressed by the harbor, which was considered one of the best ports in all the South Sea. It had good anchorage, good protection on all sides, and ample food and water, but, once again, the Spanish chose not to settle this new land and returned home. Finally, the loss of their sea power to the English and threats from the Russians in Siberia to settle California prompted their renewed interest to colonizing California.

Out of desperation, the plans for the Sacred Expedition under the direction of Jose de Galvez, Inspector General of New Spain, were to be carried out by Captain Gaspar de Portola. Portola left the Baja mission site of Velicata in May, 1769, accompanied by a fifty-five-year-old Franciscan priest named Fray Junipero Serra—this was preceded two months earlier by the departure of Captain Fernando de Rivera y Moncada. Moncada's land expedition accompanied by Fray Juan Crespi reached San Diego in mid-May, 1769. In July of the same year, Portola's expedition reached San Diego de Alcala with 74 soldiers, priests, and Christian Indians from Baja, California. Portola, leaving some of his men behind, left San Diego on a 600-mile journey to locate Monterey. By the time he returned in January 1770, 19 of the 40 men Portola left behind died. A lack of consistent food resources, heat, and drought coupled with a diminishing supply of ammunition and a restless Kumeyaay population plagued the expedition from its inception; a final blow to the missionaries was their inability to convert the Kumeyaay who resisted the Spanish. A small skirmish between the Spanish and Kumeyaay occurred on August 15, 1669, resulting in the death of five Kumeyaay warriors.

Dieguno woman in 1892 at Balboa Park
during the Cabrillo celebration
(Whaley Papers - Photograph courtesy of the Historical Shrine Foundation of San Diego)

Morale was low, and the Kumeyaay were still hostile when Father Serra received permission to relocate the mission in 1774, a few miles east along the San Diego River to a place they named Nuestra Senora del Pilar. By 1775, the first Spanish child was born in California, but not all was tranquil in the Spanish domain as Kumeyaay resentment of the Spanish reached a peak. On the morning of November 4, 1775, warriors from 40 Kumeyaay villages gathered for battle and descended on the mission. Four soldiers standing guard opened fire. The nephew and son of the Presidio commandant were wounded instantly, and Father Luis Jayme was captured, tortured, and killed. Spanish justice was swift, and the leaders of the Kumeyaay rebellion were swiftly and cruelly punished.

The mission was rebuilt with wood and thatch smeared with mud to prevent fire in case of another attack. However, it was not the Native Americans who dealt the next blow to the mission—it was Mother Nature in the form of deadly rains, years of drought, and, finally, a major earthquake in 1803 which destroyed the church. Out of the rubble came the fourth and final church which stands today.

By the early 1830s, 15,000 head of cattle and 20, 000 sheep could be seen grazing on the local hillsides, and, to the delight of the Spanish missionaries, 1500 Native Americans were baptized. Unfortunately, the success of the mission system came at the expense of the Kumeyaay. Introduced European diseases were responsible for the decimation of many Native American cultures, including the Kumeyaay—most were buried in mass graves and became merely lists on registers. In 1800, mission records indicated that of the 16,000 Kumeyaay baptized over a ten-year period, almost 9,000 died from disease and other causes.

The Mexican Era began in 1834, after the Spanish relinquished control to the Mexican government and the mission land were secularized. Mexican governor Pio Pico awarded the mission lands to a retired soldier and former mayor of San Diego named Santiago Arguello. The Native Americans were freed from bondage but had no legal rights to their land. The remaining Kumeyaay either turned to living off the land or were found destitute, wandering through the back streets of San Diego. The adobe walls of the mission buildings slowly dissolved back into the earth that gave them life while concerned members of the congregation saved vestments and art, transporting them to the large home of Don Jose Antonio Estudillo. The mission bells hung from a wooden beam and other sacred objects were hidden. The mission might have disappeared if not for Abraham Lincoln who, in 1862, restored the San Diego mission and the 22 acres surrounding it, to the Catholic Church.

The Whaley House has witnessed more history than any other building in the city. Since the 1850s, the house served as a residence, theater, boarding house, a place for musical soirees and formal balls, a court, and was the focus of a battle for the county seat. The history of the house reads like the history of San Diego in a concentrated form. The Whaley House exists due to the dream of one man, Thomas Whaley, a civic-minded eastern merchant who built the house at a cost of over $10,000 in 1857. The brick was made from native clay and river sand, the cedar for the woodwork came from the East, and the hinges, doorknobs and locks from New York. The house has survived fires, earthquakes, robberies, vandalism and disrepair, and was barely spared demolition. There are countless joys and tragedies associated with this venerable house, and it is these imprints that provide the tales of apparitions and occurrences that bring people from around the world to visit the house. Most people come hoping to catch a glimpse of Thomas, Anna, their children, or Yankee Jim Robinson.

Born on October 5, 1823, in New York City, Thomas Whaley was the seventh child in a family of ten born to Rachel Pye and Thomas Alexander Whaley Sr. The Whaley name ran through more than 800 years of English history. The family had been prominent in local and national affairs since 1067 and included well-known historical figures: Oliver Cromwell, Frances Goffe, and Major General Edward Whaley. James Whaley (Thomas's grandfather) moved his family to America in 1722, settling at Plymouth, Massachusetts. He brought with him, English flintlock muskets, homemade firing mechanisms, and English flints. Weapons were needed by settlers along the eastern seaboard to aid in taming the natives. Before the Revolutionary War, the family migrated to New York City carrying on their experiments with weaponry.

Thomas Whaley Sr., son of the gunsmith, carried on the business while serving with the New York Militia. He was sent to Washington on August 14, 1814, the day the British burned the Capitol. After the war, Thomas Whaley Sr. married Rachel Pye whose father, William, manufactured locks in Brooklyn. He was taken into the firm. About the time Thomas Whaley Jr. was born, William Pye died a death. Pye's business was left to Rachel Pye Whaley who was raising four children: John, Henry, Thomas, and Harriet. During 1832, Thomas Whaley Sr. passed away in New York, and stated in his will that his son, Thomas Jr., should receive a liberal education.

Rachel, a shrewd businesswoman, increased the family holdings through astute purchases of real estate. One of the New York City parcels she bought was located in what is now known as Central Park. Her two boys, John and Henry, eventually took over the management of the locksmith business and succeeded in obtaining government contracts In Washington, D.C., and Harpers Ferry, West Virginia. Thomas, the youngest of the boys, showed an unusual ability for business, and his mother decided to give him the best possible education so that h might eventually take over the management of the family business affairs.

Thomas went to boarding school in Colcester, Connecticut, enrolled in Washington Institute, and graduated with honors. He was sent to Europe under the watchful eyes of a tutor to travel and study for two years. Upon his return from Europe in 1846, he managed his father's business affairs and rental properties for his mother. Problems in the settlement of the family estate forced Thomas to begin a new career involving working for the Sutton & Company shipbuilding firm.

Events of December 1848 had a profound influence Thomas Whaley's life. The discovery of gold in California aroused his interest, and rumors of a newly proposed line of government steamships to California piqued the interest of his company. They planned to expand the operation to the West Coast with an office in San Francisco. Thomas Whaley was offered a ticket and the possibility of partnership in the firm if he would go; and go he did. Times were hard in the East, and the outlook was bleak around the world. Whaley was young and adventuresome, and he eagerly accepted the challenge. Off to California he went.

Dadguerreotype of Thomas Whaley
taken prior to his California Voyage on the Sutton in 1849
(Courtesy of the Historical Shrine Foundation)

Accepting a consignment of goods belonging to George Wardle, a stock of locks, window sashes, and hardware from his father's shop, and guns from Grandfather Whaley, young Thomas Whaley boarded the **Sutton**, January 1, 1849, for a trip around Cape Horn. He was also in love with a young lady, Ms. Anna Eloise De Launay. Whaley expressed his feelings for Anna in a letter to his mother, "... You might call on Mrs. Lannay [sic], you will find her a very pleasant lady. I may as well inform you that I have a particular regard for her youngest daughter, Miss Anna, indeed I love her add intend marrying her if ever I return from California a rich man . . . I may send for her. She is a pleasant and amiable young lady of very affectionate disposition and gentle and innocent as a lamb. She is only 16 or 17 years of age. You would no doubt love her as a daughter-in-law. She attends Miss Green's School on the 5th Avenue."

Unfortunately for Thomas Whaley, the trip was excruciating and slow, taking 204 days to go from New York to San Francisco. He was lucky to have arrived safely given the problems that occurred at sea as he stated in one of his letters, [sic] "Last night... Mr. Theophilus Valentine one of the forward passengers blew out his brains. Our ship was guarded in consequence. Passengers on board held prisoners. After being without fresh provisions for 24 hours they were relieved... Rough seas... Ship uneasy.. .Cry all hands on deck... Albertross... Sternboat gave way to four passengers in the Sea, quarter boat lowered, picked up one, two climbed up... Schoonmaker drowned... Sea was running mountain high and dangerous... I could not refrain from shedding a tear... But had I known the leaky condition she was in and the Character of her Captain I would never have set foot on board her especially after being forewarned by Anson that she would never round the Horn safely... little prospect of reaching "Eldorado... Believe the "Old Sutton" is like the "Flying Dutchman" doomed eternally to wander the seas over."

Thomas Whaley, a fortunate man, finally reached San Francisco on July 22nd and recorded in another of his correspondence, [sic] "150 vessels at San Francisco... Went to Rosses... Post Office not open... Wilburs & Muir... Received letters... All accounts wonderful. Incredulous... As a general thing goods worth nothing... My wagon and window sashes worth a fortune... Legitimate business had been made into a gamble by the speculators. Sidewalk deals, although there were no sidewalks, went on day and night. Auctions were held with much noise and shouting and were nearly as exciting as gambling games. No one wanted to pay a set price for anything—they liked the fun of bidding. One store catered to Indians, taking their gold weight for weight, on a scales made of sardine cans, in exchange for the raisins they loved."

San Francisco was an aggregate settlement of cloth houses, canvas tents, adobes, flimsy stores, and ramshackle saloons. The store into which Thomas Whaley moved was located on Montgomery Street between Jackson and Pacific. The agreement with George Wardle stipulated that Whaley dispose of the consignment for which he would receive $600 per month. Whaley also had his own stock of hardware and a consignment of miners' equipment from Flintoff & Co. which he would dispose of at a 10 percent commission. The operation was successful and with the proceeds, he purchased his own building on Montgomery Street and rented the Wardle store to Lewis Simons for $350. He improved his store property with the addition of a second story for offices and living quarters and had plank sidewalks constructed.

By April 1851, Thomas Whaley purchased land at Rincon point near the shipyard and erected a spacious two-story house with a balcony commanding a beautiful view of the bay. His partner, William Warner, was expecting his wife to join him, and Whaley hoped that young Anna De Launay would come along as well. He wrote his lady many letters, giving her detailed descriptions of this first house he obviously had built for her—however, it was not to be... yet!

Anna Eloise De Launay
(Courtesy of the Historical Shrine Foundation)

While managing rental property for Wardle, he also had invested in a side venture with a lawyer, Lewis Franklin. The Franklin brothers were partners in a business at San Diego. When all appeared to be going perfectly, a fire on May 3rd and 4th, 1851, hit San Francisco. In Whaley's letter to Anna Lannay [sic], he wrote, "This city was consumed by fire the night of the 3rd and 4th. The scene that presents itself is painful in the extreme to gaze upon... There are to be seen only smoldering embers with here and there tottering walls of warehouses that were thought to be proof against the flames. To give you an imperfect idea of the vast extent... it is more than a mile in one direction and about half a mile in the other... Twenty center blocks of the most dense and thickly settled quarter the town is in ashes. At least a thousand houses have been burned, the largest number ever in the United States, not even excepting the great fire in New York in 1835... The loss is variously estimated from ten to fifteen million dollars... our business men are crippled but resolve to surmount the obstacles... many a noble and courageous heart has fallen victim in their glorious endeavor to rescue from the flames the effects of others... While the tottering walls of Delmonico's were being removed they suddenly gave way and buried five poor firemen beneath the ruins... By this fire the buildings, which I erected upon Montgomery St., were destroyed... I stood watching my buildings until they fell with a crash. In a short space of minutes all that I had toiled for and which I had looked upon with so much satisfaction was reduced to cinders, and ashes was all that remained to represent the $10,000 which they cost... "

To compound Whaley's problems, Anna's mother refused to let her come to California. Anna had sent him her likeness, which he often gazed upon, and he, in return, had sent her a bag of gold dust to buy some silks and beads. The fire may have destroyed Whaley's savings but not his resolve. Upon the advice of friend Lewis Franklin, Thomas Whaley decided to leave San Francisco and seek his fortune in San Diego.

Whaley arrived in San Diego on October 4th and remarked that the climate of San Diego was like that of Italy and healthier than San Francisco. This small, old Spanish town of about 250 to 300 inhabitants, is where he came to settle. At that time, Old Town consisted of six or eight stores, two hotels, and an apothecary shop kept by an old friend of Whaley's from New York, a Dr. Painter. Painter was the only physician along with three lawyers, a Catholic church, (temporarily located in the house of one of the citizens), and nightly fandangos or parties. Whaley began again in quaint San Diego.

Although he was beginning a new life in San Diego, his thoughts were far away with his Anna, as he writes, "Not a night passes, Anna but what I look at your daguerreotype... I sleep with it under my pillow...It gives me great pleasure to gaze upon it. What if I should not know you! You may have grown tall, become very corpulent, and have adopted the 'Bloomer Costume'... If that were the case, I should not know you... I am ready to take you for better or worse, so it makes no difference in what shape you appear so long as you come."

As Whaley and Franklin established their first store and began to prosper, Whaley studied Spanish so he could do business with the local people. During November of 1851, Chief Antonio Garra of the Luiseno tribe, along with several other Native American groups, mounted an insurrection when the sheriff threatened to collect taxes from the tribes who ran cattle in the area. They attacked Warner's Ranch and Major Edward Fitzgerald and Lt. Colonel Magruder who had a small detachment of men stationed at the old mission, left to defend the region against further attacks. While the soldiers were chasing Garra, the town of San Diego was under martial law, and every man enrolled as a soldier. There were only 35 men and a few sentries left to protect the town against the Luiseno Indians, and Whaley had his six-shooters at the alert. Five soldiers were killed during the ensuing battles, and the insurrection ended with the capture of Garra. On January 10, 1852, Thomas Whaley was one of twelve designated men who were part of a firing squad at the cemetery. Thus ended the life of Antonio Garra, the Luiseno leader responsible for the insurrection. The execution was swift and normalcy returned to San Diego.

Old Town San Diego in 1877 based on Poole's survey in 1856 and Cout's survey in 1849. The Whaley House lies on parcel 38, lot 1 on the corner of Harney and San Diego Streets
(Courtesy of the San Diego Historical Society)

During March of 1852, Thomas Whaley and Lewis Franklin parted ways, with Franklin selling his interest in their general store. During April of the same year, Whaley partnered with Francis Hinton, and the two ran the "Tienda General," with great success. Their first year in business resulted in a profit of $18,600, due in part to the fact that they ran a cash and carry trade, which resulted in no bad accounts.

On August 17, 1852, Yankee Jim Robinson was caught, tried and found guilty of grand larceny and was sentenced by a jury (some say an extremely biased trial) to be hanged. The sentence was to be carried out immediately, but for some reason, the hanging was postponed until September 18, 1852. According to a news article from the Los Angeles Star dated August 28, 1852, "At the recent term of the County Court at San Diego, James Robinson, otherwise called "Yankee Jim," was tried for burglary, and sentenced to be hung. Two accomplices, Gray and Harris, were each sentenced to be imprisoned one year in the State Prison. The charge upon which they were tried, was for stealing a boat, but they are strongly suspected of horse stealing and even murder.

Yankee Jim made powerful resistance to the arrest, and was finally captured by the aid of the "lasso," which in the hands of a person expert in its use is irresistible. His execution is fixed for September 18, and he says that before that time he will make a confession that will astonish the natives. Robinson was eventually hanged; some say it happened on the very spot where Whaley's House now stands, although absolute proof is lacking. There was even mention of a curse placed on the hanging ground by Yankee Jim when he was unfairly (as some historians speculate) ushered into history; a curse that affected the reportedly Whaley family and those who followed.

By April 1853, the health of Francis Hinton took a turn for the worse, leading to the dissolution of the partnership. Whaley wasted little time in finding another partner, and teamed with Ephriam Morse to run the general store. Since business was doing well by mid-1853, Thomas Whaley was now in a position to head east, and claim his bride. Thomas and Anna were married at the Church of the Ascension on 4th Street in New York City by Reverend Seabury, on August 14, 1853.

During this time, Juan Bandini opened a new store and began selling goods for half the price that Whaley and Morse were. This began a decline in the fortunes of Thomas Whaley. The bride and groom returned to San Diego temporarily settling at the Gila House. Whaley also escorted the wives of Ephraim Morse and Charles Poole back to San Diego to be with their husbands.

In San Diego, Anna found the employment of Native Americans as house servants a custom although it was difficult to keep them "decently clothed" and disciplined. Whaley "bought" a Native American girl from her parents by giving them $100 worth of goods from his store in exchange for their consent for the girl to live with his family. The girl stayed about a month and then disappeared and returned to her parents. When Whaley went after her, the parents were willing to let her go but wanted to be paid again, and this continued as long as the kind-hearted Whaley consented to the scheme.

The San Diego & Gila Southern Pacific & Atlantic Railroad Co. was organized by Judge James Robinson and Louis Rose during September of 1854. Thomas Whaley and thirty others invested in the company. Shortly before the birth of their first child, the Whaley's moved to the Burkhardt house on Juan Street opposite the Tienda General. A boy, named after Whaley's partner, Francis Hinton, was born on December 28, 1854. At this time, Whaley purchased nine lots totaling about 8 1/2 acres in San Diego for $302. On March 18, 1854, Thomas Whaley dissolved the partnership with E.W. Morse.

During May, Thomas Whaley reopened his general store with his brother, Henry Hurst Whaley, and Henry's wife, Annie who came from New York. Henry and Annie lived with Thomas and Anna after coming to California from New York. According to some, both families quarreled and Henry and Annie

Old Town San Diego
View showing Old Chapel, Don Rafel's Cabin, Old Stone Jail, Graveyard, Whaley House, Church and Parsonage
(Courtesy of the San Diego Historical Society)

On May 1, 1855, Whaley and George Tebbetts purchased two Vervalen patent horsepower brick-making machines, complete with moulds and one force pump for $2,500. One of the brick-making machines was put into immediate use near Old Town and the other at the beach, which made it convenient for shipping the brick to other locations. Whaley wrote his mother, "... I have a fine lot..., which I shall enclose with a wall sometime this year. I am now building a granary of brick... I have 150 thousand bricks left after putting up my granary, and if I don't dispose of them soon I shall convert them all into houses and rent them. I have plenty of my own land to build upon. I have a fine rockaway carriage and a span of sorrels, with harness of silver... My wife has every comfort and luxury I can parlor is furnished with Brussels carpet and mahogany and rosewood parlor is furnished with Brussels carpet and mahogany and rosewood furniture, and a mahogany crib for little Frank. We frequently have musical soirees and our house is the resort of most of the best people in the place. My wife is the best little woman in the world, loved by all. She is proficient in music, plays, and sings."

On September 2, 1855, Thomas Whaley purchased Lot 1 of Block 480 in San Diego from the City of San Diego. During September of the same year, George Tebbetts sold his brick manufacturing business to Whaley, which Thomas Whaley continued to operate alone. On November 10, 1855, Whaley and Company dissolved. Thomas Whaley no longer desired to work with his brother, Henry who reportedly often overcharged customers, drank on the job and would verbally abuse people. The dissolution was not pleasant, as Henry challenged Thomas to a fight. The brothers parted ways under duress. A second child, Thomas Whaley, Jr., was born on August 18, 1856, at their temporary living quarters on Twain Street.

Between 1856-1858, several architectural plans for the Whaley House were drawn up, indicating that the house went through additional changes to the interior over the years. During September 1856, Whaley began building his two-story, Greek Revival residence. The bricks for the building were fashioned in Whaley's brickyard. The building was to serve as a house and a store, and was completed by May 1858. Whaley confidently stated [sic], "I feel I will have the nicest place in San Diego... I must wait patiently until it is known that this [Old Town] is to be the terminus of the railroad. I feel that San Diego with its climate and bay can become a teeming metropolis. It has the same possibilities as New York."

The Whaley House in Old Town circa 1874
(Courtesy of the San Diego Historical Society)

The house Whaley constructed faced San Diego Avenue. The downstairs portion of the house was divided into three large rooms, which extended to the back of the house. The front of the building consisted of five pairs of doors set close together, each with a wooden base about three feet high. These doors corresponded to the five upstairs windows. A covered veranda extended the full length of the front of the house.

The upper part of the structure was constructed of five sets of French windows, with the windowpanes, each about one-foot high, set in sashes in groups of two. These extended to the top of the doors that reached nearly to the twelve-foot ceiling. The upper floor was designed to be the family's living quarters, while the lower level was envisioned as a store. The width of the house was 32 feet across. The original plan was to combine living quarters with a store.

Thomas and Anna Whaley with Francis Hinton
born in 1854 and Anna Amelia born in 1858
(Courtesy of the Historical Shrine Foundation)

During this time, the granary was a separate building with a loading platform and no front windows. Two small windows on either side were the only means of ventilation at this early date. An adobe wall about seven feet high surrounded the entire lot. A gate within a high wooden frame divided the front wall in the middle, and a similar gate formed the entrance to the back corral. An adobe wall separated the back corral from the front yard; an outhouse built of brick stood in the front yard close to the dividing wall. The back corral was used to round up cattle for branding purposes. Cactus clumps stood here and there outside the wall, and a well occupied the center of the space. The adobe wall originally was whitewashed. The yard and flowers were Anna Whaley's delight, and the kitchen garden contained all manners of vegetables and herbs. Fruit trees included orange, cherry, fig, and pomegranate. There were two cedar trees in the back yard, and Anna planted the pepper trees herself. There was also a fan palm on the property.

On August 22, 1857, the Whaley House was completed, and local newspapers called the structure one of the finest in southern California. The house was furnished with mahogany and rosewood furniture, Brussels carpets and damask drapes. The Whaley House was a showplace during this time. The Whaleys had a rockaway carriage, which comfortably held six people, and a span of reddish-brown horses, called sorrels with silver mounted harnesses in which Thomas transported his family and envious friends.

During September 1857, Thomas Whaley opened his new store on the lower level of the house. Whaley was inclined to take cash over credit, offering discounted merchandise for such transactions. His favorite motto was, "Quick returns, small profits." He had a rat-proof granary and numerous supplies, but few people came to buy. It didn't take Thomas Whaley long to realize that his store was too far away from the plaza. During September of 1857, Whaley was commissioned County Clerk. During October, Whaley moved his business into the wood-frame storefront of Mrs. Kerren near the Plaza (the social and economic center of Old Town). This building was most recently used by Pendleton and Company. Whaley was assisted in his new store by Hay Ringgold.

The year 1858 ushered in numerous changes for the Whaley family and few were good. Tragedy struck the Whaley House on January 23, 1858 when their second son, Thomas Jr., died. The pain of this loss was tempered somewhat by the birth of Anna Amelia Whaley, in the house on June 27, 1858. However, on August 21, Whaley's fortunes took another turn for the worse when his store caught fire and burned to the ground: arson was suspected. During the fire, Whaley lost over $3,000 in merchandise. Those who helped Whaley remove merchandise from the store, came late due to a rumor that there was gunpowder inside; a false claim that prevented the withdrawal of numerous valuable items before the fire worsened. Instead of valuable merchandise, the first items taken out were whiskey barrels.

Further setbacks occurred when Whaley's investments turned a loss. Since he could only rent a portion of his house for $40 per month, and numerous people owed him money that he was unable to collect, Whaley's financial fortunes were at an all time low. The losses forced Thomas and Anna to consider moving from their house and San Diego for awhile, and they left for San Francisco at the invitation of Major George H. Ringgold. Before leaving in January 1859, Whaley turned over his affairs to Frank Ames, a

Wells Fargo Agent. His holdings at the time included the house, property in San Diego, brickmaking machines, and bricks. After moving to San Francisco, Anna's mother, sister and brother came to live with them.

On March 31, 1859 while in San Francisco, Thomas Whaley was appointed United States Commissary Storekeeper under Captain M.D.L. Simpson, thanks primarily to the influence of his friend, Major George H. Ringgold. On October 31, 1859, Whaley terminated his relationship with Wells Fargo Agent, Frank Ames. Census information for 1860, listed the following boarders in the Whaley House: Robert E. and Sarah Doyle, a mail agent from New York; James E. Mason, a mail carrier; Samuel A. Ames, a mail carrier; and, Gabriel Parades from New Mexico. The Doyle family was eventually forced out of the house due to non-payment of rent.

By July 1860, Whaley hired lawyer and Justice of the Peace, Augustus S. Ensworth to manage the Whaley House, where Ensworth also resided. For over two years, he kept the Whaleys apprised of the deteriorating condition of the house. Initiating as many improvements as he could afford, including repairing the leaking roof, he could not prevent the corral wall from collapsing. On November 5, 1860, Anna Whaley gave birth to George Hay Ringgold Whaley, who they named after their dear friend.

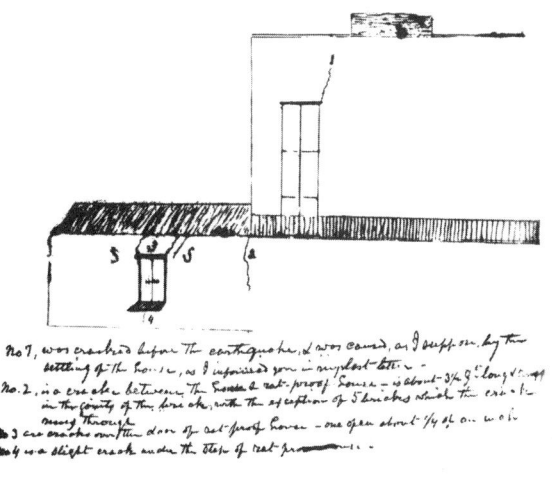

A sketch of earthquake damage to Whaley House in 1862
(Courtesy of the Historical Historical Shrine Foundation)

On May 27, 1862, while the Whaleys were still in San Francisco, a powerful earthquake rocked San Diego, and many houses in town became uninhabitable or badly damaged including the Whaley's. Ensworth sent Whaley a photograph of the house, describing the event as "Awful with the tremors continuing for many days." On October 14, 1862, Violet Eloise

Whaley arrived, the second Whaley child born away from their San Diego home.

A drawing of Violet Whaley by Robin Sweeton of SOHO

Around this time, Republican Alonzo Horton purchased 960 acres of prime land in present-day downtown San Diego, and began preparations to develop a new townsite. Political control hung in the balance. Old Town and New Town inhabitants became more antagonistic during this time. The Republican majority of New Town wanted to take control of the political future of San Diego by having the official records moved from Democratic Old Town. Alonzo Horton was the founder of New San Diego and a vocal proponent of this shift in power.

The third Whaley child to be born in San Francisco was Corinne Lillian Whaley, who entered life on September 4, 1864. While still in San Francisco, Major Kirkham, Whaley's superior, informed Thomas that due to numerous complaints filed against him in Washington, he would be dismissed and face a dishonorable discharge. Whaley avoided this disgrace by resigning his post. He claimed his innocence from all charges before his resignation was accepted. If things weren't bad enough, his business at home took a plunge, leaving him with serious financial indebtedness. To care for the family, he took a position in February 1866 as an issuing clerk in the U.S. Army Quartermaster's Corps. By September 1867, this position was terminated.

On July 31, 1867, Whaley received orders to proceed to Sitka, Alaska Territory, to establish a base and take possession of the Territory for the United States, while Anna and the children remained behind in San Francisco. This was yet another setback for Thomas, because not only did he receive less money than his prior positions afforded, but he also was required to leave his family. Beginning on September 3, 1867, Thomas Whaley took charge of three government transports with stores in Sitka until the United States formally took over on October 18, 1867. Whaley assisted on raising the American flag on the island of Japonski, opposite Sitka.

During 1867, Anna and the children returned to San Diego. She welcomed the change of environments, because the economic stress was affecting her health. Anna stayed with Major George H. Ringgold's wife, Mary, and Anna's mother, Victoria DeLaunay. Anna spent considerable time remodeling the house, and slowly repaired the earthquake damage to accommodate her and the five children. According to Corinne Whaley, the new look of the house was warm, comfortable, and inviting.

The parlors were the reception rooms for all the balls, and all Old Town would attend them. The stairs led up the back. The kitchen was a lean-to built on the back porch and connected with the dining room through the window. A pantry separated the dining room from a large front room, which we called the office. The same room was used as the headquarters for General Thomas Sedgewick during the railroad development. This room was also used as a sewing room.

The large room to the north, called the "big room" by the family, the annex by others, was used for other purposes. It served as the courtroom from 1863-70, with the county records being kept upstairs in the main building. The furniture consisted of a circular railing almost the width of the room, on the back of which was the judge's chair resting on a raised platform. A canopy hung at the back of the chair on the wall. The furniture consisted of chairs and benches. The room also functioned as a location for political meetings, a billiard room, dairy, kindergarten, Sunday school, store, and residence.

On November 25, 1867, Thomas Whaley was unanimously elected as a councilman in Sitka, Alaska. During January 1868, he received word that his mother had sold some family property and would split the $40,000 among her children. The catch was that Thomas would have to go to New York to obtain his share. In February, Thomas, Anna, and their son Frank sailed for New York. The younger children stayed with Victoria DeLaunay in San Francisco.

By late summer, Thomas and family returned to San Diego with monetary resources, courtesy of his mother's generosity. Alonzo Horton was busy putting New Town on the map as the Whaleys arrived back in Old Town. Aware that New Town prices for merchandise were extremely high, Whaley set his sights on reopening his Old Town store. With his newfound capital, Whaley restocked his store and initiated improvements to his dilapidated home. Thomas repaired the roof, replaced the rotting floors, attached a granary to the house, replaced windows, changed the front entrance from a loading platform, put in front and back doors, and otherwise readied the house for Anna's return with his children.

A meeting of stockholders of the San Diego and Gila Southern Pacific and Atlantic Railroad Company was held at the office of W.H. Cleveland in San Diego on October 10, 1868. At the meeting, Thomas Whaley, Louis Rose, and D.B. Kurtz were appointed to submit the names of 13 stockholders for election as Directors of the Company. They selected the following: Louis Rose, Thomas Whaley, George Hyde, A.E. Horton, O.S. Witherby, J.S. Marmasse, Jeff Gatewood, William H. Cleveland, William N. Robinson, G.A. Pendleton, E.W. Morse, James Pascoe, and George Lyons.

FOR SALE OR TO LET.

MY TWO STORY BRICK HOUSE, at Old Town, San Diego, commanding a fine view of the Harbor, within 700 feet of the Plaza, on the principal street leading to New Town, having a front of 32 feet, and a depth of 42 ft. with a one-story wing attached 31 x 27 ft., also of brick. Size of lot 150 x 217½ ft. divided into two large corrals, having arched gateways 10 and 12 feet wide, a well of good water and force pump. The buildings are substantial, and with an outlay of $1500 may be made the finest and most comfortable in the Southern part of the State; suitable for a Hotel, Residence, or Business purposes. I will sell the premises as they now stand, or put the same in complete order and finish, for any responsible party desiring to take a lease.

THOMAS WHALEY.

For further particulars, enquire of
WETMORE & CURTIS,
Franklin House.

Old Town, San Diego, Oct. 24, 1868.   4w

TO CAPITALISTS.

STORE WANTED.—I will agree with any person who will erect a building suitable for my business, at New Town, to lease the same upon such terms that will pay fair interest on the amount invested.

THOMAS WHALEY,
oc24:2t]   Old Town, West side Plaza.

Also on October 10, 1868, Thomas Whaley reopened his General Store, with this alluring announcement, "For Sale Cheap For Cash - dry goods, clothing, etc.- Received direct from the East by Thomas Whaley - West Side Plaza, Old Town." Whaley's General Store also sold a large assortment of calicos, mourning prints, Detaines, Alpacas, Furniture, Chintzes, brown and bleached sheeting and shirting, long cloths for pillow slips, brown and blue drills, blue and white checks, brown and bleached jeans, cambric linings, paper muslin's, fine blue, white and scarlet Shaker flannels, family white blankets, towels, handkerchiefs, hoop skirts, gloves, children's caps, boys clothing, Shaker socks, business suits, Marseilles vests, diagonal and Belknap overskirts, fancy and Wamasutta white shirts, and, linen bosoms, etc."

On November 1, 1868, Thomas Whaley leased the second floor of his house and the use of the corral to Thomas W. Tanner for $20 in gold coin, allowing him to take down the second story's twelve feet of studding, commencing at the east brick wall of the house, for the purpose of making an exhibition room. He was allowed to remove a portion of the east end railing of the balcony for the purpose of erecting stairs for theatrical productions. The Tanner Troupe operated out of the upstairs bedroom, where there was a small stage and seating for up to 150 people. The Troupe offered moral, chaste, and versatile entertainment, consisting of drama, farce, comedy, singing and dancing, laughable burlesques, Negro delineation's, etc. Unfortunately, Thomas Tanner died within 17 days of the opening.

NEW ADVERTISEMENTS.

THEATER.

THE RENOWNED
TANNER TROUPE!

Proprietor, - - - T. W. TANNER

THE MANAGER has the honor to inform the citizens of San Diego, and Public generally, that, having Leased the upper part of the BRICK HOUSE, he has fitted up the Hall for the purpose of offering to the generous Public a short season, of his Moral, Chaste and Versatile Entertainments, consisting of Drama, Farce, Comedy, Singing and Dancing, Laughable Burlesques, Negro Delineations, &c., and hopes his untiring efforts to please, will meet with a Liberal Share of Patronage. He will offer his

FIRST EXHIBITION
On Wednesday, December 2nd.

☞ For Particulars see Programmes.

ADMISSION,.....................50 Cents
Children Half Price.
Reserved seats.... .. ..75 Cents

Doors open at 7, Performance to commence at 8 o'clock, precisely.

Courtesy of the Historical Shrine Foundation

There was a meeting of the Board of Directors of the San Diego and Gila Southern Pacific and Atlantic Railroad Company in San Diego on December 5, 1868, where Thomas Whaley was appointed Stock Commissioner as well as being appointed to the Finance Committee along with Mr. Gatewood and Mr. Robinson. On December 12, 1868, Anna Whaley and the family arrived in Old Town by steamer. On December 19, 1868, Thomas Whaley as Stock Commissioner, began offering subscriptions for company stock to be received by Whaley, "...at my office in the brick building on San Diego Avenue." 10% of the stock subscribed for had to be paid at the time of subscription.

During January 1869, Whaley's General Store on the corner San Diego Avenue and Harney Street advertised wholesale and retail merchandise at the lowest market rates for cash, including, dry goods, millinery, embroideries, laces, hosiery, boots, shoes, hats, curtain damasks, shades, carpets, Chinese matting, wines, tobacco, wood, willow ware, and wash boards. A newspaper advertisement on February 20, 1869, mentioned that Whaley and Crosthwaite, successors to E.W. Morse, formed a co-partnership that ran a merchandising store for wholesale and retail cash purchases, including hardware, cutlery, iron, steel, and timber.

On June 26, 1869, a meeting of citizens at Franklin Hall appointed Thomas Whaley and others to make arrangements for the upcoming American Independence day celebration which would revolve around an excursion and picnic at Rose's Canon, one mile east of La Jolla. On June 30, 1869, the Union newspaper listed individuals who paid county taxes, with Thomas Whaley paying the lowest tax at $132, and A.E. Horton paying the highest, at $8,228. On July 19, 1869, the Union Republican Party Convention of the County of San Diego met to nominate for the ensuing general election in the two-story brick building belonging to Thomas Whaley.

During August 1869, the County of San Diego signed a two-year lease for the courtroom in Whaley House, guaranteeing the Whaleys $65 a month. The lease permitted the county the use of the big room and the three upstairs rooms for storage of their records. The accommodations were the best possible solution to the problems of the evicted county officers. Whaley had put up a dais and railing at the north end of the room. Here, the judge used to sit while he held court.

A September 18, 1869 newspaper article stated that this [event] was, "...one of the brightest in the history of the place, destined to be the Pacific terminus of the second Trans-continental Railway of America." Hon. William. H.. Seward and traveling party, Hon. S.B. Axtell, Member of Congress, Hon. L.G. Roots, Member of Congress, Gen. W.S. Rosecrans, etc. were in attendance. Thomas Whaley was one of Committee appointed to prepare reception.

On October 4, 1869, The San Diego Board of Supervisors paid Thomas Whaley, $130 for use of his house as a courtroom. A newspaper article on November 8, 1869 noted that "Whaley, & Crosthwaite are selling off their extensive stock of goods at cost." On February 10, 1870, the **Union** newspaper detailed that Rev. L.H. Cox will hold Divine Service at Whaley's brick building on Sunday next at 11 o'clock a.m. and at 7 o'clock p.m. All are cordially invited to attend."

On March 17, 1870, a newspaper article references the fact that, Whaley & Crosthwaite, wholesale and retail dealers, leased Horton's Hall in South San Diego [New Town] for their grocery, crockery, china, glass and Queensware, liquor, dry goods, clothing, boots arid shoes, carpeting, and hardware business. The June 1870 census listed the following information for the occupants of the Whaley House: Thomas (46); Anna (32); Anna (11); Violet (7); Lilly (5); Francis (15); George (9); and S. Yow (16) a domestic from China.

Courtesy of the Historical Shrine Foundation

The **Union** newspaper of July 14, 1870 had this to say about the brewing feud between Old Town and New Town political opponents who were fighting for control of the location of the county seat. "Removal of the County Records - The Board of Supervisors have passed an order directing the removal of the County Records from Whaley's Building in Old San Diego to the Express Building in New Town, and designating Horton's Hall as the future place of meeting for the Courts. This action was taken in answer to a petition signed by nearly all the citizens of New San Diego praying for such removal on the ground that the latter was the most central point and that a great majority of the people of the county would be accommodated thereby.

During October 1870, Thomas Whaley was granted a license to sell spirituous and other liquors in the Court House Building, Old Town through January 1871. On October 6, 1870, the Board of Directors of the San Diego and Gila Southern Pacific and Atlantic Railroad Company elected new directors for the ensuing year, with Thomas Whaley being elected. The group felt that work would soon commence upon the rail line. On April 1, 1871 The District Court and Judge Morrison ordered the removal of the records and courthouse furniture to the southern part of the city in order that the April term of Court could be opened without delay.

This was followed on April 4, by a proclamation by the San Diego County Board of Supervisors, who ordered that the Sheriff and Supervisor French take charge of, and proceed to move the Court Room furniture to the new court house at 6th & G, a brick building owned by Alonzo Horton and rented by the County for $95 per month. The Board also ordered that the County Clerk proceed at once to move the papers and records of his office to the new rooms, further ordering that Thomas Whaley be notified by the Clerk that as soon as his building shall be vacated by the County Officers, the County will no longer be responsible for the rent of the same after they shall be so vacated.

The shift in power from Old Town to New Town reached its peak in early March, when one of the most active proponents of the Old Town faction, County Clerk George Pendleton, died. A last stand was made by Judge Thomas A. Bush and Sheriff McCoy to keep the records in the Whaley House. Old Town boosters guarded the records against theft with firearms and a cannon. Newly appointed County Clerk Scott, a pro-New Towner and others waited for the right time to strike. While Thomas Whaley was out of town and while other Old Town proponents considered the situation under control, on the evening of March 31, the New Town contingent under Scott and his gang took express wagons to the Whaley House, broke into the courtroom, loaded the records in a wagon, and carted them over to 6th and G Streets where they were stored on the second floor of the Wells Fargo building. The transfer of power had unceremoniously passed from Old Town to New Town.

1906 reenactment of the night-time removal
of the Court House records from the Whaley House
(Courtesy of the Historical Shrine Foundation)

A visibly upset Thomas Whaley returned from his trip to find that not only had his house been broken into and all the court records removed, but that the county would no longer be paying him to store records in his house, even though the lease had not expired. On April 14, 1871, Whaley wrote to the Board of Supervisors claiming he was owed rent from County for brick building formerly occupied as Court House, and proposed that he be allowed to rent the building to other parties, deducting the amount so received from the rent due from the County. Whaley's demanded compensation never came, and the controversy signified the end of Old Town dominance over San Diego political affairs. It was no longer the county seat, and its glory had departed.

During August 1871, Whaley again wrote the county regarding payments due him for broken glass in the house and rent due for April, May and June. This was to no avail.

On October 4, 1871, the San Diego and Gila Southern Pacific and Atlantic Railroad Company had their annual meeting of stockholders and the following directors were elected: C.L. Carr, E.W. Morse, J.S. Mannasse, Louis Rose, Thomas Whaley, Gustave Witfeld, Wm. N. Robinson, Thomas S. Sedgwick, A.E. Horton, James McCoy, J.G. Estudillo, M, Schiller, and Bryant Howard.

During February 1872, the Pioneer Society was organized. Members included: Thomas Whaley, W.B. Couts, Jose Estudillo, George Lyons,

Marcus Schiller, James Connors, and E.W. Bushyhead. Jose Estudillo served as the secretary.

On May 9, 1872, Thomas Whaley announced himself as a candidate for city trustee of the First Ward. One newspaper article stated that, "Whaley is a good man, but the fact that he is ardently supported by the bankers will cause many of his friends to vote for Mr. Estudillo., whose election was assured in any event." Another article said that "Jose G. Estudillo will have a clear field before him, and will leave his opponent so far behind in the race that he will never think of running for office again." The election results listed on May 10, 1872 stated that Jose Estudillo had 50 votes, while Thomas Whaley garnered only 17.

Social Party

INVITATION.

San Diego, Cal. 1872

M___

You are respectfully invited to attend a PARTY to be given at the house of THOMAS WHALEY, in Old San Diego, on the .... 187_.

Very Respectfully,

Courtesy of the Historical Shrine Foundation

An article in the **Union** dated July 2, 1872, stated, "A large number of friends of Miss Annie Whaley were invited to participate in a party given her at the residence of her father, at Old Town, on Saturday night last. The gathering was to celebrate the young lady's birthday, and was merrily enjoyed by all who attended."

On August 1, 1872, another article in the **Union** said, "Emulating the example of the Grant boys, the Greeley boys of Old Town organized a club the other day, and elected the following officers: F.M. Whaley, president; E. Evans, v.p.; J James Connors, secretary; Wm. Connors, treasurer; Albert Smith, captain; M. Stewart, standard bearer - organization of Democrat boys."

During the Depression of 1873, Whaley & Crosthwaite's business venture failed. Thomas Whaley was deeply in debt, and appealed to his mother for a loan. Whaley set off for New York to help his mother settle his father's estate (his father died in 1832) which stipulated that when the youngest child reached 20, the proceeds would be divided up among family members. Since the youngest child had long since reached the age of 20, the estate was settled and Thomas received $5,000. This went to pay his debts in San Diego. Whaley remained in New York as an agent for Edward P. Young, a Trans-Atlantic brokerage merchant, and managed Young's properties.

An article in the **Union** dated April 29, 1873 stated, "We are glad to learn that Mr. Thomas Whaley has recovered from his recent severe illness, and is now able to be out." Less than a week later on May 4, 1873, the **Union** noted, "We were pleased to see Mr. Thomas Whaley on the street today. He has nearly recovered his usual health." By the end of May, Thomas Whaley, and Mr. and Mrs. E.W. Morse of San Diego headed east for three or four months on the steamer, Arizona. While Thomas was still in New York, Anna Whaley held a dance for the young boys and girls of Old Town on July 4th. Whaley wrote from New York that he was healthy again and enjoying his trip. He was also convinced that a number of visitors would be coming to San Diego in the fall and winter months.

The Whaleys son, Francis Hinton Whaley at 18, became a local agent for **Pacific Monthly**, a magazine for boys and girls that published in San Francisco. During 1873, the voters register lists: Thomas Whaley as being 44 years of age, a merchant from New York. On July 8, 1874, a reunion took place in Anna Whaley's house, with dancing going on until late. On December 24, 1874, a note in the newspaper states that Frank Whaley, president of the Clavelle Social Club, is in charge of a Christmas Tree party to be given at Old Town this evening. This is a private gathering, and cards of invitation will be presented at the door.

On March 31, 1875, the Clavelle Social Club met at the residence of Thomas Whaley. The officers were Francis Whaley, William E. Connors, Alexander Lyons, and George Lyons. The San Diego Historical Society was invited to one of the group's events at the Whaley House where there was a pleasant dancing party. Music was supplied by the band of the club, and it received numerous compliments. After the dance, the band serenaded the young ladies of the place, and was greeted with a light in the window wherever they went.

On October 20, 1875, the newspaper noted that "Thomas Whaley, who has been absent in the East nearly two years, returned to San Diego by steamer." On July 4, 1876, The Old Town folks celebrated the 4th of July with a picnic in Rose's Canon and in the evening there was a dance at the house of Mrs. Thomas Whaley. Everyone had a very happy time.

On October 31, 1876, Frank Whaley left for the Centennial. The **Union** called Frank, "... a bright young gentleman who was graduated as a fellow of 'art preservation' in the **Union** office has entered upon the publication of a neat and interesting literary weekly named, **The What Not**, in San Bernardino."

During November 1879, Thomas Whaley was back in San Francisco, attempting to procure employment with the Quartermaster Department, and solicited contributions for lands for the Atchison, Topeka and Santa Fe Railroad. He was unable to secure a position, and returned to San Diego in low spirits. According to locals, his family was in dire straights, as he had no position and no money. His property was held by his good friend, E.W. Morse, and he was delinquent on the tax rolls. His only income was roughly $25 a month paid in city script for his services as clerk for city trustees.

Unfortunately, the script was only redeemable for 40 cents on the dollar. Fortunately, his son Francis Whaley sent money and was able to keep the family from starving. His depression affected his family who complained of his idleness, poverty, despair, and abuse, particularly toward his son, George who wanted to be a musician. George was finally driven from the house, no longer able to tolerate his father's anger. He found a place downtown where he played the violin and adopted his mother's maiden name.

The Whaley House in Old Town circa 1880s with upper balcony, five upstairs windows, the railroad line in front of the house, and no front porch railing.
(Courtesy of the Historical Shrine Foundation)

On March 4, 1880, George Whaley made his first public appearance as a violinist at Horton Hall, where the **Union** reported, "Considering .the short time he has been practicing, the music he draws from the violin is really wonderful. George began practicing two years ago and is self-taught."

On October 2, 1880, Thomas Whaley was commissioned as Notary Public for San Diego County, with his office on the corner of Fifth & E Streets. Later in October, Whaley formed a real estate firm with E.W. Morse, and C.P. Noell at 5th & E Streets in downtown San Diego During 1881-1882, Thomas Whaley was the city clerk. On July 15, 1881, Francis Whaley published the first edition of the **San Luis Rey Star**, an Oceanside newspaper. He learned the trade from interning at the **San Diego Union** office in Old Town. On October 19, 1881, Francis Whaley, who was said to have extensive legal experience, was appointed Justice of the Peace at San Luis Rey. On April 27, 1882, Judge Frank Whaley was noted as the head of the **San Luis Rey Star**.

On January 5, 1882, Violet Eliose Whaley and George T. Bertolacci were married in Old San Diego by Rev. Dr. Bunker along with her sister, Anna Amelia Whaley who married John Thomas Whaley, a first cousin and son of Henry Hurst Whaley. On September 24, 1882, Thomas Whaley decided to run for the job of County Treasurer. On October 5, 1882, Thomas Whaley celebrated his 59th birthday. This was on the same day that his granddaughter, Mabel Eloise who was born to Anna Amelia and John T. Whaley.

In the files of the **San Diego Union**, it was noted that Violet Whaley Bertolacci was granted a divorce on April 12, 1883, only a year and three months after being married. During June 1883, Lillian Whaley became the first girl in a class of six to graduate from Russ High School, which eventually became San Diego High School. In August of the same year, Lillian was hired as an assistant teacher in National City. Francis H. Whaley was appointed a Notary Public for San Diego County on March 30, 1884.

Photograph courtesy of Alex Sill, West Hills, California

During 1885, The Trans-continental railroad was connected to San Diego. A great tragedy also took place at the Whaley House that year. The events were documented by Margaret Heron James, from the Escondido Family Genealogy as, "Tragedy at the Whaley House." A **San Diego Weekly Union** headline dated August 27, 1885, stated, "Tragedy struck the Whaley household again in 1885. The headline read 'Through the Dark Portals, Violet Whaley Shoots Herself Through the Heart and Finds the Rest That Earth has Refused... At 10 o'clock Wednesday morning, the people of this city were startled by the report that a young lady living in Old San Diego had committed suicide by shooting herself through the heart. Investigation proved thc story to be only too true, and learning an inquest was to be held at once, a representative of The Union secured a conveyance and drove to the scene of the tragedy, the residence of Mr. Thomas Whaley, his second eldest daughter, Violet, being the unfortunate victim of self-destruction."

"When we arrived the body was all prepared for examination by the Coroner's jury, when they should be summoned. The dead reposed on an improvised cot, neatly draped, and the calm face looking out from the laces loving hands had placed about the throat and brow showed little of the heated battle that had raged about the heart until chilled by the leaden messenger of death— the fatal pistol ball. The long, jetty locks were combed back from an olive brow, high and broad, indicative of mental power, capable of extreme joy in success, or a frenzied despair in adversity," "She looked sadly beautiful in death Indeed, a Violet has fallen from the parent stem. Only 22 years of age, yet a victim to melancholy. Three years ago she was married, but unhappily, against her parents' advice and to a worthless fellow, with whom she lived but two weeks. Since that time, she has been living with her parents and two sisters at North San Diego, or Old Town. A divorce was procured from her faithless husband, Edson, who had several aliases, and she returned to her maiden name; that marriage blighted her life and its curse has built her tomb. Refined and intelligent, and a passionate-lover of the beautiful in nature, she also worshiped the arts, and music was her passion. But the piano is now silent, and the guitar will never more 'wake to her touch."

"A note was found upon which she had written a few frenzied sentences, saying her life was a lie, that she was fated, life was intolerable to herself, and it would be better for her friends when she was dead, The wording of the note showed she was 'laboring under great mental excitement when it was written."

> Mad from life's history,
> Swift to death's mystery;
> Glad to be hurled
> Anywhere, anywhere, out of this world
> But let the curtain be drawn,
> she has gone to meet her God,
> He shall judge of the tired spirit hastened to its creator

Lillian Whaley provided testimony at the inquest held on the body as follows: "I reside at Old San Diego. The person lying here is Violet E. Whaley, age 22 years. I last saw her alive about two o'clock this morning. She left her room about 6, dressed, went out and remained about half an hour. Father went down to get his horse, then came up and asked where Violet was. After he went down the second time he opened the back door and called to her and immediately after mamma and I heard the shot. Coming downstairs, I found papa had brought her in, apparently dead. He took her into the parlor. I knew she was shot because I could see the blood. My sister threatened to take her life on the 5th of July this year. I think she was tired of life. She thought no one cared for her and her life was a burden. She attempted to take her life at that time by jumping into a cistern out here. She took no interest in anything since that time. She was under Dr. Gregg's treatment. She was anxious to have health, but was tired of life. She had been married but was divorced and took her maiden name. She slept by the side of the bed where mamma and I slept. There were no bad feelings in the family. We did all we could to make it pleasant for her. I am positive that she had my father's pistol this morning. Yesterday or the day before, she asked father for a bunch of keys among which was one to a box in which she heard him say long ago he had a pistol locked up. She went to father's room, got the pistol and took it into an adjoining room, placing it in the bureau. She had been misleading us for two or three mornings by getting up and going down, and coming back again. This morning she went as usual, but remained so long as to arouse my suspicions and father's. Mother thought nothing of it. Going out, she passed through father's room, to the room where she hid the pistol. I heard a pistol shot about 6:30. She shot herself while in the privy."

Thomas Whaley's testimony follows: Age 61, residence San Diego, real estate dealer. Deceased was 22 years old, a native of this state, born in San Francisco. She lived at home with parents. I last saw her in my room this morning. She passed in and out again about 6 o'clock. I heard her unlock the door, go down stairs, and unlock back door. Shortly afterwards I got up and dressed and hurried down into backyard. I thought she might be in water closet. I called to her and asked if she would be out soon, and she said no. I walked up and down the backyard may be a couple of minutes and then asked again if she would be out soon. She said no. I went into adjoining closet and then went to stable and attended to my horse. I went back to my room, washed, finished dressing and came downstairs again. I went into the room and sat down to breakfast, being in a hurry to get downtown before the heat of the day. I thought Violet might like a peach, so I took one. I rose and went to the door and asked her if she wanted a peach. As I called out, I heard the pistol shot. That was about 6:30 a.m. I sprang instantly forward and went in the closet. I found Violet sitting upon the lower seats. I took her in my arms and carried her into house. As I entered, I called to her mother, that Violet had shot herself. I took her into parlor and laid her upon the lounge.

The Whaley House in Old Town with no upper balcony, five upstairs windows and no front porch railing in front of the house.
(Courtesy of the Historical Shrine Foundation)

She was alive when I laid her on lounge. I don't think she lived more than 10 or 15 minutes. She did not speak or groan. My impulse was to go instantly for a doctor. Mrs. Whaley suggested I had better go down to the Altamiranos family as they could go quicker. This I did. I don't think she was alive when I came back. I looked around water closet but could find no weapon. I raised the lids and saw the barrel protruding. I think it was my revolver. I have looked in box and found my revolver gone. I kept it in box with private papers. The revolver had been there a year or eighteen months. It was small revolver with six or seven chambers that had been loaded for three years. It is about 32 caliber. The day before yesterday Violet came to stable and asked for my keys saying she wanted to open a little box. I gave them and asked her to return them as I would want them in New San Diego. When she brought them back, I asked her if she had opened the box, and she said no. Again yesterday morning she got the keys and when she returned them and was asked if she had opened the box, and she said yes. I told her she was fortunate as there were but two keys on the ring. She was then as cheerful as she had been for some time. On July 5th, I was harnessing my horse and heard a scream issuing from the cistern. I went there and found Violet holding to the pipe. I asked if she could hold on. She said yes. I ran to the house and told my wife. Violet had jumped into the cistern. When the shooting took place, there was no one present but my wife and two daughters. Violet had shown no particular life or interest for some time. She was naturally lively; loved music; played piano and guitar. She seemed to take more interest in such things lately and we thought she was getting better. Found a note in back porch saying she was tired of life.

The Jury's verdict was presented as follows, "We, the jury summoned to inquire into the cause of the death of Violet E. Whaley, find that her death was caused by her shooting herself through the heart with a pistol held in her own hands; while laboring under mental aberration:

Signed, John N. Young, Foreman
Lua Sune
S. A. Atino,
John Burton

Salmendo Estudillo,
Patrick O'Neill,
Ramon Osuna,

In the same newspaper was an article about Violet's funeral. "The funeral of the unhappy Violet Eloise Whaley took place from the Episcopal Church, Rev. H. B. Restarick officiating, at 2 o'clock yesterday afternoon. The services were very sad and impressive, and called many an unshed tear to the eyes of those present. The coffin was enshrouded in floral offerings, and a beautiful garland of white lilies, tulips and roses reposed on the casket over this heart of the dead. The church was filled by friends of the deceased, and of the family, who had gathered to pay their respects to the dead. From the church the remains were borne to Mount Hope Cemetery for interment, followed by a large number of carriages. At the grave a prayer for the dead went up from all hearts, as the minister with a few well-chosen words committed the body beneath and her soul to God. She now sleeps the sleep of death, but let us believe the Violet shall bloom — again—beyond the dark river, and the sweet perfume of a chastened spirit shall be wafted back to earth to bless her stricken parents, sad brothers and weeping sisters."

Early photograph of the Whaley House with the small upper balcony, three upstairs windows and railroad line in front of the house.
(Courtesy of the San Diego Historical Society)

The **San Diego Union** published the following response from Thomas and Anna Whaley on August 23, 1885 as follows: "We desire to express our heartfelt thanks for the many kindness' shown us by loving and sympathetic friends, both Spanish and American, during our recent terrible bereavement. To Mr. Restarick, our generous pastor, for his kind consolation: to Mr. Mason and the school children of Old Town, for their thoughtfulness in singing their parting songs at the late home (Whaley House) of their beloved friend: and to the press of San Diego and National City for their consoling notices, we extend assurances of our grateful remembrance. Wishing all our friends happiness and lives free from the trying ordeal, such as has been our experience, we remain, Thomas Whaley and Mrs Thomas Whaley"

During 1885, Thomas Whaley became a City Trustee. In November of the same year, Thomas Whaley commenced building a one-story frame house, 30x38, on his property near the junction of E and State Streets in San Diego, becoming the family residence for many years. On August 24, 1885, it was noted in the local newspaper that Francis H. Whaley was retiring for reasons of poor health.

Thomas Whaley retired in 1888, having served as City Clerk, Notary Public and real estate representative for several years. On December 31, 1888, Francis Hinton Whaley married Susan E. Murray, the daughter of Senator & Mrs. J.P. Murray of Mendocino in Mendocino, California. A newspaper clipping in 1889 noted that the Whaley House was occupied by Mr. W.M.Barnes, a mine owner from El Paso, Texas. On November 22, 1889, Francis and Susan Whaley became proud parents of a daughter.

Thomas Whaley
(Courtesy of the Historical Shrine Foundation)

On December 14, 1890, at the age of 67, Thomas Whaley died at 933 State Street in San Diego.

On May 12, 1893, Anna's mother, Victoria DeLaunay, a native of Rouen, Normandy, France, died at age 90 at the State Street address.

On December 18, 1905, Anna Amelia Whaley, the daughter of Thomas and Anna Whaley, died in Modesto, California.

In 1909, a dance was held at the Whaley House in Old Town. Hosted by Anna Whaley, 50 couples attended, where old time guitar and violin music filled the house for first time in 25 years.

From 1909 until 1910, Francis (Frank) Whaley lived in the Whaley House and began restoration of the building, which had been abandoned for a number of years.

During 1912, the remaining Whaley family members were listed as follows: George H. Whaley, musician; Lillian Whaley, assistant at the Public Library; Francis H. Whaley; Anna E. Whaley (widow of Thomas) resided in restored Whaley House which is now utilized as an Old Town tourist attraction (the restoration of the Whaley house coincided with the restoration of the Casa de Estudillo now promoted as Ramona's Marriage Place, and the establishment of the San Diego Electric Railway down San Diego Avenue)

Courtesy of Alex Sill, West Hills, California

On February 24, 1913, Anna Whaley, widow of Thomas, died in the house in Old Town. Anna was 80 years of age, and survived by Francis, George, and Lillian C. Whaley.

On November 19, 1914, Francis Whaley, the first born child of Thomas and Anna Whaley, died in the Whaley House. The funeral was held in the house. Francis ran **the <u>San Luis Rey Star</u>** in 1880s; was the Justice of the Peace in Old Town; was a familiar figure at Old Town; and he interested tourists in San Diego's early history. During his later years Francis lived with his sister, Corinne, at the family home.

During 1915, George H. Whaley, musician, and Lillian C. Whaley, an assistant at the Public Library lived in Whaley house.

On January 5, 1928, George H. Whaley passed away, and Lillian resided in the Whaley House alone.

From 1932 until 1935, Lillian C. Whaley lived in the Whaley House with her cousins, Mr. & Mrs. Frederick James and their son, Frederick Jr. During 1935, Lillian entered a nursing home due to ill health.

The Whaley House prior to restoration
(Courtesy of the San Diego Historical Society)

On August 10, 1953, the Whaley House was placed under a Court Order for immediate liquidation to provide for physical care of Corinne Whaley. A progressive Old Town realtor named Heffner, listed property for sale. The property was considered a possible site for a motel. Local activists rallied to save the Whaley House from destruction.

On September 14, 1953, Lillian Corinne Whaley died in San Diego. She was a member of the first graduating class of San Diego High School, a schoolteacher at San Luis Rey and National City and assistant librarian at the Carnegie Library in San Diego.

The deteriorating house of uniquely classical architecture was on the verge of being scrapped. If not for the tireless work of its admirers who borrowed money to preserve it at the 11th hour of its existence, the memories of a bygone era would be left only to history books and personal accounts. As San Diego was on the verge of being abandoned by the Spanish in 1770, which took a last-minute miracle to save, the Whaley House faced a similar fate. It was also rescued from demolition. Its devoted sponsors accomplished the near impossible task of raising funds to preserve the house as a testament to San Diego's lusty youth. In 1957-1960, the Board of Supervisors of the County of San Diego agreed to purchase and renovate the house.

Reconstruction of the Whaley House with a view of the deserted courtroom.
Fireplace and entrance to the wine cellar lie in the background.
(Courtesy of the San Diego Historical Society)

Credit for the initial preservation efforts go to the late June and Jim Reading, the Board of Supervisors, the Society of California Pioneers of San Francisco, and members and volunteers of the Historical Shrine Foundation. June Reading sadly passed away in 1998, and is no doubt watching over her beloved house.

The current caretakers, the County of San Diego and Save Our Heritage Organization, now devote their time and energy to the restoration of one of the most unique and important landmarks in southern California.

Photograph of The restored Whaley House
(Courtesy of the Historical Shrine Foundation)

Plan of the Whaley House
Downstairs Rooms

1. Courtroom
2. General Store
3. Parlor
4. Study
5. Guest Room
6. Hallway
7. Dining Room
8. Porch

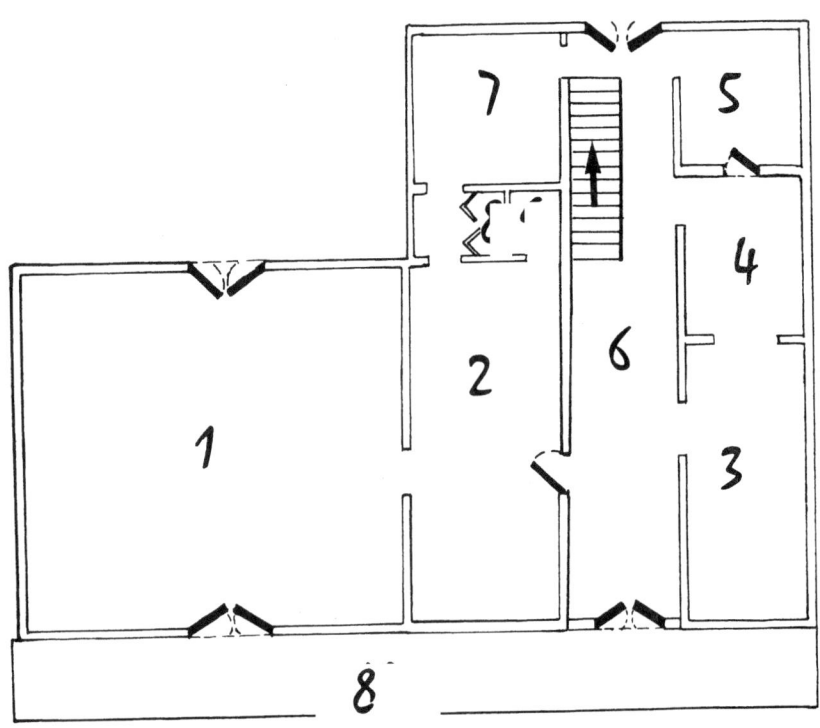

Plan of the Whaley House
Upstairs Rooms

1. Theater
2. Theater
3. Bedroom
4. Bedroom
5. Hallway
6. Master Bedroom
7. Dressing Room
8. Balcony

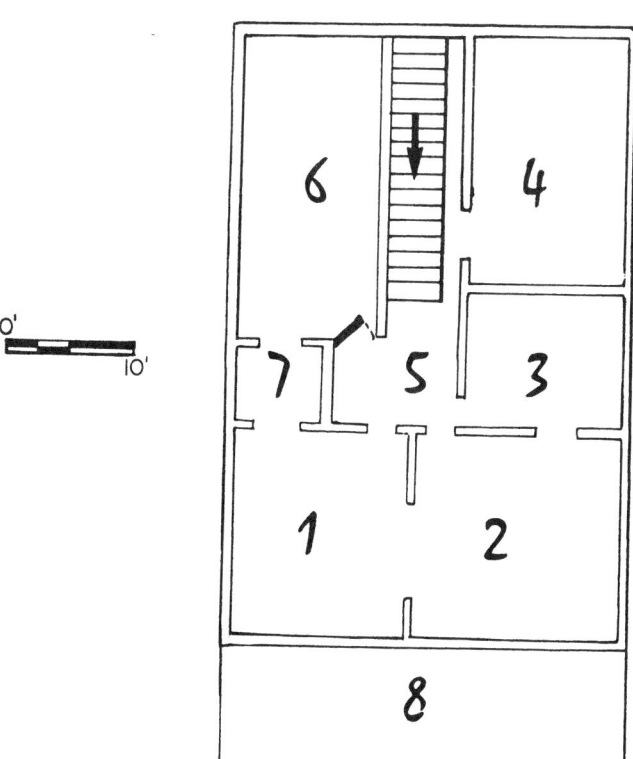

A Textbook Case for Hauntings

They come at night often. And often they come into your most private, intimate time: sleep. It is as if unconsciousness—like madness—is some sort of in-road to where they live and play. But they also show themselves in broad light making their appearance even more mysterious by not being so mysterious as to use darkness for a cover. They manifest themselves in many guises, using all your senses. Auditory apparitions seem to be the most common accounting for about 60 percent of the experiences, but all the senses are involved including that unnamed sense that simply tells you something is not quite right by sending that special chill. And they manifest themselves just about anywhere—at the foot of your bed, across a sun-showered field, through a window or door, or sometimes as just light or shadow. But, we know they especially show themselves at Gettysburg. "They," of course, are "ghosts." "Spirits" may be a better, less volatile term, but we're talking about the same thing: a sound, a smell of something that is long gone; a vision, a touch out of time and beyond reason of someone who is dead. And, perhaps, "dead" isn't the right word either with its connotations of final and eventual decay. If the spirit is the very essence of the person and the body is something it just lives in and breathes out of for a while, then maybe the word for the moment of cessation of the living body in terms of what the spirit does is "to move on. "

Mark Nesbitt, **Ghosts of Gettysburg III** (1995)

Possible face in the former downstairs study
Photograph by Ellen C.
(Courtesy of the Historical Shrine Foundation)

Who are they? What do they want? What are they? Why are they still here? There are loads of questions but unfortunately very few answers— even after decades of research and scientific investigation. Agreement and disagreement, a natural dichotomy exists when ghosts and the paranormal become a topic of conversation among the living. Perhaps it is because the topic is so personal, like politics and religion. The very essence of the discussion lies in whether or not one believes in life after death and whether we have a soul which transcends physical death. To be sure, the issue of transcending death has been bantered about in philosophical, psychological and religious circles since the first human being "passed away."

Whether deaths comes in the heat of battle; in an emotionally-charged situation prompted by hatred, rage, jealousy or revenge; whether alone or in the comforting arms of a loved one, or surrounded by others, the question of what happens next, is most certainly on everyone's minds. The rituals surrounding death are numerous. Bidding farewell to one who has passed away takes many forms. The journey into the unknown begins at birth when we must face our mortality almost immediately—through our developing religious convictions—to dealing with the death of someone close to us. The question of whether we have a soul, a life force, an eternal energy consciousness may be resolved during one's lifetime, yet what actually happens to this life force at the moment of death becomes foggy and distorted. If we have a soul, where does it go? What is the journey like? Do we remain behind to right our wrongs? Is there a limbo, a purgatory, or worse, a hell where we must wait until greater power grants us access to a divine afterlife? Do the scores of movies, plays or books about the subject even come close to describing what lies beyond the veil of this physical reality?

Misty form rising from the bed in fhe former upstairs guest room
(Now the older children's bedroom)
Photograph by Doreen Turner (Courtesy of the Historical Shrine Foundation)

Ghosts exist or for lack of a better word, co-exist in the physical realm, which for us is this planet and our domain. For centuries they have defied logic and eluded scientific explanation. They are an enigma as well as a profound mystery awaiting an explanation that will satisfy "non-believers." To those who believe, they are as real as you or I in the flesh. No amount of argument to the contrary can change the believers minds, for they are convinced that they have experienced something profound, mysterious, enlightening and elusive. The encounter has allowed them to pierce the veil of eternity and briefly contact other dimensions; a portal between life and afterlife where the thin thread of reality and illusion vanishes for an instant. This highly personal encounter is usually instantaneous, and affects only a fragment of an individual's total sensory potential, yet it leaves a lasting impression that can oftentimes change one's religious belief. For some, seeing a ghost can be as awe-inspiring as any religious experience. They have connected with something otherworldly, unexplainable, intangible— even angelic in some instances. Whatever the label for this phenomenon, the experience leaves a lasting impression.

We should not fear ghosts, but have respect, for in most instances that energy does not exist to harm us, but possibly to teach, to guide, or ask us for assistance in helping them reach "the light;", to show us the potential for surviving death for those who need assurances that something better lies beyond pain and suffering—or, perhaps if we see them as evil they will not disappoint. If we in truth have a soul, a spiritual energy, then we are akin to those twilight dwellers, those restless denizens of the hidden dimension, except for our bodies which we too shall shed when we embark on our journey after life. Looking at the possibility of encountering a spirit without fear is difficult for most—even the thought sends a chill down the back; however, a healthy respect for the possibility of an afterlife encounter may mean walking with trepidation into an old deserted house on a moon-lit night. Not everyone is frightened, but all are curious, because everyone likes a good mystery, a puzzle to solve; and the puzzle of whether there is life after death as evidenced by paranormal phenomena may be the last great mystery out there to solve.

A discussion of ghosts or hauntings will always involve a physical backdrop, like a set in a movie, replete with costumes and make-up. It will also entail a script, where invisible performers act out their scenes which are recorded on invisible celluloid to be replayed when the proper set of conditions are in place. Some people either have a predisposition to the paranormal (acting like transmitters), or are extremely sensitive to the psychic wavelength or paranormal energy, and are fortunate enough to catch glimpses of these "premiers" which have been stored away in a vault that does not depend upon time or space to start the projector. Again, the context (history, time, and location) provides the establishing point for understanding the phenomena; without it, we are truly at a loss for an explanation as to why certain people "remain behind." Just because we cannot see, something doesn't mean it isn't there; and just because we cannot explain something, doesn't mean it doesn't exist. Faith and belief can always be counted on to bridge the gap between reality and illusion, and creativity and pragmatism. Are ghosts, mirrors for mankind, mimicking the plethora of emotions, actions and responses exhibited by the living for providing messages or insights into the meaning of life itself on this physical plane of existence? Could they be messengers who come like the ghosts of Christmas past, present, and future to warn us, to enlighten us, to bring us hope, or show us what it may be like if we do not change our ways?

Some ghosts appear as demons, others as angels. Some repeat patterns while others warn, throw tantrums, celebrate or appear sad, confused, and even disoriented. From an emotional standpoint, Ghosts-r-us, imitating the living in every way. They are the epitome of the unknown, the mysterious, uncertainty, fear, longing, goodness, and love. They are also reminders that the flesh will get weak and the physical environment is only temporary, but perhaps the soul remains incorruptible and eternal. If ghosts are mirrors for us, because they once were like us, then we should look at them not with remorse or pity, but with kindness and love and wish them God-speed to complete their metaphysical journey to the light of oneness with all things, while we ponder our own predicament, and come to terms with our own mortality.

The Whaley House appears as a working laboratory for the study of the paranormal, one of the few places where the history of hauntings is alive and active, not simply an annotation in a book citing the last apparition as occurring sometime in the 16th or 17 century—thus, relegated to a folk tale or legend. What happens inside the house gives those who believe in the concept of the paranormal continuing hope that due to the special energy emanating within the house, researchers may be able to capture convincing proof that will lay the skeptics to rest with regard to the matter of whether or not we survive physical death.

From the history, we move to the hauntings, we now enter another dimension where some feel that death is merely an extension of life, separated by a very thin veil. Here, in this nether world, those once of flesh and blood, continue on their appointed rounds without the physical constraints that saddle us. If this concept is true, then Thomas, Anna, Violet, and many more who occupied the Whaley House in life, continue to visit their former abode, crossing paths with us, the living and manifesting as a wisp of wind, a gentle touch, a whiff of perfume or cigar, a shadow on the wall, a stray note on a personless piano, or a faint whisper that bids the visitor welcome!

Thomas Whaley House Museum, Old Town, San Diego

The following information was provided by Save Our Heritage Organization (SOHO), who has been actively involved in serving San Diego County since 1969.

This two-story Greek Revival style brick residence in San Diego's Old Town, was designed by Thomas Whaley and completed in 1857. The home, acclaimed as the "finest new brick block in Southern California" by the San Diego Herald, contained mahogany and rosewood furniture, damask drapes, and Brussels carpets. Whaley established his general store in this residence, and solicited cash customers only. The Whaleys moved to San Francisco but returned to San Diego in 1868. Whaley family members would live in the house for nearly a century.

From October 1868 to January 1869, the Tanner Troupe Theatre operated out of the front upstairs bedroom. The San Diego County Courthouse utilized the former granary in August 1869 and rented three upstairs rooms for records storage. After the establishment of New Town San Diego by Alonzo Horton in 1868, the town focus changed to present day downtown San Diego.

During a March 1871 raid, courthouse documents were removed from the Whaley House and taken to Horton's Hall on 6th and F in San Diego. After the County's exit, Whaley connected the former granary and courtroom to the residence, changed windows and doors, and altered the front portico.

On October 31, 1956, the County of San Diego purchased the historic Whaley House, and undertook a major renovation of the property. During November of 2000, SOHO accepted responsibility of administering to the daily operation of the Whaley House from the County of San Diego. A number of changes have been to the interior since that time. Inappropriate furnishings have been removed or changed to faithfully portray the house as it was from the late 1860s to the 1880s. Their spirited inhabitants are apparently satisfied with the changes, as they continue to make their presence known to visitors and staff on a regular basis.

The Whaley House is open from 10am to 4:30 every day except Tuesdays. Admission: adults $5.00, seniors $4.00, and children $3.00. Tickets can be purchased in the SOHO Museum Shop next door. This two-story Greek Revival style brick residence on San Diego Avenue, designed by Thomas Whaley, was completed in 1857. The Whaley House is operated by SOHO.

The Ghost of Yankee Jim Robinson

*The following information was extracted from a Souvenir Program, entitled **The True Story of the Ghost of "Yankee Jim"** by Frances Bardacke, which was reprinted from San Diego Magazine. The authors were granted permission to use this information in this book by the Historic Shrine Foundation.*

If the ghost of Yankee Jim Robinson wanders through the halls of the Whaley House, I have yet to meet him there. Although I am a firm believer in the policy of live and let live even after death, I don't easily see ghosts. However, the theory that Yankee Jim's presence is still felt on the premises is something else again. I find Yankee Jim's haunting the most persistent I have yet encountered. His name and origin have never been established and his place in history books is haphazard, at best, yet he has never let San Diego forget him completely. He moved in on the Whaley Family when they built a house on the sight of his hanging. Is it possible that a ghost with such a strong personality didn't have a history before August 13, 1852! Could the carnivorous gold fields of California have swallowed him whole, leaving no traces of the big, imposing, six-foot-three desperado!

Stairs looking toward the first floor
(Courtesy of SOHO)

I may not see ghosts, but certainly, something kept nagging at me. Early this spring I took a trip up north, and back in Time, to see if I couldn't discover who Yankee Jim was before he moved down to San Diego and took up residence in the Whaley House. I started in the libraries, checking every James Robinson and Yankee Jim of the Gold Rush. I read the manuscript of the pioneers and the notes and scrapbooks of the compulsive chroniclers Benjamin Hays and Hubert H. Bancroft. I read State records, personal letters, and the contemporary fact and fiction of old newspapers. Some where I ran across my great-grandfather but didn't have time to pay my respects.

In the Bancroft Collection, among the documents of the California Government of Monterrey I found a Santiago Robinson who signed a petition for entry into California in 1842. Santiago, a Spanish version of James, was the name Padre Holbein had put on Yankee Jim's death certificate. In one notation he was referred to as an Americano, in another as de las Islas Bermudas. Larkin, the American consul at Monterrey, writes in his records that James Robinson, a native of the Bermudas and mate on the American schooner the Julia Anne, was discharged in 1841 and in 1842 petitioned to enter California and was granted a one-year entry. That was the closest I got. I was looking for a sailor because it seemed to me only a sailor would try to steal a thirty-ton schooner to make a getaway. Most landlubbers "borrowed" horses. But I was looking for a Nova Scotian bluenose or an English Sidney-duck, who had somehow earned the nickname Yankee Jim.

I gave up looking for the man and decided to check the town Yankee Jims in Placer County. Thirty miles east of Auburn, up on a ridge between the North and Middle Forks of the American River, there is a town called Forest Hills. Five miles north where the twisting road to Colfax crosses a dirt road that seems to go no place in particular is a rock marker that reads: Yankee Jims - Gold was discovered here in 1850 by "Yankee Jim" a reputed lawless character and by 1857 [the] town was one of most important in Placer County. The first mining ditch in this county constructed here by H. Starr and Eugene Phelps. Colonel William McClure introduced hydraulic mining in this area in June of 1853 - State Registered Landmark No. 398.

What was in 1855 the sixteenth-largest town in California now consists of six families. The libelous, off-hand way they spoke of the Town's founder convinced me that the big bandit in the red shirt couldn't have been haunting them. Most people and histories insist he was an escaped convict from Sydney and the number of places he was supposed to have been hanged for his evil deeds are, to press a point, legend. Finally, in the Placer County Directory of 1861, I discovered "Yankee Jim and his companions, six in number, at Yankee Jims Dry Diggins during the winter of 1850." That led me to a story by Mr. Currier, told to Mr. Fairchild and reported in The History of Placer County by Myron Angel and M. D. Fairchild, printed in 1882.

Mr. Benjamin Currier's story goes like this: In [1849], because the winters were so severe, and unguarded gold strikes were so easily lost, "dry diggins,' which were up on the ridges and not liable to flooding-out, were at a premium. That year rumors reached Barnes Gap on the North Fork that there was a rich strike up on the ridge to the South and that a character named Yankee Jim was bringing large nuggets into the trading camp from there. Mr. Currier and five friends decided to trail the mysterious Yankee Jim to his camp and set out at night innocently explaining that they left after dark because they didn't want anyone to follow them. Yankee Jim had a reputation for giving followers the slip, and they lost him, but they moved in on two other miners at Shirt Tail Canyon. While the others were panning gold, Ben Currier, thinking, I suppose of the coming winter, kept on searching. One day exploring up towards the ridge in Busby Canyon, he found a man asleep under a bark shelter. When the miner woke up he seemed suspicious and told Currier he was worried because he had no more bullets for his gun. Currier offered to get him bullets and the man said that if he would keep his discovery a secret he would make it worth Currier's while. Mr. Currier didn't tell his friends and brought back some spare bullets and in gratitude the big stranger told him his name and offered to share his strike.

Courtroom
(Courtesy of SOHO)

He then told Mr. Currier that he it was whom they called Yankee Jim and said he was a native of the State of Maine. He also told his newly-formed acquaintance his proper name and the town of his nativity. These facts were all noted at the time in Mr. Currier's Journal, which is now in Boston, and are not remembered, else this work would be the first to rescue from obscurity and forever perpetuate the true name of that historical character, as well as locate his nationality. Common belief has obtained that he was an English Convict, in early days called "Sydney-Ducks," but Mr. Currier is of the firm opinion from his "patois" and knowledge of the New England States that he really was a Yankee and that for a number of years before the discovery of gold he had "combed the beach" along the California Coast, having previously run away from some ship."

Yankee Jim must have been fair game, for soon Ben Currier had told his friends and a coveted digging was a secret no longer. By 1850, according to one his story, it was "inundated by upwards of a thousand stalwart miners" and Yankee Jim had disappeared, his name and birth place forever lost in some diary back east. Only at the end of the account does it suddenly became interesting again. There, with a typical Northern Californian geographical error, is the story of the intent to pirate the Plutus; the story that even San Diego didn't know about until last winter. "As to the fate of Yankee Jim, there have been several accounts, the most probable of which is that he was hung by orders of an irregular Court at Los Angeles Sept. 18, 1852, for an attempt to steal, in the Harbor at Wilmington, the Pilot Boat Plutus with the intention of putting to sea, with the probable intent of engaging in piratical acts."

[The] Legend in Placer County may have substituted Los Angeles for San Diego, but the story of Yankee Jim's attempt to steal the pilot boat, the Plutus, is the same as the eyewitness account that J. Judson Ames wrote in the San Diego Herald of August 27, 1852.

Sybil Leek and Hans Holzer Meet the Whaley House Spirits

Funeral humor occupies a very special place within the human consciousness. No matter how sophisticated the culture or the individual, the need remains to render death less fearful with a little tentative ridicule. Perhaps laughter is itself an affirmation of life. Macabre jokes are always in vogue. A perennial favorite is the one about the boy who disrupts mourners at a burial service by rushing about crying, 'Programs! Programs! Get your programs! You can't tell the dead ones from the lives ones without a program!" For June Reading, director of the historic Whaley House in San Diego, the problem of determining the lives ones is no joke. After more than thirty years in a haunted house, she takes the apparitions that inhabit the showplace in her stride—though, admittedly, it's confusing to see someone wandering about and not know whether she or he is a living ticket holder or a specter from the original cast.

Antoinette May, **Haunted Houses of California** (1993)

Dr. Hans Holzer's coverage of the Whaley House hauntings, including the seance with English medium Sybil Leek in 1965 are well documented in his books:**Where the Ghosts Area: The Ultimate Guide to Haunted Houses** (1995); **True Ghost Stories** (1992); **America's Restless Ghosts (1992)**; and **Great American Ghost Stories** (1988). We appreciate his permission to extract the seance information for this publication.

Orbs on ceiling of the courtroom
(Courtesy of SOHO)

According to Holzer, a seance in the Whaley House was scheduled for Friday evening, June 25, 1965 with the famed psychic Sybil Leek, accompanied by Regis Philbin, and Holzer's wife Catherine. Leek entered the house after dark, followed by Holzer who allowed Leek to get her "clairvoyant bearings" prior to the trance session. The event was to be taped by a camera crew while Catherine Holzer assisted with the tape equipment. June Reading, the director of the Whaley House [who is now deceased], was responsible for arranging the event as well as bringing together about a dozen people who had seen unusual things in the house, witnesses who Holzer was anxious to interview individually. As Leek gathered her psychic impressions, Holzer went into the courthouse room to conduct the interviews—the excitement in the atmosphere was bound to stir up any ghost present! After the interviews, Holzer began looking for Leek who was wandering throughout the house attempting to pick up psychic impressions without interruptions.

After a brief search, Holzer found Leek seated, deep in thought in one of the old chairs which used to be in the kitchen—it was now downstairs in back of the living room. Holzer was finally able to break her train of thought and have her move on to the kitchen area. Sybil told Holzer that while she was standing in the entrance hall, looking at the post cards, she made it only half way up the stairs before a ghostly young girl came down and headed toward the kitchen—Leek following close behind. It was so real, that Leek thought it was Regis Philbin's daughter. It was the last thing she recalled prior to being brought back to reality by Holzer. Philbin's daughter had not been on the stairs and Leek then volunteered a description of the young girl as having long hair, and wearing a long dress. The little girl made her way to the table in the living room while Sybil found a seat in the rocking chair.

Upon further interrogation by Holzer, Leek commented that there was a great deal of confusion associated with the house—some of associated with an upstairs room which has been structurally altered. Leek confirmed two focal points of activity and that at least four ghost frequented the Whaley House. Leek picked up on the same spirit of a little girl as did William Richardson's group who visited the house in August 1965.That report did not reach Holzer until September, well after this seance— so Leek could not have read his mind about the occurrences.

Leek continued by stating that while deep in thought in the living room she obtained an impression of a child who died while he was very young, whereupon she obtained a date of 1872—The Readings exchanged glances. With that, Holzer, Leek and the other adjourned to the courtroom and the trance sequence began. Slumped over in a chair, Leek first picked up the parched voice of an entity who said the year was 46, and that he and everyone else around him had a bad fever and required water. Holzer calmed and reassured the spirit who would not identify itself. With that, Leek immediately picked up on a tremendous amount of confusion and the name Anna Bell who died very suddenly at the tender young age of 13 and said something about her chest. Leek said that the child understands very little about what is happening to her but her mother comes to visit. The house according to the spirit was used for buying and selling things. Leek said the child would not hurt anyone and remains tied to the kitchen area.

Suddenly, an angry male spirit came through. The name began with a C, or Calstrop, and said he was around 32 years-old and five feet ten. He wears a green coat, sports a mustache and side burns and frequents a room upstairs—the bedroom at the left at the top of the stairs. Leek picked up the fact that he had a business in the house with things that come from the sea. He is worried about papers, gave the date of 1872 and said that dividing the house was wrong. He died in the house and is confused and unhappy—but he wants the house all to himself and knows he is dead. The entity began laughing through Leek, and said it was funny that people come into the house thinking it is theirs—because it isn't. Holzer asked the spirit to pass over, that his urgent matter is no longer important. Leek said that the man was now upstairs. Leek continued getting information, such as the fact that her just walks around, does not like new things or any noise except when he makes it. He said his mother plays the organ and her name is Ann Lassay... Lannay. He died in 1889 and he like roaming around the house (actually, Whaley died in 1890, but according to Holzer, ghosts have difficulty recalling exact dates, but remember circumstances and emotional experiences well) Leek said the man continually worries about the house and the other papers taken from the house which are four miles away. He wants the papers returned to him and if he doesn't get the whole house back, he will make matters worse for the living (by triggering alarms, making noise, open windows, and fooling with the electricity). He was adamant that he is still the master of the house.

Several wispy forms in the courtroom
(Courtesy of SOHO)

Leek as the male entity continued responding to Holzer's questions, saying that when people come to visit, he walks around the garden. When asked about who inhabits the kitchen, the entity responded that a twelve-year-old child remains there to meet her mother, and his death was a tragedy, caused by the child ingesting something from the cupboard that killed her—an acid. Leek's entity said that the girl was in the way in a family of boys and that her father didn't care as much about the girl as he did about the house.

Holzer, when realizing that the male spirit would not go peacefully into the light, reassured it that the house was in effect, his. This act of placation didn't work as Leek said that he was a vicious spirit who would have his revenge on the house, even though Holzer explained that his enemies were all dead. The fact that a grave injustice was perpetrated against him made him all the more adamant to right the wrong—apparently, even if it took him, or his spirit eternities to do so. With that, Leek was brought out of her trance and back to normal. Holzer asked the Readings about the accuracy of what transpired and found out that the injustice that this man (by now it was concluded that the voice belonged to Thomas Whaley) was referring to, could have been the County's agreement to lease the courtroom from 1869 to 1871, with Whaley supplying the furniture and constructing two windows. The contract was voided without further compensation when New Town, under the direction of Alonzo Horton, became the new seat of power and the records were forcefully removed from the Whaley House. Whaley's appeals were never heard—a great injustice to a man who was such a dynamic force in Old Town. Power shifted from Old Town to New Town, and although the years passed, and eventually so did Whaley, his spirit lingered.

As for the young male ghost who inhabits the upstairs nursery, Holzer and the seance determined that several children died in the house, but no one could say for sure who it actually was—Leek's contact with a young male child's presence was a personality of someone who may have died of a bad fever, gave the faintly pronounced name of Fedor, and spoke of a mill where he worked. Asking June Reading to make some sense out of this information, she replied that the courtroom once served as a granary around 1855 to 1867. As far as the Russian spirit, it has been documented that there was a considerable otter trade along the Southern California coast prior to the American occupation of the area. The Russians established wells in this area and came to trade otter pelts. Holzer was utterly amazed, conceding that there was no way Sybil Leek could have known such obscure facts. Reading continued by saying that this would have taken place in the 1800s, after the Spanish had occupied the area.

Asking Reading if there was anything else she would like to comment on, Reading replied, that the references to the windows opening upstairs, and the ringing of these bells could not have been known by Leek since she had no time to acquaint herself with the stories, nor talk to anyone else about the occurrences in the short time she was around people. According to Holzer, the puzzling statements about "the other house" would also be resolved. As he and Sybil Leek were walking through the garden, inspecting the rear portion of the Whaley House, they discovered still another wooden house standing in the garden. Questioning Reading regarding this second house, Holzer was informed that it was called "'The Pendelton House." In order for this historic structure to be saved from destruction by the impending freeway, it had to be moved— it never belonged to the Whaleys although Thomas Whaley once tried to rent it.

According to Holzer, "no wonder the ghost was angry about the other house—it had been moved in his property without his consent. The name beginning with the letter "C" or Calstrop was still a mystery. Although all the other information coming from Leek fell into place, this name was elusive. "Then the light began to dawn, thanks to Mrs. Reading's detailed knowledge of the house," claimed Holzer. Reading proffered that "It was interesting to hear Mrs. Leek say there was a store here once," and Reading elaborated, "There was a store here at one time, but it was not Mr. Whaley's...It belonged to a man named Wallack...Hal Wallack." Reading said that it was in the 1870s that this man rented space from Whaley for six months, before selling out. Holzer then found out from Reading, that the disturbances really began after the second house had been placed on the grounds. Was that the straw that broke the ghost's patience, according to Holzer?

Later, Leek made her way to a wall adjoining the garden, a wall where there was no visible door. However, Leek insisted that there had been a French window there. This too was confirmed by the Readings. In a straight line from this spot, the group wound up at a huge tree. Leek stopped and explained that Thomas Whaley and his mother often met—or are meeting, as the case may be. Holzer was not sure whether Mr. Whaley had taken his advice to heart and moved out of what was, after all, his house. But as Holzer stated, "Why should he! The County had not seen fit to undo an old wrong."

Holzer and Leek left the next morning, hoping that at the very least they had let the restless one know someone cared. A week later Regis Philbin checked with the folks at Whaley House. Everything was lively—chandelier swinging, and rocker rocking. June Reading contacted Holzer to let him know that the otherworldly activities continued at the house. Evidently the child ghost was also still around, for utensils in the kitchen had moved, especially a cleaver which swings back and forth on its own. "Surely that must be the playful little girl, for what would so important a man as Thomas Whaley have to do in the kitchen! Surely he was much too preoccupied with the larger aspects of his realm, the ancient wrong done him, and the many intrusions from the world of reality. For the Whaley House is a busy place, ghosts or not" concluded Hans Holzer.

On replaying his tapes of the seance, he noticed a curious confusion between the initial appearance of a ghost who called himself Fedor in his notes, and a man who said he had a bad fever. It was just that the man with the fever did not have a foreign accent, but Holzer distinctly recalled "Fedor" as sounding odd. Were they perhaps two separate entities! Holzer's suspicions were confirmed when a letter written May 23, 1966—almost a year later—reached Mr. Holzer. A Mrs. Carol DeJuhasz wanted him to know about a ghost at Whaley House—not Thomas Whaley or a twelve-year-old girl with long hair, but instead, she was concerned with an historical play written by a friend of hers, dealing with the unjust execution of a man who tried to steal a harbor boat in the 1800'S and was caught and hanged in the backyard of the house. DeJuhasz thought that his ghost ought to be there.

A number of people tell Holzer of tragic spots where people have died unhappily, but rarely does he discover ghosts on such spots just because a tragic death occurred. He was therefore not too interested in Mrs. DeJuhasz's account of a possible ghost. But she thought that there should be the ghost of Yankee Jim Robinson at the Whaley House since when he was captured, he fought a saber duel and received a critical wound to the head. Although alive, he became delirious and was tried without representation. sick from a fever, he was sentenced to death and subsequently hanged in the yard behind the Court House.

The Theater
(Courtesy of SOHO)

As Holzer states, "Was his the ghostly voice that spoke through Sybil, complaining of the fever and then quickly fading away!" It was William Richardson who provided a further clue or set of clues to address this puzzle. In December of 1966 he contacted Holzer to report some additional experiences at the Whaley House. According to Richardson, this series of events began in March while his group was helping to restore a historic old house which had been moved onto the Whaley property to save it from destruction. During their lunch break one Saturday, several of the group were in Whaley House. Richardson was downstairs when Jim Stein, one of the group, rushed down the stairs to tell me that the cradle in the nursery was rocking by itself. Richardson rushed upstairs, but the chair wasn't rocking. He was just about to chide Stein for having an overactive imagination when the chair began rocking—it rocked for a short time and then stopped. The cradle is at least ten feet from the doorway, and a metal barricade blocks tourists from entering the room. No amount of walking or jumping had any effect on the cradle. While it rocked, Richardson remembered that it had made no sound. Coming into the room, Stein rocked the cradle at which time Richardson was conscious of the noise it made. The old floorboards were somewhat uneven and this in conjunction with the wooden rockers on the cradle made a very audible sound—The odd thing was, when the Whaleys lived there the carpeted the entire upstairs. This might explain the absence of the noise.

According to Holzer, the Whaley House became the setting for an historical play in June, which focused on the trial and hanging of Yankee Jim Robinson. The presentation took place in the courtroom as well as on the grounds of the mansion. The actual trial and execution had taken place in August 1852—five years before the Whaley House was constructed. Yankee Jim was hanged from a scaffold which stood approximately between the present music room and front parlor. Soon after the play went into rehearsal, things began to happen. Richardson was involved with the production as an actor and therefore had the opportunity to spend a number of hours in the house between June and August. The usual footsteps were heard by most of the cast and crew—many were interested in the ghostly phenomena. As Richardson, Barry Bunker, George Carroll, and his fiancée, Toni Manista were dressed in period costumes most of the time, the ghosts should have felt right at home. Toni played the part of Anna, Thomas Whaley's wife. She said that she often felt as if she were being followed around the house—a feeling they all had at one time or another.

One night in particular, Richardson was sitting in the kitchen with his back to the wall, when he felt a hand being run through his hair. Thinking it was one of the other cast, he quickly turned around—but there was nothing to be seen. Richardson said he always felt that it was Anna Whaley who touched him. It was his first such experience and he felt honored that she had chosen him to touch. Additionally, according to Richardson, there is a chair in the kitchen made of rawhide and wood with a seat made of thin strips of rawhide crisscrossed on a wooden frame. When someone sits on it, it sounds like the leather in a saddle. On the same night, Richardson was touched, the chair made sounds as if someone were sitting in it—not once but several times. When something strange is about to happen, Richardson and others noticed that a change in the room temperature is usually a precursor to an event—the kitchen, according to Richardson, is no exception—really getting cold in there sometimes.

Richardson went on to say, that "Later in the run of the show, the apparitions began to appear. The cast had purchased a chair that had belonged to Thomas Whaley and placed it in the front parlor. Soon after, a mist was occasionally seen in the chair or near it. In other parts of the house, especially upstairs, inexplicable shadows and mists began to appear.

George Carroll swears that he saw a man standing at the top of the stairs. He walked up the stairs and through the man. The man was still there when George turned around but faded and disappeared almost immediately. " Richardson and others also smelled cigar smoke during the summer months when the house was opened in the morning, or at times when no one was around. According to historical records, Thomas Whaley was very fond of cigars and was seldom without them.

Richardson's amazing accounts continued with the sound of footsteps being heard in the house "The heavy steps of the man continued as usual, but the click-click of high heels was heard on occasion. Once, the sound of a small child running in the upstairs hall was heard. Another time, I was alone with the woman who took ticket reservations for Yankee Jim... We had locked the doors and decided to check the upstairs before we left. We had no sooner gotten up the stairs than we both heard footfalls in the hall below. We listened for a moment and then went back down the stairs and looked. No one. We searched the entire house, not really expecting to find anyone. We didn't. Not a living soul," stated Richardson. Concluding, he told Holzer, "Well, this just about brings you up to date. I've been back a number of times since September but there's nothing to report except the usual footfalls, creaks, etc. I think that the play had much to do with the summer's phenomena. Costumes, characters, and situations which were known to the Whaleys were re-enacted nightly.

Yankee Jim Robinson certainly has reason enough to haunt. Many people, myself included, think that he got a bad deal. He was wounded during his capture and was unconscious during most of the trial. To top it off, the judge was a drunk and the jury and townspeople wanted blood. Jim was just unlucky enough to bear their combined wrath. "His crime? He had borrowed (?) a boat. Hardly a hanging offense. He was found guilty and condemned. He was unprepared to die and thought it was a joke up to the minute they pulled the wagon out from under him. The scaffold wasn't high enough and the fall didn't break his neck. Instead, he slowly strangled for more than fifteen minutes before he died. I think I'd haunt under the same circumstances myself," stated Richardson. "Two other points: another of the guides heard a voice directly in front of her as she walked down the hall. It said, 'Hello, hello.'" There was no one else in the house at the time. A dog fitting the description of one of the Whaley dogs has been seen to run into the house, but it can never be found."

Holzer states that usually, ghosts of different periods do not "run into" one another, unless they are tied together by a mutual problem or common tragedy. The executed man, the proud owner, the little girl, the lady of the house—they form a lively ghost population even for so roomy a house as the Whaley House, except that it does get confusing now and then when someone is seen walking about the house and no one is sure if the person has bought an admission ticket. Surely, Thomas Whaley wouldn't dream of buying one… and he is not likely to leave unless and until some action is taken publicly to rectify the ancient wrong.

If the county were to reopen the matter and acknowledge the mistake a long time ago, then Holzer is sure the ghostly Mr. Whaley would be pleased and let matters rest. The little girl ghost has been told by Sybil Leek what has happened to her, and the lady goes where Mr. Whaley goes. As far as Yankee Jim, Holzer suggests he be tried again and found innocent of stealing the boat, and according to Mr. Holzer, there is that splendid courtroom at the house to do it in. Holzer concludes by saying that "Maybe some ghost-conscious county administration will see fit to do just that. I'll be glad to serve as counsel for the accused, at no charge."

Large orb along with numerous other orbs in the courtroom
(Courtesy of SOHO)

Another Perspective of the 1965 Seance

Ghosts and spirits are as old as mankind, and they are a part of our existence; of who we are. Whether they can be scientifically explained or not, ghosts remain a part of every culture, a testament to the fact that we cannot control everything, or know everything, and some things must be taken on faith or left to a higher source to ultimately explain. Most of us like a good mystery, and ghosts still represent one of the best mysteries around.

Rob and Anne Wlodarski (2001) **Dinner and Spirits**

The following commentary on the Sybil Leek/Hans Holzer seance held inside the Whaley House was provided courtesy of the late June Reading and offers a non-psychic perspective of the spectacular event.

Hans Holzer came to the Whaley House on Friday, June 25, 1965, bringing his charming wife Catherine, Regis Philbin and his wife Casey, Channel

10 photographers and English medium, Sybil Leek. At Mr. Holzer's request, I had gathered together members of our volunteer group, who had witnessed the variety of phenomena at Whaley House—there were 12 in number and included: Charles, Jessie and Rusty Keller, who were members on the Board of Directors of the Historical Foundation; Suzanne Pere, who had been working with me on the manuscript collection, and who seemed to be sensitive to the activities; Grace Bourquin, our Saturday volunteer, who had witnessed an apparition (a figure of a man); Lawrence Riveroll, who had seen an apparition of a small lady dressed in a hoop skirt at the balustrade of the parlor; my mother Lillian Allen who had experienced the breeze on the stairs; Jim Reading, my husband, who was involved with the windows opening, and the alarms ringing at all time of the night; Bernice Kennedy our Sunday worker, who had been present when the unexplainable sounds at the front door occurred, and myself, June Reading who had experienced most of the sounds and phenomena.

Stairs looking toward the 2nd floor
(Courtesy of SOHO)

Regis and Casey Philbin, had attempted to spend the night in the house with Colonel Bill Rankin in November 1964, but were frightened by what was believed to be the apparition of Anna Whaley, Thomas Whaley's wife. Mr. Holzer selected the group after reviewing the "haunting" documentation, and specifically asked to interview only those individuals who had been connected with the House for a period of time, and who could be trusted not to have fabricated their stories. The selected individuals were ushered into the courtroom, the place where so many of the unusual events took place. There, Mr. Holzer would tape record his interviews with the various people regarding their experiences in the Whaley House—it was like an informal social gathering of old friends.

Everyone was seated in the jury box, and over the next 45 minutes told their stories to Mr. Holzer. Though I was sitting in the front row at the time, I thought how solemn each person was, and how intent they were in giving Mr. Holzer the exact details of each paranormal experience. These people, responsible for making the Whaley House known to the general public, were now sharing additional information about the house—a tribute to its haunted past. It is amazing to me how a lot of seemingly unimportant occurrences, facts when presented for the first time, as it was for most all who were vitally interested in Mr. Holzer's serious approach, began to see a pattern in the proceedings—when everyone was finished, we had quite a story, much of which dovetailed. For the first time, we were all together at the Whaley House and talking in unison about our experiences, that we had seen or heard, always in the afternoon or daylight hours, as it seemed the natural thing here, as these were the house when the family were occupied in normal tasks, rather than in the dead of night.

After the group divulged their stories Holzer said that I would only be introduced to Mrs. Leek only after the seance.

Mr. Holzer then came and asked me abruptly "to get everybody out of the house," and that he would not "put her [Mrs. Leek] in a trance until everyone leaves." The task of informing all those who had volunteered their time to discuss their experiences, to leave so abruptly fell on me. The fact was, Mrs. Leek would not enter a trance state until the house was cleared and Mrs. Leek was isolated from everyone else. The disappointed volunteers, thinking that they were also going to be able to meet the world-famous psychic, had to file out of the house—their task was complete.

Several of us went into the courtroom to await Mrs. Leek who was acclimating herself to the house. Mr. Holzer had told Mrs. Leek to write postcards, and wander about the house until she felt comfortable in any one of the rooms she came to, and when she found a room she felt at ease in, to sit down, and relax, let any thoughts come into her mind, and prepare herself for going into trance. When the time was right everyone met in the courtroom. Mr. Holzer had recorded what Mrs. Leek said in the kitchen, took pictures of her sitting in one of the chairs out there, and said that it was time to begin the session.

As it turned out, later, I could understand Mr. Holzer's reluctance to have a group of people stay for the seance. A Hypnotic trance if done properly, is nothing for curious people to see. First of all it is a rather frightening experience to witness, as the subject does appear in a deathlike state, and most people aren't prepared for the change in appearance. I'm not talking about entertainers, but the kind of hypnosis that a doctor uses to treat a patient, or correct conditions. It has to be done carefully—the subject is completely under the control of the hypnotist, and if during this session, which in this case was to last almost an hour, there is any disturbance from the audience, it may be difficult to arouse the subject from the trance-like state he or she is in. What is done for entertainment on stages is not like this. Evidently there is no way of putting a person in a light trance-like state, but Mr. Holzer put Sybil Leek into a very deep state. As she went under his influence, and having worked with him, she was perfectly at ease and trusted him completely. It was easy to set how dangerous and how serious he was. Catherine, sat at the tape recorder, quietly, nearby, as Mr. Holzer, bent over Sybil, talking to her quietly and steadily. Regis Philbin sat next to Mrs. Leek with the Channel 8 with microphone in his hand, waiting to catch her first words.

Mist in the former upstairs sitting room (now the theater)
Photograph by Doreen Turner (Courtesy of the Historical Shrine Foundation)

As I watched Regis, Casey and I sat at the back of the courtroom, in the last row of chairs, as spectators. Suddenly, I saw Regis's coloring change, and he became intent upon the face of Sybil Leek. Had looked at her unbelievingly, and saw as both Casey and I, her facial muscles began to look as though an invisible hand was changing the contour of her face, which seemed to lengthen. In the meantime, her healthy color which normally appears ruddy, began to pale, and she became ashen. Her head, which at the onset of this session was upright, began to fall backward, until at length she looked as if her neck could no longer support her head. With her eyes closed, she looked as if she was certainly near death. Had I not known what to expect to some degree, I was sure we had a very sick person seated in that chair, as if someone was experiencing a heart attack. She was as still and quiet as someone who was unconscious from a stroke.

Mr. Holzer, by now, had risen to his feet. Because Mrs. Leek was completely relaxed and her head had fallen so far back, he had to lean way over the edge of the Captain's chair with the microphone in order to speak to Mrs. Leek. Noting her position, and watching Mr. Holzer's movement and Regis Philbin's startled expression, I knew Mr. Philbin was experiencing a seance for the first time and he was obviously frightened, yet so excited by what was taking place that he had forgotten that his job was to hold up the microphone up—I could sense that the time was right for Mr. Holzer's questioning to begin because Mrs. Leek was in such a deep trance state. I knew this trance-position could not be faked having learned enough about the human body from my pre-med days at the University of Minnesota to know that it would have been inhumanly possible for anyone to place their head in such a contorted position, except for having a broken neck—nobody, not even a contortionist could do it. Here was a real, honest-to-goodness, hypnotic state.

Mr. Holzer seemed to have an intense power and will to command the trusting Mrs. Leek who claimed to be a witch) into the trance-state. Her trance-state was so deep, that Mr. Holzer had difficulty in making contact with her. Her first words uttered indicated that she had gone back beyond the period of the Whaley House and its inhabitants. When the first voice came through, it was weak sounding, as if someone was in pain—the spirit claimed to be Russian and came from 1746. It was a fact we knew little about, but the spirit continued by saying that he was a member of a party of Russian sea otter hunters who had camped on the property where the Whaley House now stands. It couldn't be confirmed whether this Russian was injured, because his voice was so faint that the conversation became incoherent. Historically, we knew that Russian sea otter hunters had encamped near the San Diego River. Aft, but not much else.

After this line of questioning, there was a pause as Mrs. Lee rested. Mr. Holzer then asked her about the spirit in the kitchen, Mrs. Leek said that the spirit belonged to that of a small child with reddish hair, who had died, but was not one of the Whaley children. She was too young to contact, having died before she learned to communicate. This was probably a child belonging to the Whaley's neighbors who used to run in and out of the house. Mrs. Leek said that it is this spirit who moves things in the kitchen, including the meat cleaver, cups, dishes and rocking chair or the kitchen chairs—whenever there is sufficient energy present, things move in the kitchen. I began to wonder if any of the inhabitants of the Whaley House would speak out. Just then, there was another silence.

In my desire to hear from the Whaleys, and perhaps because I was concentrating too much to hear from them, I was letting myself in for a disappointment—after all, these things were of a spontaneous nature. Just as I was projecting disappointment, the silence was shattered by what appeared to be a man's voice, issuing from Mrs. Leek. The words "I feel that an injustice has been done me," were not those of Sybil Leek, but of Thomas Whaley! Of all of us in the room, only I could have known those words. They appeared in letters he had written to the Board of Supervisors, in 1871, following the removal of the County records from his house while he was away on business. No one had access to the Whaley collection but me, and this material which had not been published, was safely locked in filing cabinets in the house.

During this time, Whaley actually spoke through Mrs. Leek. He admitted to opening the windows, causing the bells to ring (i.e. the alarm) and he wanted everyone to know he was still the Master of the house, complaining about the bolt at the back door, saying it made it difficult for him to enter the house. He asked about his papers, and seemed concerned over the theft of the County records, because in the excitement of the moment, the thieves had taken some of his personal papers. Just how important the paper collection was to him, I realized more fully later (in a portion of his 1849 journal, he recounts an incident involving Captain James Wardle and Dr. Johnson, and winds up by saying if someone took his journal, he would not hesitate running that man through with his sword or shooting him).

Mrs. Leek continued the seance by mentioning Anna's maiden name, the fact that the room has been used for feed or grain, saw a store in operation in the courtroom (Wallach's name was mentioned—he operated a store in the courtroom for 6 months), and later commented on Whaley's connections with shipping. She asked if the house had been altered, about structural changes, said that straight out from the music room there was something buried in a box (this agreed with our experiments with a Ouija board—i.e. Lawrence and I used it sometime ago and I thought this was silly!), Anna, Thomas, and two others are present in the downstairs portion of the house all the time. Many other names were said, but none of us had the opportunity to hear the playback of the tape recording, which would have helped.

The next day, I introduced Mr. Holzer when he addressed the Parapsychology Foundation on Adams Avenue. He had a bad moment when he was baited by two people who were either trying to prove Mr. Holzer a fraud, or were attempting to make a name for themselves. At a later meeting, which Jim and I attended he publicly apologized for what he had said. Holzer has had the last laugh however, as he handled a difficult situation with tact, and without losing his temper. But when the Parapsychology Foundation wrote again asking him if he would speak upon his return to San Diego, he said that there would be a $500.00 fee. That finished his appearance before them for time. This meeting with Mr. Holzer resulted in a lot of public recognition for the Whaley House, and an extremely busy summer, the best we have had to date.

The Phantoms of the Opera Group

People either believe in ghosts or they don't. They are either afraid of them or they are not. But there is a paradox here, for those people who believe most deeply in the possibility of contact between the living and the dead are those who are most likely to regard ghosts as benign and comforting presences, while people who don't really believe in ghosts are most likely to regard them as some sort of horrible visitation and are absolutely terrified of meeting one.

Daniel Cohen, **The Encyclopedia of Ghosts** (1984)

The following story was provided by our friend, Dolly Boyd of Calabasas, California.

It was during the Summer of 1965 that several of us involved in the San Diego Civic Light Opera were sharing "true" family ghost stories when the subject of the Whaley House in Old Town, came up. Although I had heard many ghost stories from my parents growing up in California during the 1920s, I had no personal experiences at 17 years of age. One of the chorus members, Bill Richardson, had been a docent there and knew the caretakers, the Readings. He brewed an ingenious idea one night at rehearsal and shared his plan with us. We negotiated front row tickets to opening night of "Little Me " in exchange for an all night visit to the Whaley House. What a coup! Incredibly, the Readings agreed—with the stipulation that they accompany us and that we have some other adult supervision as well. Most of us were between the ages of 17 and the early 20s, with a couple of older cast members who were as curious as the rest of us.

The San Diego Starlight Opera
(Courtesy of Dolly Boyd)

We picked a magic number of 13 attendees, and met at the Readings house after the performance, about 10:30 in the evening on a warm Friday night, August 13, 1965. Everyone in the group brought pencils and paper to record any unusual activity which might occur during the night long gathering. We all met in the courtroom to hear a brief history of the house; the rooms we were allowed to enter; and how we should properly conduct ourselves in this, one of the most famous haunted houses not only in San Diego, but in the United States.

We seated ourselves around the large table in the courtroom which was also San Diego's first granary and morgue—Perhaps is was our youthful energy and exuberance, but it wasn't long before we had the table groaning as it bounced a little with our hands spread out over the table. My suspicious brother, David Calderon, stood aside to watch the spectacle, when he noticed the chain barrier which separated the actual judge's bench from the visitors began to sway back and forth as though someone was swinging it with gentle fingers, but with enough force to keep it in motion—he was one of maybe four skeptics out of the 13.

In the parlor, I observed the crystals hanging from the base of a hurricane lamp tinkle, first on the left side and then move to the right side. After the episode with the hurricane lamp, and with uncharacteristic bravado, I felt the urge to go upstairs, to the master bedroom where paranormal activity had been reported in the past. The San Diego Union newspaper sometimes reported police activity there such as the windows in the room opening from the inside and setting off the burglar alarm). I situated myself on the floor near the bed, because I had read that the bedclothes often are mussed in the morning and need straightening, and within a short period of time observed the rocking chair to the right of the bed begin rocking slowly back forth, as though someone were sitting in it.

I hopped up to touch the chair and see if I could feel anything when it stopped abruptly. When I pushed it, it rocked with quick, short "rocks" and stopped moving gradually. When my concerned brother entered the room, as he was looking all over for me. As I began telling him about the chair, our conversation was interrupted by the chandelier directly overhead swaying as though someone was holding it to one side, then the other, and then twisting it to the right and left—of course there was no one but my brother and I in the room. My skeptical brother picked up the chair to see if there were any wires or strings attached—we found nothing that could account for the movement.

About that time we were summoned downstairs to the courtroom to report any unusual findings—and boy, did I have some stories to offer! I can't recall how the "little table" came into the picture, but it was about two-foot by two-foot square and about 30 inches high and began to tip and move as soon as I put my hands above it. Someone suggested that I ask it questions, and get it to "tap" out answers, such as, one tap for "yes", two taps for "no," and so on. I felt silly talking to a table but I began asking it questions anyway. The answers proved to be astounding.

It tapped out that "it" was a little red-haired girl who died from accidental food poisoning. Mrs. Reading was unusually surprised and left the room to get Thomas Whaley's diary. She returned to show us the entry where he wrote of that an 11 year-old girl had died in the house by accidentally ingesting something that proved fatal. Then the table began scooting along the floor and I kept having to prove that I was not pushing it, let alone even touching it, when it led the group to the entrance of the kitchen and stopped. Then one of the utensils that were hanging in the kitchen began to sway. It was at that point that I decided to call it an evening. I hurriedly grabbed my belongings, yelled for my brother, and fought with the others to get out the door first! It was after 3:00 a.m. when I departed — I was completely exhausted. I don't know if anyone stayed behind with the Readings.

Curiously, I saw the little table on a local television show hosted by Regis Philbin several months later. I had heard that he and a camera crew tried to spend the night, but was unable to keep their wits about them for an entire night. I will never forget that adventure and will always wonder how that little table moved along the wooden floor without benefit of someone's pushing it—or maybe "someone" did!

Another friend in the local theater, George Carroll, worked on an original production staged on the Whaley House grounds entitled, "The Hanging of Yankee Jim." He worked with the lighting crew and spent many hours in the upstairs master bedroom while installing and operating the spotlights on the actors below in the yard. As is common in theater productions, hours are long and late and he attempted many times to catch a catnap on the settee between the front bedroom windows. He complained to me that something kept waking him up, and on one occasion, he was awakened by his own coughing and choking on cigar smoke. The room had no visible smoke, and yes, Thomas Whaley smoked cigars.

Another Perspective of the Phantoms of the Opera Group

> "Do you believe in ghosts!" As I sit in bookstores, autographing books, that is the question asked of me more often than any other. To tell you the truth. I don't know how I feel about ghosts, but I've witnessed some happenings that were not explainable, and I have talked with some well-educated, highly respected people who told me they have en countered ghosts. I have found no reason not to believe them.
>
> Nancy Rhyne, **Coastal Ghosts** (1989)

The story of the Civic Light Opera visit to the Whaley House as told in a prior discussion by Dolly Boyd was also witnessed by William Richardson and the late

Mrs. June Reading. The following account details the perspectives of both June Reading and William Richardson, Richardson's account also appearing in Hans Holzer's book, Great American Ghost Stories (1963).

June Reading places the date of the all night session on either July 23 or 30, 1965. It was a Friday night and she and her husband were guests of William Richardson, attending the StarLight Opera Company production of "Little Me." This was followed by an all night session at Whaley House. Carolyn Whyte and her friend conducted the meeting and it was a success. The energy produced by those eager youngsters caused much phenomena, tables moved, an apparition appeared to one of the skeptical boys, and we saw a shadow in the study, the flickering light at the window, and had many indications or spirits.

Dining Room
(Courtesy of SOHO)

Bill Richardson came in the next Sunday and played the tape he had made on the proceeding, which turned out very well. Plans were made to have a class, but Carolyn White did not follow through, although she is very good, and handled the explanation of psychic phenomena so well. Perhaps she will come again, maybe during the Christmas season when things are manifesting.

William Richardson's perspective is as follows. He asked the director (June Reading) to allow several of his friends from the Starlight Opera, a local summer musical theatre, to spend the night in the house. At midnight, on Friday, August 13, everyone met at the house. Carolyn Whyte, a member of a San Diego parapsychology group and a member of the Starlight Chorus, began the proceedings with an introductory talk about the history and what to expect. At this point, everyone went into the parlor and waited anxiously for something to happen.

The first experience was that of a cool breeze which blew through the room. It was felt by several of the people and was noticeable given the fact that all the doors and windows were locked and shuttered tight—no breeze could have been coming in from the outside. The next occurrence was that of a light appearing over a boy's head. The light traveled from his head across the wall, where it disappeared. Upon investigation, the arc of light was found to have disappeared at the portrait of Thomas Whaley, the original owner of the house. Footsteps were also heard several times upstairs.

At this point the group separated into smaller parties and scattered to different parts of the house. One group went into the study which is adjacent to the parlor, and witnessed a shadow on the wall surrounded by a pale light which moved up and down the wall, changing shapes as it did so. There was no source of ambient light in the room and a person could pass in front of the shadow without disturbing it.

Another group was upstairs when their attention was directed to the chandelier that began to swing around as if someone were holding the bottom and twisting the sides. One boy was tapped on the leg several times by some unseen force while seated up there.

Meanwhile, in the downstairs parlor, an old-fashioned lamp with prisms hanging on the edges began to act peculiarly. As several people watched, several prisms began to swing by themselves. Some would stop and others would start, but they never swung simultaneously. After looking for a draft, everyone was convinced that there was no breeze in the room, which could have accounted for the strange action of the prisms. At this time the entire group returned to the courtroom. Carolyn White suggested that the group try to elevate the large table in the room psychically. The group sat around the table and everyone placed their fingertips on the table.

Orbs and mist in the former kitchen (now the dining room)
(Courtesy of the Historical Shrine Foundation)

A short while later it began to creak and then slid across the floor approximately eight inches. Finally, the table lifted completely off the floor on the corner where Richardson was seated. Later, a small table was brought into the courtroom from the music room. Again, the experiment was to see if the table would tip or move. With just their fingertips on the table, it tilted until it was approximately one inch off the floor—it then fell. They stood the table upright and tried the experiment again using their fingertips and almost immediately it began to rock. Since a code had been worked out for "yes" and "no" a conversation with the table began. As this was occurring, a chain across the doorway in the courtroom was almost continually swinging back and forth and then up and down.

Through the system of knocking, it was discovered that the ghost was that of a little girl. She did not tell us her name, but she did tell us that she had red hair, freckles, and hazel eyes. She also related that there were four other ghosts in the house besides herself, including that of a baby boy. The conversation with her spirit lasted for nearly an hour. At one point, the table stopped rocking and started moving across the floor of the courtroom, into the dining room, through the pantry, and into the kitchen. This led us to believe that the kitchen was the place she felt most comfortable in, or where she stayed most of the time. The table then stopped moving and several antique kitchen utensils on the wall began to swing violently—they swung for the rest of the evening at different intervals. The table then retraced its path back to the courtroom and answered more questions.

At 5:00 a.m. everyone decided to call it a night—a most interesting night. When the group of 15 began their night at the Whaley House, there were a few real believers, several who half believed, and quite a few who didn't believe at all. After that evening, there was not one among the group who was even very doubtful in the belief that some form of after life existed.

Misty form near bed in former upstairs master bedroom
Photograph by Steve Kompier (Courtesy of the Historical Shrine Foundation)

California's Most Haunted House

There is something marvelous beyond the horizon of death and the limit of our sight. It becomes personal knowledge when our minds ore coaxed out of the shadows of the purely material world and into the brilliance and brightness of the world of the spirit that lies just beyond the limit of our sight.

H.P. Lovecraft

The following story was excerpted with the permission of Richard Senate from his book entitled, **The Haunted Southland** *(1994)*

The Parlor
(Courtesy of SOHO)

His face grew red, and he began to visibly shake and gag. Could it be that the psychic researcher was feeling the ever-tightening noose of a hanging that took place in 1852? Thomas Whaley built his impressive red brick house in Old Town San Diego, in 1856 on a low hill with a view of the harbor. Mr. Whaley didn't know, or didn't core that he was building his mansion on the site of the municipal execution grounds. Almost from the first the house was rumored to be haunted by ghosts of hanged criminals. Today, the Whaley House has been converted into a museum dedicated to the early pioneers who developed San Diego. The stories of phantoms have continued to circulate. Today the Whaley House is said to be the most haunted house in all of California. Many of the greatest ghost hunters in all of the land have conducted investigations at the historic home, and each one has come away convinced that something mysterious does indeed walk the halls of this building.

Psychic researchers have on numerous occasions informed those tending the Whaley House, including site manager June Reading that it is one of the most active haunted houses in the world, a fact that she heartily agrees with. Over the last three decades hundreds of visitors have experienced the unknown in the house. They have seen moving shadows, heard laughter and music, observed rocking chairs rocks by themselves and felt chilling cold spots. Writer and parapsychologist Hans Holzer investigated the site and saw a figure at the top of the stairs, a figure he believed was the restless ghost of Thomas Whaley himself. His research team also uncovered evidence of several other phantoms in this old house. At one time a local television crew did a documentary on the place. The host, a very young Regis Philbin, saw o face appear on one of the walls during the taping. Other ghost hunters who have investigated this one haunt include Suzy Smith, noted author on the supernatural, and Antoinette May, psychic researcher and writer. They too came away convinced that the brick pile was filled with unexplainable phenomena much as possible, not wishing to stimulate an overactive imagination into conjuring up a self induced hallucination. The team arrived like regular tourists.

The first went into the courtroom. Thomas Whaley had rented out part of his house to the local courts as trial space. Many strange things have taken place in that room over the last few years, including visitors seeing a heavy chain swing by itself. I must confess that the moment I stepped into this room I felt a well-defined chill creep up my spine. I watched the chain but it rested, unmoving. The rest of the team began to spread out on their own in groups of two and three, until I was left in the room quite alone. I was hoping to relax and feel some of the reported supernatural residents of the old place. I didn't get to rest more than a minute or two. One of the team came charging in with wide-eyed fear. Mr. Senate," she said. "you got to see this." He pulled my arm and jerked me towards the stairway to the second floor. Another member of the team tried to stop us on the up, claiming that some force had attempted to trip her on the stairs! But the first team member had me firmly by the arm and would not release me. He pulled me along while the others followed. At the top of the stairs two others were waiting, looking into one of the rooms. they were watching something with hypnotic interest. I was pushed before them, and watched as one or the rocking chairs moved back and forth a few inches. I could detect no wires or strings in the room. A glass pane separated us from the room—a normal thing in a historic house museum filled with valuable antiques—no one was in the room, the windows were closed, yet the chair seemed to be moving.

Another couple came forward, stating that they had seen two small girls in one of the rooms and had watched as the figures vanished away. They were as white as a sheet and shaking from the unexpected encounter with a real phantom. "We saw them" the young woman said clutching the arm of her husband, a burly construction worker, "They were just standing there by the window looking out. They were dressed in long white gowns, like nightgowns. Her husband nodded his head in agreement adding, "They turned and looked at us and then they became transparent and were gone. The couple had joined the group as a lark—the look on their faces indicated that they had really gotten their money's worth. Another team member came running up from the stairway. "There's someone breathing in the Kitchen" she yelled. "There is nothing there but you can hear them clearly." I commented that it might be the ghost of Anna Whaley, the wife of the builder, who died in the house in 1913.

I began to write out their experiences until another member—a member who identified himself as a complete skeptic—ran up to me red in the face. He told me to come with him on the double. Because of the look on his face followed. Gone was the sneer of the non-believer, to be replaced by a look that indicated wonder, and perhaps even a trace of fear. He took me to the archway that lead into the music room, on the first floor and bid me to stand under the arch. "What do you feel?" he asked. I didn't feel anything, and told him so. "Did you feel anything around your neck," he asked. I didn't and asked what he had experienced. In a disjointed narrative, he explained how he had stood under the arch and felt something tighten around his neck.

It had happened twice, each time he stood under the arch. I asked if he would try it once again. He agreed and as he took his place under this arch he gasped and seemed to struggle with something twisting around his neck. I pulled him from the archway as he turned purple. He didn't know the history of the house. He didn't know that the archway was built on the exact site of the scaffold used to hang 'Yankee' Jim Robinson in 1852—his crime, stealing a rowboat. The hanging had been a botched job from the start. A drunken hangman had failed to measure Jim's legs and instead of quickly breaking his neck, Jim slowly, painfully, strangled to death. The self-proclaimed skeptic had become a believer.

He had come on the ghost hunt only to please his wife and saw it only as a lark—until he felt the rope that took the life of 'Yankee' Jim. Over the years, more events have been recorded in the historic Whaley House. Though no one encountered the mustachioed man in the dark frock coat, believed by many to be the wandering ghost of Thomas Whaley himself, or smelled his distinctive Havana cigars, the group was convinced that the stories of supernatural goings on were true.

Of the thirteen members of the San Diego investigation, everyone, skeptic as well as believer, experiences something out of the ordinary at the Whaley House. The team concluded that this mansion truly lived up to it's reputation as a real haunted house.

A Psychic View of the Whaley House

For most people, nothing is more terrifying than having an experience that flies in the face of common sense and science. We grow up in a world of high technology, computers, television, and space science, where everything that happens has a scientific explanation or at least promises a rational, sober explanation. When we confront the unknown in the form of disembodied footsteps and voices, or the sudden appearance of someone who is known to be physically dead, we can be terribly unsettled and frightened.

Dr. Philip Stander and Dr. Paul Schmolling, **Poltergeists & The Paranormal** (1996)

The following story was provided by psychic, Michael J. Kouri, who resides in Pasadena, California

During April 1989, I arrived with two friends, not having set foot in the Whaley House for several months. I immediately felt at home, something that happens every time I visit the historic landmark. However, on this particular day, the vibrations were much stronger than during any prior visit. Upon entering the front hallway and speaking to the Docents on duty, the three of us stopped in the parlor areas and peered into the room over the wrought iron enclosure. One of the Docents came over and asked if any of us played the piano—a nudge from my friend and the Docent ushered me into the room. Seated in front of the marvelous, old piano, the Docent informed me that it belonged originally to the famous pianist Jenny Lind. As I tried to figure out what I should play, I began to feel a very cold chill come out of nowhere and envelop me—although the front door was closed.

The Parlor
(Courtesy of SOHO)

Still uncertain as to what I should play, a tiny voice seemed to whisper in my ear to play "Jesu Joy of Man's Desiring." I looked quickly over my shoulder to see who made the request, but to my surprise, no one was next to me. My two friends had wandered down the hallway and were looking at the study with the Docent. Asking for the voice to repeat its request proved fruitless—there was only stillness.

As I began to play the song, that soft voice began singing the words. The sweet sang in perfect rhythm to the tempo that I was creating. At that moment, several other visitors appeared with the Docent to listen. Not only could I see their reflections in a nearby mirror, but I could also feel their presence. As I continued playing, I began to feel a presence standing directly behind me, and to add to the eeriness, I could also feel a pair of hands resting on my shoulders—yet I knew that no one else was in the room with me, at least no humans. I wasn't frightened, just a little confused because I wasn't really picking up vibrations in the room.

Finally, the Docent came into the room and asked how I liked the instrument. After stopping, she ushered me into the study where another piano was. Again, the voice whispered to play Jesu. So I began to play once again. This time,I asked the Docent and my friend if they could hear a voice calling out. They both looked at one another questioningly then replied "No, what are you talking about." Just as quickly as the voice came, it ceased. As I was leaving the parlor room, the Docent asked me why I had chosen Jesu Joy of Man's Desiring, because it was one of Anna Whaley's favorite pieces of music. I couldn't tell her that a little voice told me to play it, so I shrugged my shoulders and moved on with the tour.

Another incident occurred in October of 1992 and took place in the kitchen—it was a room I hadn't paid much attention to in the past. I was visiting the house alone and decided as part of my exploration, to inspect the kitchen area. This particular day was very humid outside, not unusual since San Diego occasionally had Indian summer conditions in October—a late season heat wave. As I peered beyond the southern glass partition, I observed another guest looking through the northeast partition. As we were both looking around the room, the little rocking chair began to rock back and forth on its own. This was immediately followed by a child's laughter. The giggling continued for quite some time. Astonished, we all watched this manifestation and called out to the Docent to come and have a look. As quickly as it began, the rocking and laughter stopped.

Just as I was about to leave the room, I heard a little voice, like that of a child, whisper very slowly, "MICHAEL, MICHAEL." I was again drawn back to the kitchen partition to look in. At that moment, a Docent came up behind me and oddly, asked if my name was Michael, to which I replied, yes, it was." As she stood by my side and I began to ponder not only her odd question, the strange little voice, the rocking chair incident and a child's laughter, the meat cleaver as well as a few of the other utensils on the kitchen wall began to sway back and forth on their hooks as if some unseen force had walked by and ran their hand along them, causing their movement. The Docent and I watched in silence and awe as the utensils continued to sway. Within seconds there began a slow materialization of what appeared to be a child with her arms wrapped around a man who was clearly sitting in the tin bathtub. The impression of the ghostly pair became more pronounced each second we stood there. Both of us couldn't believe what we were witnessing, as goose bumps covered my arms. The Docent remarked that the spirits appeared to be drawn to me, and I responded that whenever I came to the house, unexplainable things seemed to happen. As far back as I can remember, I have heard ghostly voices echoing inside the Whaley House. Sometimes I have heard a deep baritone voice of a man bidding me farewell, until next time or welcoming me when I arrive at the house.

Another episode occurred during a Thursday afternoon visit to the house in 1995. My truly gifted psychic friend, Sharon and I were visiting San Diego on a sightseeing excursion when I suggested we visit the Whaley House, since she had never had the opportunity to spend time inside. After a quick lunch across the street, we were walking toward the house when we observed a man dressed in black, period clothing standing on the outside second story balcony facing the street. As we walked closer to the house, we also noticed that the figure appeared to be looking at them, following their every move. As we reached the sidewalk area in front of the porch, the man waved his hand while bending over the balustrade. Sharon and I both heard a deep baritone voice come from the man as he laughed and then vanished before our startled eyes. Sharon immediately commented that she could feel very strong vibrations emanating from the front porch of the house, and the entire property gave off a strong energy.

Before entering the house, we strolled around to the back of the property where other tourists were milling around. It appeared as if the other people were huddling over something, so we walked over to take a closer look at what the commotion was all about. The three visitors appeared to be looking at a bush, but upon closer inspection, we noticed that they were witnessing a very unusual specter, that of a transparent cat—everyone there could see right through it. The event then turned even more bizarre, for as we stood and watched the cat run across the yard, we began hearing the sound of a dog barking. Before you could say WHALEY, the transparent cat was being chased by a ghostly dog. The pursuit ended when both animals circled the back stairs then disappeared right though as solid wall of the house—all these events took place before we set one foot inside the house. We couldn't imagine what else could top this.

We decided it was time to go inside, which we did by going in at the main entrance. Once we entered, the ghostly scene of the ghostly cat being chased by the spectral dog through the hallway greeted us and both vanished as the chase led into the courtroom—wow! We also immediately noticed the strong smell of cigars in the house. As we walked toward the back of the house, the odor grew more intense, becoming strongest as we reached the study. The smell remained for a few seconds, then disappeared. At that point, Sharon began to go into a light trance and I knew that the presence of a child was nearing the kitchen directly behind where I was standing. Sharon began to describe a horrifying scene in which a man was bringing a small girl into the kitchen through the back door. He placed her in a chair in the middle of the room where she was screaming in pain. A woman dressed in old-fashioned clothing seemed to be attempting to comfort the little red-haired girl. Sharon snapped out of the trance-like state and said that the strange reenactment had come to an abrupt end.

Ball of light and unusual light shapes
in the former kitchen (now the dining room)
(Courtesy of the authors)

Leaving the kitchen area, we ventured upstairs. While looking at an extensive collection of antique dolls, I decided to snap a few shots for my mother who loved old dolls. Then Sharon and I moved over toward the master bedroom where again we both heard that deep, baritone laughter emerge from the house. I called out into the hallway, but there was no response. My left hand began to tremble (something that usually happens when I'm about to have a psychic encounter) and Sharon and I tried to make contact with the spirit. One of the Docents came upstairs to tell us that she was feeling extreme cold spots in the hallway between the kitchen and the study. Just hen, the laughter began again. The startled Docent fled downstairs. We took many photographs and then left the house. Later, when we had the pictures developed, two distinct images appeared on film. One was the form of a woman, appearing pregnant, standing by a cradle in the nursery room; the other was that of a ghostly woman wearing a fancy looking hat while gazing out of the upstairs window. These photographs as well as many others can be viewed in the courtroom of the Whaley House—all were taken by amateur photographers.

June A. Reading: "I'm sure there's a pattern to all of this"

> *The subject closest to my heart has always been and will always be ghosts and hauntings. In uncovering the evidence, one discovers real proof of the survival of the inestimable human spirits after death and, in the more common ways of recording, snippets of the past are literally brought back to life. In understanding more abour ghosts one understands more about the human psyche, about our hope and fears and what makes us tick.*
>
> Natalie Osborne-Thomason, **Psychic Quest** (2002)

This story was extracted from the San Diego Evening Tribune as well as the September 1962 issue of Fate Magazine. The late June Reading granted us permission to use this information for our book.

According to the late June Reading [the former curator of the Whaley House at the time], about 10:00 a.m. one April morning in 1960, heard footsteps coming from upstairs. She had first heard the sound of someone walking across the floor a week before the Whaley House opened to the public as a Museum. County workmen were still painting some shelving in the hall, and during the week prior to the opening, often arrived before she did, so it was not unusual to find them already at work when Reading arrived.

On this particular morning, however, she had planned to furnish the downstairs rooms, and so she hurried in and down the hall to open the back door awaiting the arrival of the trucks with the furnishings. Two men followed her down the hall: they were going to help with the furniture arrangement. As she reached up to unbolt the back door she heard the distinct sound of what seemed to be a person walking across the upstairs bedroom floor. At first, she paid no attention, thinking it was one of the workmen. But the men, who heard the sounds at the time she did, insisted Reading go upstairs and find out who was in the house. After first calling out, and after getting no reply, she started to climb the stairs. Halfway up, she could see that no lights were on, and noticed that the outside shutters to the windows were closed. Reading made some comment to the men who had followed her, and turned around to descend the stairs. One of the men jokingly said that the spirits must have come to have a look at the furnishings and everyone promptly forgot the matter. However the sound of walking continued.

Study and Parlor
(Courtesy of SOHO)

For the next six months Reading found herself continually going upstairs to check and see if someone was actually there (residents of Old Town were apparently very familiar with this sound of footsteps on the roof, having heard it for many years). Even Corinne Lillian Whaley, the youngest and last Whaley to live in the house, and died there in 1953 at the age of 89, was said to have heard the same sounds on a number of occasions— it was all part of the otherworldly legacy of the Whaley House.

Similar events happened during the day, sometimes when visitors were in other parts of the house, other times when Reading was busy at her desk trying to catch up on correspondence or bookwork. On occasion the footsteps would sound as though someone were descending the stairs, but would fade away before reaching the first floor. No one could ever account for the mysterious sounds of unseen people walking, although the ghostly Whaleys were always prime suspects. According to Reading, on other occasions during fall 1961, windows in the upper part of the house began to open unaccountably. Horizontal bolts were finally installed on the three windows in the front bedroom in the hope that this would alleviate the problem. Additionally, burglar alarms were installed as an added security measure to help deter would-be burglars and pranksters.

The burglar alarms only seemed to exacerbate the situation and upset the spirits. After the burglar alarms were installed, they would begin going off in the middle of the night. Much to the chagrin of the local police, San Diego Burglar Alarm Company, and the Readings, someone had to frequently go in late at night and check the house after the alarms were triggered. Usually, nothing would be disturbed. However, on one occasion, the house get vandalized, and that was in 1963 when several items from the kitchen display were stolen.

Again in fall of 1962, while Reading was giving a talk to 25 school children, she heard what sounded like someone walking on the roof. Even one of the children interrupted her to ask what the noise was. Excusing herself, Reading ventured outside, down on the street to see if workmen from the County were repairing the roof. Satisfied that there was no one on the roof of the Whaley House, she resumed the tour—the mystery behind the footsteps was never explained, by natural causes or otherwise.

During September of 1965, Reading was in the house with Mrs. Kennedy and William Richardson when they experienced sounds as if the front door were opening. Every time they checked to see who came in, there was no one there. This was accompanied on several occasions by sounds of people walking on the front porch, but upon further inspection, no one could be seen. The interruptions seemed to occur many times over a three-week period at all hours of the day—it was a frustrating experience to have to be constantly interrupted by unseen visitors.

Reading was attending to the house during October 1965, when visitors reported seeing the crystals on the parlor lamp moving. She reached the area in time to see the phenomenon. She theorized that it has something to do with the Whaley story that is told to guests, since the event occurs at least once a week, usually in the afternoon—its called keeping the spirit alive.

On one November morning, 50 students from Chula Vista High School descended on the Whaley House, and June Reading remembered that the teacher confided that they were interested in the ghosts of the Whaley House. She began her talk in the courtroom, giving them both history and ghost stories. There were exchange students, three teachers and a bus driver present. The driver preferred to stand at the back of the room as he had been sitting all day. Reading went on with the talk, standing in front of the council table, facing the students. After a long talk, at which time the children and adults were engrossed in what she was saying, Jim (June's husband) and June divided the children up and started on separate tours of the house. Toward the end of the tour, the bus driver who had been quietly watching the proceedings from a good vantage point, took June aside and told her that during her talk the chain suspended from the railing at the side over to the post at the wall, had begun to vibrate up and down while she stood talking, and then began to swing back and forth. June quickly asked him if he could recall what she had been saying when this event took place. He replied that June was telling the class about Thomas Whaley venturing to California on a dangerous voyage around Cape Horn.

The session lasted until about 11:30 when the children boarded the bus. During that time, they saw the meat cleaver in the kitchen move. The Bus driver said he would be definitely come back to the house. He also told Reading that he was sure some of the teachers in the group had witnessed the movement of the chain.

The Parlor
(Courtesy of SOHO)

This sudden and unexplained movement of the courtroom chains has happened before when June talked to groups of visitors. On one occasion, the chain was seen moving back and forth when a San Diego Burglar Alarm repairman brought his entire family over for a tour of the house. One minute they were being lectured about the house and the next moment the chain began swaying.

During September of 1965, around 4:30 P.M., after Mrs. Kennedy had left, Reading and her husband were alone in the house. She began to realize that the kind of talk that is given, along with the energy produced by a group of people who are interested in the paranormal usually triggers an episode. In Reading's own words, "... it occurs to me that if a person dies while engaged in an activity that is important, and doesn't have an opportunity to complete the task, he or she could be, in the spirit world, trying to finish the business." This would fit the bill for Thomas Whaley who died without completing or resolving some important tasks.

Consequently, perhaps he feels compelled to try and complete it in the afterlife. Reading always wondered if she might help him in some way. However, She did not want to drive him away from the premises. Reading stated, "I enjoy knowing he and Anna are around, though I don't understand some of the other manifestations. They are not typical of Whaley's actions nor Mrs. Whaley's, and if Holzer's surmise is correct about the little girl in the kitchen and the Russian who camped on the property, these people may be interfering with what Whaley wants to do. But Tom ought to appear to me, because I know so much about him, and his activities, like his quiet sense of humor, and want to be friendly, provided he doesn't take offense. I hope he knows that I intend to do what is right, and wish him to be pleased. I have always felt that because of our birthdates and Violet's occurring in October there was something we had in common, and tackled problems in a similar way."

According to Reading, visitors and staff not only see ghosts but sometimes capture strange 'ghostly' images on the photographs they take, and send them to her for her ghostly photo gallery—the pictures were placed in a glass case in the courtroom for all to see. Reading was been fortunate to see a man wearing a black frock coat and a pair of pantaloons, with a broad-brim black felt hat upstairs. His face wasn't turned toward the staircase and he faded away. She knows it was Thomas Whaley because she has his passport with his physical description, and knows personal details about him from his journals. Reading was also upstairs with another guide when they heard a man's laughter, a baritone laugh—most likely belonging to Thomas Whaley.

She had another experience with music boxes that are kept in the music room. There has been several occasions when the sound of the music boxes can be heard playing in the background—the music, however, is not from the time period of the box, but from music played a long time ago. Reading has received reports of organ music emanating from the courtroom where an old fashioned organ is situated.

One hot and humid August afternoon there was a great deal of static electricity in the air and a visitor called down to Reading from one of the upstairs rooms. Reading hurried upstairs and both women stood in amazement as something resembling fireflies were floating around in the room—Reading had never seen anything like that before and it never happened again. Reading immediately put in a call to the local Parapsychology Foundation, described the firefly-like manifestations and was told that they may be ectoplasmic tubes. The woman continued, saying that the tubes often form a figure if enough are present if there are enough present. As the women watched in stunned silence, they were finally able to make out the features of what looked like half of a figure standing near the edge of the bed. The figure seemed to be folding clothes or a similar activity.

Reading said that the Whaley House caters to almost ten thousand schoolchildren a year, and the eager children want more then anything, to see ghosts. Sometimes they are not disappointed and have reported seeing apparitions, the chains in the courtroom move by themselves, smelling cigar smoke and perfume, hearing unexplained footsteps and feeling cold gusts of wind brushing by them on hot summer days.

Mist in the former kitchen (now the dining room)
Photograph by Doreen Turner (Courtesy of the Historical Shrine Foundation)

There was a time when a man from New Jersey, came to the house with his Polaroid camera. He walked into the courtroom with Reading and snapped several pictures. Peeling back the film on one of the exposures, both were startled to see a cloudy, white energy form about eight inches across the length of the judge's bench—it resembled a large, heavy piece of yarn. According to Reading, there is a lot of that happening in the house, and sometimes it can be seen. She also witnessed an energy form develop in the study, near Thomas Whaley's desk. The filmy ectoplasm would fluctuate from being visible to invisible over a long period. It would occasionally move, but never really become anything complete or recognizable.

According to Reading, "What an opportunity presents itself here, for spirits to help mortals while one is trying to re-create the past they lived in and give a visitor a picture of what life was like. If the spirits of the departed knew, I am sure they would be interested, and I know Thomas would want to help. I even wish I had a chance to meet Lilly, who was, I am sure now, ahead of her time in intelligence, and reasoning. Well, I tried to see her, but got no response. But the closeness I feel is for old Tom, and his time, which I feel is very important to our day and times, and from his information we can better appreciate what we are and what we have achieved, as inhabitants of San Diego. I am sure there is a pattern to all of this, but if I don't strike the key soon, I shall get discouraged. I have tried hard."

After Hour Hauntspitality

> *A ghost is a paranormal manifestation. It may take the form of a visual apparition, a disembodied voice, the feeling of a cold spot, or a psychic scent not of this world. The key to all of these extrasensory encounters is that they are all believed to be caused by someone dead.*
>
> Richard Crowe, **Chicago's Street Guide to the Supernatural** (1966)

The following account was provided by three individuals who choose to remain anonymous. We know these individuals personally, and can vouch for their integrity and the fact that following information is legitimate. The participants, for purposes of anonymity will be named Ricky, Lucy and Fred. The stories are told by Ricky, base on the events that took place on August 23, 1998, and August 24, 1998 as follows:

It was Saturday, August 23, 1998 at around 11:30 p.m. The outside temperature was a comfortable 70 degrees, and it was even warmer inside, where there was no air conditioning, and lighting was minimal. There were no other people in the house, since it was after hours and closed to the public. When we entered, it felt like a tomb inside, as the air was oppressive and deathly still. First, a slight digression. Earlier in the afternoon, Lucy and Ricky met with Fred in the structure north of the Whaley House and adjacent and to the east of the Derby-Pendelton House. As the three were discussing the haunted nature of the Whaley House, they were introduced to Maria, and Maria Carmen, both of whom were working on research of their own involving the Derby-Pendelton House. Fred was in the back portion of the house, which was moved from another location some years ago. This structure was consistently rumored to have several spirits inside.

What set the stage for later events, began with our entrance into a kitchen/ storage area which leads into Fred's office. Fred entered first, followed by Maria, and Ricky. Upon entering, Maria and Ricky sensed a presence. The air was electrically charged, and the hair on our arms and the back of our necks stood on end. The interior of the building was deathly still, and musky, yet everyone could feel that they were not alone. Within seconds,

Maria and Ricky felt as if someone or something brushed by them. They called the others in, and Lucy and Maria Carmen followed. Everyone felt the same energy or force in the kitchen area. It was as if several pairs of invisible eyes were on all of us.

Adjacent to Fred's office, opposite the kitchen, is another room used for storing Whaley records and files. As we were discussing the continuing feeling of being "passed though" by some force, the rocking chair in the storage area began to move back and forth a few times, then stopped. Repeatedly we felt as if someone unseen was in the room with us, passing by each of us as we were relating our feelings about the incident.

The Parlor
(Courtesy of SOHO)

Fred told us that, on a number of occasions while working alone in the building, he would hear the sounds of pots and pans moving or crashing to the floor, but would never find anything out of place, or anyone else in the room. He had occasionally felt as if someone else was in the room with him, yet it never bothered him. He did say, however, that he had never experienced a continuous flow of energy and feeling of being watched as he did that day. For about 20 minutes, we all felt a presence in the room. Then, as quickly as it had come, the spirit left. With that, Fred predicted that it was going to be an exciting night. Fred, Lucy, and Ricky decided to spend some time in the house late at night after closing, so as not to be disturbed.

Little did we know how true Fred's prediction would be until 11:30 p.m. rolled around. After having dinner, we decided that it was time to see if we could "pick up" anything in the house. We sauntered over to the back door of the house, disengaged the alarm, entered, and turned the alarm back on. We walked down the hallway toward the courtroom. We didn't feel frightened, or apprehensive. It felt as if we were being invited into a friend's house, except that the friends had been dead for over a hundred years. We heard no unusual sounds, nor did we smell Anna's perfume or Thomas Whaley's cigar. We did however, feel as if every step we took was being watched by unseen eyes.

The three of us decided to go into the courtroom and see if we could contact the Whaleys. Having been involved in several seances in the past, we thought that we would try to contact the spirits by using a simple "yes" and "no" knock code when a question was asked. No one in the group had ever played the part of a medium before, so getting someone into a "trance-like state" was not considered an option. We wanted to keep control and keep it simple provided "they" were willing to cooperate. We chose a small table on the left side of the courtroom bench. We grabbed some chairs and made ourselves comfortable. We placed our hands on the table and said a prayer of protection, to surround us in God's light and allow only positive spiritual energy into our circle. It didn't take long for a response from the "other side."

Lucy had never participated in a seance before. She did not consider herself particularly psychic, nor in her wildest imagination did she consider herself a medium; however, within five minutes, her precepts were shattered. After we all held hands and closed our eyes, Ricky felt a chill, and an electrical energy engulf the area surrounding the table. My eyes immediately opened, as did Fred's. To our amazement, Lucy began moaning in pain, and her left hand slowly became contorted. It was as if an unseen hand was taking each finger (beginning with her little finger), and closing then one by one until a fist was formed. Lucy's hand then began shaking. Her eyes were closed and the expression on her face suddenly turned from one of peace, to anger. Lucy was no longer in control. Fred and Ricky immediately sensed a male presence, powerful, angry, and strong. Lucy continued to moan as her head moved back and then forward, coming to rest on the table. By now, both of her hands we clenched tightly.

Fred asked if the spirit was Thomas Whaley? The moaning spirit with a deep, resonating voice responded with an emphatic, "Yes!" Before was could ask another question, the spirit blurted out "Angry," "They had no right," "Resolution." "Must resolve." "Must!" We assumed at that point, that the spirit was referring to the night that Thomas Whaley's house was illegally broken into in March, 1871, while he was away on a trip to San Francisco. A question to verify our suspicions triggered an, "Of course," "Them," "Thieves." "They took it!" We asked if there was anything, we could do to help. Lucy's hands quickly slammed down on the table very hard, three times, and the voice bellowed out, "Justice." "Want justice." Ricky demanded that the spirit not abuse Lucy's body, but only speak through her. Lucy then sat upright, and in a tiring voice demanded, "Set record straight... justice." Fred asked if he also wanted monetary compensation. "No money," boomed the voice. "Not about money." "Justice." "Retribution." "Took papers." "Mine." ... took mine... want apology... return to me." Ricky then asked, "What about what happened to Anna?" That question elicited sadness and restlessness from the spirit. As the spirit of Thomas said, "Must do honorable thing," Lucy slumped forward, and that portion of the session was concluded. As Lucy came out of her trance, Fred and Ricky looked on in stunned silence. Regrouping, we asked Lucy if she remembered anything. Lucy said, "No, but I am very tired, and my hands are killing me!"

Trail of orbs in the upstairs theater
(Courtesy of SOHO)

We told Lucy what had transpired, and she couldn't believe it! "I'm not a medium, and this has never happened to me before," she told Fred and Ricky. As long as I've known her, she has never had anything like that happen. She did say that she felt strange, as if she were half-asleep and half-awake. She was holding her left hand, which was now hurting her quite a bit. We related how her hands had hit the desk three successive times with a force that could have only come from someone who was very strong and very angry. We told her that she had somehow conjured up Thomas Whaley, and he was trying to tell us that his spirit was not at rest because of what happened the night his house was broken into while he was away.

We reasoned that perhaps Thomas Whaley is awaiting the return of his stolen private papers. He is still hoping for an apology from someone for the wrong perpetrated on him and his wife and children. It must have been terrifying for Anna, and extremely frustrating for Thomas. With the theft of the court records the era of Old Town's political dominance of San Diego ended. Thomas Whaley never received so much as an apology from those responsible for breaking into his house, and robbing him over 120 years ago.

As Fred, Lucy and Ricky sat in the dimly lit courtroom thinking about what had occurred, we also wondered what really happened that night. What must Anna and the children have gone through? We reasoned that there was probably still so much energy in the house because there were so many unresolved issues, so much trauma, much of it pertaining to the night of March 31, 1871. To our surprise, we learned that it was also Anna Whaley's birthday! We tried to regroup to see how we all felt about continuing. Lucy was reluctant, fearing that she would become a medium once more against her will. We assured her, that if she protected herself and asked to be the receptor, it wouldn't happen again. We hoped that this time we could actually initiate a question and answer period through knocking or tapping.

As we joined hands again after a protective invocation, we patiently sat in silence. Not a sound penetrated the room. We waited, and waited, and continued asking if there was anyone else in the house who wished to speak—only silence. The minutes ticked by. Then, it happened to Lucy again! Lucy's hand slowly contorted, and clenched. Her head went backward again. Then a voice came through. It was a more somber, and sad, tone—not angry. The intonation was definitely feminine and of someone in pain. We asked, "Who are you?" "Anna" was the name that reverberated throughout the courthouse. We continued, "Why are you in so much pain?" A soulful wailing was followed by, "They came into my house." "Frightened." "Died." "Who died?" we asked. "I died," "Men in house," "Guns," "My children," were the responses. We realized that Anna was picking up where Thomas left off. Through Lucy, Anna was describing the events of the night the 'New Towners,' broke into her house while Thomas was away. "What are they doing to you.," we asked. "Stairs, man with gun, I'm dead, dead!" was her painful response. She was distressed and unnerved. We were reliving the past with Anna Whaley.

As the questioning continued, we were able to discern that four men broke into the house while Anna and the children were upstairs asleep. She woke up at the sound of the courtroom doors being forced open, and by the time she woke up the children, two men had approached her as she was coming down the stairs. One man held a gun to her chest as she positioned the children behind her. From what were could decipher, Anna kept saying that she was "dead," no doubt because she thought that the man with the gun was going to shoot her, and possibly the children. Her fear was transmitted through Lucy to us. She could hear other men downstairs in the courtroom, but the two men would not let her go.

We then asked what the men were doing:, "Beating me." "My children." And "Hurting me." "Dead." Suddenly, Lucy's hands were thrust outward as she screamed, as if trying to push someone away Then in agony, she yelled out, "Get away." "Stay away, leave us alone!" Thinking this was a continuance of the break-in episode, we asked, "Are the men still hurting you?" "No, not them." "Negative spirit, in house, stay away, get away from us." At which point, Ricky invoked the name of God, and the Holy Spirit to have the negative spirit to be gone, and to leave Anna and us alone! This seemed to work, as Anna's spirit calmed down. Anna now continued, "Tired, very tired, here." "Remain in house." "Must guard it."

We then asked about Thomas: "Is Thomas with you?" Lucy replied, "No, not with me." "Many others here," she added. Anna pleaded again to "go home," to be released, saying that she was very tired. When Lucy's body jerked, there was a charge of electricity in the air, and the spirit was gone before we could ask additional questions. We thanked the spirits for communicating with us, and Lucy came out of her trance-stated. She stated that her hands were "killing her" from all the pounding.

As soon as Fred and Ricky pulled themselves together, they began putting everything back in order. Lucy and Ricky decided to take a stroll upstairs and sit outside the master bedroom. We thought, after all that had happened, Anna might show herself at the top of the stairs. We shouted downstairs for Fred to turn off the upstairs lights so that we could sit in the darkness for a few minutes. We saw all the lights go off downstairs, as well as in all the rooms upstairs except for the light in the hall and master bedroom. No matter what Fred tried, that light would not go off. He couldn't understand it, saying that he never had a problem-getting switch number 17 to turn off. We took it as a sign that we were not supposed to remain in the house any longer, so we prepared to leave. Perhaps if we had stayed, much more would have happened, and it may not have been something we could have handled after the courtroom seance. Or, maybe Anna would not have been able to control the negative spirit she mentioned during the seance.

We quickly walked downstairs and out the front door, quite sure that the night of the infamous break-in was indelibly etched in the psyche of the Whaley House. Thomas, Anna, their children, and other spirits are still active, and very much a part of the energy that remains in the house. The other spirits who inhabit the house may be any number of individuals who visited it, or died in the house over the years: Native Americans, Yankee Jim, the Whaley children; a neighbor child who died in the house; former enters... who knows!

Lucy left hoping that would be her last psychic encounter with the Whaleys. Upon leaving, we noticed that Lucy's hand was literally black-and-blue from being slammed into the desk, and her ring had been hit with such force that it was noticeably bent! This was not to be her last encounter of the weekend, however.

The Second Encounter
The Whaley House: Sunday, August 24, 1998: 11:00 a.m. - 12:30 p.m.
Sunday Conditions: Warm, roughly 74 degrees inside; crowded downstairs (approximately 10 visitors, including docents).
Lucy, Wanda, and Ricky upstairs in front of the Whaley's master bedroom (Sunday).
Area of occurrence: At the foot of the stairs in front of the master bedroom, and to the right of the nursery.

The following day (which was actually the same day given the fact that we left the house at 1:30 a.m.) would produce another surprise. We returned to the Whaley House around 11:30 a.m. in order to pick up our camera which we left on a hallway table the night before. When we arrived, Fred was there and we discussed last night's encounters and asked if he had seen our camera when he opened in the morning. He had not. This was very disconcerting, since it was an $800.00, 35mm, Ricoh camera.

Theater in upstairs
(Courtesy of SOHO)

Thinking that the camera may still be in the house, somewhere, we enlisted the support of several staff, and thoroughly searched every nook and cranny in the house. No one had been in the house except Fred since our seance ten hours earlier, and he had been the first one in the house that morning. The mystery continued.

We recounted the night before, and everyone remembered the camera resting on the hallway table prior to us leaving. We all remembered that Ricky took my notebook, pen, tape recorder, and a water bottle—but not the camera—Ricky had forgotten it. Essentially, we were blaming the spirits for confiscating our camera and either hiding it, or taking it within them into another dimension. As we were mulling over the situation, a woman, her husband, and daughter walked in. Since we were discussing the situation in the hallway, and the family was only a few feet away, the woman overheard what we were talking about. The woman chimed in saying that this sort of thing is not unusual where haunting occur. Usually they affect the film, but they have been known to hide or take material possessions.

The woman, who we'll call Wanda, told Ricky and Lucy that she was a psychic, and had visited the Whaley House 30 years ago near Christmas Day, 1968. They had been visiting Old Town and chanced to stop at the house which was open. They had never read about the house, nor had they heard anything about its haunted past. Upon arriving, Wanda said that as they walked into the courtroom 30 years ago, they saw the courtroom, not as it was in the 1960s, but in the 1860s. The lights were suddenly candelabra with lit candles. She remembers taking a picture and when it was developed the candles were in the photograph—she is not sure what happened to the picture. Continuing, Wanda said that as the family approached the courtroom bench, she witnessed a partial apparition of a woman standing off the left of the bench. Wanda later found out that the woman she saw and described to docents, was that of Anna Whaley. Wanda said that the woman was trying to tell her something as she slowly dematerialized before her. Continuing on their tour, they had two other encounters; one in front of the Jenny Lind, which started playing as they looked on, and the other in the master bedroom upstairs, where a partial apparition appeared in bed.

As we discussed our impressions of house with Wanda, Fred left, and Wanda's husband and daughter went on their own tour of the house. At this point, Lucy and Ricky shared some of our experiences the night before. Without giving her specific details, Wanda stated that she believed it was Thomas and Anna who came through last night, and that Anna was here right now. Also, Wanda believed that it was the Whaleys, who took our camera, would probably "give it back" at some later date. She was also convinced that something else very profound would happen today. With that, we all entered the courtroom. There were several people there already, walking around. The instant we approached the area where the break-in took place in 1871, we all stopped. A chill and an electrical change filled the air. Our hair stood on end—we were in a cold spot in a highly charged space approximately five-feet-by five-feet. It was bizarre!

As we were absorbing the moment, we turned to the far corner of the room, to the left of the courtroom bench (where we had conducted the seance hours earlier), and noticed a greenish-white haze float above the floor. An indefinite outline began to form, then the haze rose to the ceiling and vanished. As we stood there with several other people who looked on in disbelief, we shifted our focus overhead, to the ceiling of the courtroom. To our amazement, three, greenish-white, hazy forms floated on the ceiling directly above us! As Wanda, Lucy, and Wanda's daughter stood in a circle, Ricky ran to get Fred. We all watched for about five minutes as the three amorphous shapes swirled and hovered overhead. It was amazing—we could almost make out faces. The women stood holding arms as they were definitely in a vortex of energy, also the apparent focus of the phenomenon. For the next thirty minutes, the individual ectoplasmic forms circled on the ceiling and near the north door in the courtroom—the 1871 break-in door.

Wanda told us, that, as she stood in the circle, she felt Anna in the room telling her about the terrifying night. What she attributed to Anna was almost verbatim what came through Lucy in the seance, except in detail. According to Wanda, Anna said she was awakened late at night by the crashing sound of a door being broken into downstairs. She rushed to gather the children, who were awakened, and then began to cautiously descend the steps. Before she even reached the halfway point, two men accosted her at gunpoint. She was pistol-whipped and beaten. She feared that the man with the gun would shoot her, or worse, that the children were going to be killed. In that instant, Wanda said that Anna left her body, and was dead.

As Wanda continued relating the events to us, she insisted we follow he upstairs. As we ascended the steps, and reached the ninth or tenth step, suddenly, Wanda began falling backwards, as if she were being pushed. It took all my strength to hold her upright. For about ten seconds, Wanda was being shoved back, while Ricky was shoving her forward, yelling at whatever force was doing this too her, to release her and let her move forward. Finally, we were able to make it to the top of the stairs. Wanda was gasping for breath as if she had been strangled. As we reached the top of the steps, and faced the master bedroom, Wanda cried out, "She's there, in the bed, do you see her, Anna is in the bed." To our amazement, we saw a visible depression in the bed for about five seconds; then the bed flattened out. Wanda claimed to be staring right at Anna, while Lucy and Ricky only saw the depression in the bed.

Within seconds after Wanda's sighting, she began to breathe heavily, and say, "She's in the bed, that's where she came from when the men came. Yes, Anna, we hear you. She jumped out of bed when men came in". Wanda moved toward the nursery and Lucy and Ricky continued to focus on the bed. Wanda kept talking as if she and Anna were facing each other. "Anna I hear you. I know. We're sorry, Anna, we hear you."

At that moment, Lucy began to cry out and sob. Wanda immediately went over to her and said that Anna has taken over Lucy's body, trying to show us exactly what happened that night. As Wanda grabbed Lucy, her body began convulsing, flailing her arms about in the air, and sobbing uncontrollably. Within seconds, Lucy, supported by Wanda, collapsed on the floor directly in front of the master bedroom, the exact spot (according to Wanda) where the men had accosted her. Anna, through Lucy, continued to sob. The sound was so painful, and gut-wrenching, that Wanda and Ricky could barely contain themselves. According to Wanda, we were reliving Anna's nightmarish encounter with the men who invaded her sanctuary at night while her husband was away. Lucy repeated, "It's gone, it's gone." We never found out "what" was gone, but something was taken by force that night.

Wispy forms in the courtroom
(Courtesy of SOHO)

Wanda asked Anna to calm down and tell us what happened. The sobbing stopped briefly, then she began wailing again. Lucy's body was writhing as if she were forced down, or being held down. By now, Wanda and Ricky both had hold of her, so that she wouldn't hurt herself. The pain was evident in Anna's intonation and etched on Lucy's face. The she let out a loud scream and broke free of both of us. He hands we flailing at an invisible enemy, and her legs kicking for her life—the cries of a woman undergoing an unbearable trauma. Wanda and Ricky grabbed Lucy again and held her tightly as she continued to scream, kick, and flail with tremendous force. She was fighting for her life.

We kept telling Anna repeatedly, that it was not her fault. This brought Lucy out of her trance-state, and Wanda said that Anna was now standing in front of the nursery. She was trying to see if the children were okay. Lucy was still crying as the incident concluded. A hellish night, on her birthday with the children, her house broken into, her life threatened, and no one to believe her, except perhaps the children who witnessed it. Lucy somehow, tapped into the event, and perhaps because she is a woman, and was trusted by Anna, became her spokesperson to finally let the secret out after all this time.

Who were these men? Why did they attack Anna? Why was there never a formal apology from those who committed this crime? Did the children carry scars from that night to their graves? Did Thomas finally hear the truth about that night from his wife? There is still much to do to set the record straight. Perhaps this was an important beginning!

My Whaley House Experience

Perhaps the strongest explanation for the ghost's continued popularity is its implied optimism. A spirit has literally conquered death and come back to prove it. It is both a clue and an invitation to a world beyond our own limited reality, an offer to broaden our awareness to encompass everything and anything that just might be possible. And who can ignore that kind of challenge?

Antoinette May, **Haunted Houses and Wandering Ghosts of California** (1977)

The following story was excerpted material was courtesy of www.freakopedia.com.

The Legend Begins: On September 18, 1852, Yankee Jim Robinson was hung for the fouled attempt of stealing a ship. This was not your normal hanging and maybe a bit of injustice took place to cause the ghost to hang around all this time. First of all Yankee Jim's partners only received jail time while he himself received death. At 2 o'clock p.m. on the day of his hanging, Yankee Jim was asked, with the rope already around his neck, if he had any last words. With that Yankee Jim went into a long speech that silenced the watching crowd. By law all hanging had to be completed by 3:00 p.m. so Jim continued his speech in hopes he would go over the allowed time buying himself an extra day. However, the Sheriff had other plans, so in mid sentence Yankee Jim was hung. But a ghastly error had been made. The scaffold had been built for shorter men. The toes of Yankee Jim scraped the ground. Yankee Jim Robinson slowly strangled to death. Days later after himself witnessing the hanging Thomas Whaley bought the land where Yankee Jim was killed. This is where the Whaley House still stands today.

Dining Room
(Courtesy of SOHO)

This is just one of the many stories I had heard about the Whaley House prior to my visit. Doing some research on the legends of the Whaley House and my interests peeked even higher. So when given the chance to visit this wonderfully historic house, I jumped at it. On a nice cool Saturday afternoon, I made my way down to the beautiful Old Town San Diego. As a history buff, I found this whole area fascinating and only wished I had more time to spend there. Wanting to make the best of my time I went to the Whaley House purchased my ticket and went inside the house. I was lucky enough to enter just in time to hear one of the people from SOHO give everyone a speech about the history and legends of this wonderful house.

As I sat there in the courtroom area of the house listening a strange thing began to happen, the left side of my face began to twitch uncontrollably. At first, I thought this was just muscle spasm but the weird tingling feeling and twitching began to move all the way down my left side. At one point it became so uncomfortable that, I almost had to get up and leave. My flight or fight kicked in and I choose to fight the strange thing happening to me and sat there continuing to listen.

Hearing some of the first hand accounts helped set the mood as I began to walk through the house. As I left the courthouse area the tingling/twitching on my left side subsided the further away from that room I got. After exiting the courtroom I entered the General Store. This is the area that Mr. Whaley once used as his original business. You can now you can find books of picture people have taken of the house that have supposed ghost seen with in them. Also you can read through a book that has articles from Websites with stories on the Whaley House. From there, I entered the Dining room where a beautiful silver coffee set sat. This was the first thing that caught my eye, I mean it was hard to miss something so shinny in what would other wise be a dual room.

Then I headed upstairs to the Theater. This room and a staircase from the outside leading up to the second floor was made just for the purpose for renting out to the Tanner Troupe. Renting out rooms such as to the theater group and the courtroom and such was how Mr. Whaley helped make ends meet during hard times. Although there is seating for only 42 the stage was designed to allow the audience a full view of the actors performing. The Tanner Troupe performed a variety of dramas & comedies. Mr. Tanner died shortly after the theater opened and it was closed some months later. While standing in this room with my back to the stage, the hairs on the back on my neck stood up like something brush across the back of my neck. This feeling only occurred when my back was to the stage. Is this maybe the ghost of Thomas Tanner? I she still watching over his theater? Well Mr. Tanner's ghost should be happy because after 133 years the SOHO people have re-opened the theater for providing entertainment and history.

The next room to visit was the Master Bedroom. This was the largest of the bedrooms and was beautifully decorated. While taking pictures of the bedroom I all of a sudden noticed that a curtain to my left was moving like somebody was kicking it. I was lucky enough to capture it on video. Now there was no window open in the room so was there a breeze coming from somewhere else? Or is this something more ghostly? If it was just the wind then why did it suddenly stop?

I then moved on to look at the children's bedroom. I personally didn't see anything special about this room but from many of the stories I've heard about things happening with the children and with in the room, I did begin to get the creeps. From there I moved on to the next bedroom which held 2 beds and is said that impression on one of the beds are commonly found as is somebody is sitting on it. Then I headed downstairs to continue my investigation

The downstairs bedroom is where most of the Whaley children where born. It is also the room where Lillian Whaley (Thomas & Anna Whaley's daughter) lived most of her life. Rumors have it that she didn't like to go upstairs due to she felt like there was ghost up on the second floor, mainly the ghost of Yankee Jim. More so as Lillian grew in age it became hard for here to clime the stairs and it just made it easier by her to stay in the downstairs room. The next room I moved on to the study. The desk and everything on it (which is pictured above) belonged to Thomas Whaley. Cigar smoke can sometimes be smelled with in the room along with the upstairs. Leading from the Study was the Parlor where much of the entertainment was conducted. It is rumored that Regis Philbin sat on that couch in this room and ended up witnessing the ghost of a young lady.

I then backed out into the hallway, and made my way to the back of the house to the garden and grounds. While walking around the back yard my wife, happen to take a picture up at the house from the back. When we got home and down loaded the pictures from the camera we say something very interesting in the window of the extra bedroom upstairs. Can you see it? Can you something that looks like a child staring down from the window?

I completed the tour with a walk around the grounds looking at the different plants and some of the other buildings that have been brought to the property for historical value. Finally, I ventured into Anna and Thomas's rose garden. Here I made my final comments. Do I believe this house is haunted? YES! If you ever get the chance prove it to yourself. In final note, I want to thank everyone at SOHO for his or her contribution in preserving this historic home and land. With out people like them living and standing history would surly be lost.

Not welcome at the Whaley House

> Ghosts come from all social classes: the rich and famous and the poor and obscure. They are found in mansions, slums, new houses, apartments buildings, discount stores, restaurants, office plazas, grocery stores and places where tragedy and murder took place. They are found in places where there is no tragedy or history providing a clue as to why the ghost is there. Ghosts walk through walls, step up to the second floor using stairs that were torn down twenty years ago, and gaze out at us from windows. They are helpful and turn the oven off just as the pies are about to burn. They are harmful and start fires that could have burned the house down. They are cheerful and play practical jokes and thay are terribly sand and weep endlessly in the night. Ghosts are everywhere and they are nowhere. They simply refuse to sit down and grant investigators an interview.
>
> Barb Huyser, **Small Town Ghosts** (2003)

This account was submitted by Paul from Arizona to Thomas Wolke at www.cloudplanet.com Check out the site which provides eXceptionally eXtraordinary eXperiences.

On April 9, 1999, while visiting San Diego, California, for a wedding, I had a chance to visit the infamous Whaley House. After studying the paranormal for many years, I was very familiar with it's history as one of America's most noted haunted houses because of it's constant activity and multiple entities. Well, about 11:05 that morning, I got more than I ever expected. I talked to the curator of the museum (a woman I will call Jane), upon entering and signing the guest book. I told her of my interest in the house, and asked her if there were any "cold spots" in the house. Without a moment of hesitation, she responded, "second stair from the top." She told me to wait until other visitors came down from the upstairs where the bedrooms were before I went up alone. Jane said if "anything was going to happen", it would be more conducive to have an empty atmosphere. She said it is times when the house is quiet and she's alone that she has witnessed paranormal activity.

So, I slowly took each of the long stair steps one at a time. Everything was very quiet. When I got near the top I stopped (remembering what Jane had told me about the second step). First, I slowly passed my hand (palm side down) across the third step. It was room temperature. Then I reached over second step and repeated this across the first step. Same result. Now, I would know if Jane was telling the truth, since I once felt a cold spot before in Chicago. I slowly passed my hand across the second step. It was ice cold!

I thought my mind was playing tricks on me, that I had talked myself into feeling it, so I tried it again and again, with the same results over and over. Then I decided to do some inspection in and around the second step to check for any trickery, such as hidden air conditioning vents, etc. I found nothing. Cold spots usually are between 10-50 degrees Fahrenheit. This one was cold, that's all I knew. I stepped over the second step, maybe out of respect for the dead, like when walking around graves rather than stepping on them.

I then proceeded directly to the Whaley's master bedroom to observe and shoot a picture. It had been a sunny day and there had been enough light filtering into the room to not use any flash, so I chose not to. After, snapping one picture, I walked out of the room and into the hallway, directly adjacent to the nursery, where I was hoping to hear little Annabelle bouncing her ball, as others had heard.

Then suddenly, in a split second, a tremendous, cold, numbing sensation passed through the left side of my body from back to front! It came from the room I had just left. I stood still, not realizing what had just taken place. Then, my heart started pounding. I was more scared than I ever had been in my life! I believe an apparition, specter, spirit, or whatever you want to term it "walked through me." It could have been "Yankee" Jim Robinson, who has been known to "roam through" the hallway upstairs.

The Parlor and Study
(Courtesy of SOHO)

As history tells us, this is the spot where the gallows were torn down and the Whaley House was erected in September of 1856. Incidentally, Jim Robinson was the last soul to be hanged on those gallows, but because of his tall stature, suffered a long agonizing death. He took approximately ninety minutes to die, cursing and fighting while suffocating, until he took his last breath. After, gaining my composure, I decided to slowly walk back downstairs. Note: I never saw anything as it passed through me, I only felt it. I nervously told Jane what had happened to me, and to my amazement, she was not surprised. She told me to document the events while still fresh in my mind, so I did.

Jane then took me into the parlor and opened a desk drawer to reveal black and white pictures taken over the years in various rooms of the house, all containing ectoplasm, vortices, and other unexplained manifestations. These have not been published in any book, including "The Haunted Whaley House" written by Robert and Anne Wlodarski. End of story? Not quite. When I had the film developed from that camera, much to my horror, I found what I believe to be ectoplasm on the picture I took upstairs of the master bedroom! I had taken other pictures throughout the house, none of which showed nothing abnormal. I have since sent this picture to a man I cannot name who is currently documenting material to make a video of California's haunted houses, with the Whaley House at the top of the list. I think he will use my picture, as he has indicated to me. All I know is that I have shared a very personal experience with all of you who read this. In none of it have I lied or fabricated in anyway. The Whaley House is for real ! I will never return there again, as I feel I was not "welcomed" there.

A Convocation of Souls

Do I have a clue where all this will take me? No, but that's part of the fun of life. I will keep doing what I do and just see where it all leads. Of course, I would love to be able to someday say, "Here is incontrovertible scientific evidence on the existence of ghosts. This is exactly what they are, and how you can detect, measure and communicate with them." Until that day comes, I'll keep sticking my meters into dark corners, and at the end of the day pull all the cobwebs out of my hair and just tell a good story about it all.

Linda Zimmermann, **Ghost Investigator Volume 1: Hauntings of the Hudson Valley** (2002)

Rob and Anne Wlodarski of G-Host Publishing and the International Paranormal Research Organization (IPRO) organized the event at the Whaley House on the night of May 5, 2001. With the aid of several psychics from the Orange County Society of Psychic Research, including Michael Kouri, Pat Bryan, Veral Pitsenbarger, Peggy Stahler, and former Travel Channel producer, Michelle Garforth, cameraman Matthew Cope and his wife Debbie, the authors and eight members of Save Our Heritage Organization (SOHO), the group conducted a full investigation of the house as well as a communication circle that followed the walk-through.

During the evening leading up to the seance, the psychics were allowed to visit all the rooms, and gather their impressions of the spirited clientele. Most of these gifted individuals were interviewed on camera by travel hostess, Michelle Garforth. Bruce Coons of SOHO, who provided the historical backdrop to the house and hauntings, was also interviewed by Michelle during the day. The entire event was audio and videotaped by Matt Cope of Sacred Mesa Productions and Rob Wlodarski of Mayan Moon Productions, also manned a camera for the event. SOHO member and newsletter author, David Marshall, wrote the following article, summarizing the evening's events.

David Marshall of Save Our Heritage Organization (SOHO) prepared an article about the events that transpired during the paranormal investigation and subsequent seance. The article appeared in the SOHO Newsletter of June, 2001, and is presented below with the permission of SOHO, and Mr. David Marshall, Architect, Milford Wayne Donaldson, FAIA - Phone: (619) 239-7888 allowed us to use this article in our book.

The Parlor
(Courtesy of SOHO)

On a warm May night as the sun sank behind the Pacific, we began our efforts to communicate with the dead. Around a large wooden table sat five renowned haunted house investigators and several curious SOHO board members, like myself. We were sitting quietly in the glow of candlelight waiting for the evening's main event, The Convocation of Souls.

The host was Michael Kouri, paranormal investigator, psychic, author and medium. Kouri and his associates, most of whom are members of the Orange County Society for Psychic Research had submitted a proposal to SOHO to conduct an investigation of the long rumored ghosts. The co-organizer of the event was Rob Wlodarski. An archeologist for 30 years, Rob and his wife Anne run G-Host Publishing and together they co-authored the popular book The Haunted Whaley House: A History and Guide to the Most Haunted House in America. Their intent was to monitor and record paranormal activity as part of an ongoing investigation. Also in attendance was a small crew to videotape the event. Television journalist, anchor and thrill-seeker Michelle Garforth, who has done work for The Travel Channel, The Discovery Channel and ESPN, was also there, eager to witness the Whaley spirits.

At the dark table Michael laid out the ground rules (or below-ground rules) for all of us who were new to this, open your mind, don't be scared, hold hands, don't cross your legs and try to think of "yes" or "no" questions that the spirits might want to answer. Michael spoke calmly and noted that we should watch our toes and keep away from the table legs because "the table has been known to raise and lower" during the normal course of events. We were also told to remove all watches and metal jewelry because we could inadvertently get "burned by the energy" of the spirits. If anyone got scared during the event, Michael said they should just leave the room, preferably not screaming. The table was littered with tape recorders, a digital thermometer, an electromagnetic field meter, a compass, feathers, three candles, and a toy cradle that hopefully would be manipulated by our ghostly guests.

After our orientation, Michael spoke directly to the spirits. They were told to communicate by raising or lowering the flame of the middle candle or by moving the table or other objects in the room Michael closed his eyes and declared, "there is a lot of presence in this room." It was about 9pm and our Convocation of Souls had officially begun.

Funnel from in doorway of the former study (now a guest room)
(Courtesy of Authors)

One by one we went around the table, each of us asking questions. Many of the initial questions were to determine who among the list of famous dead was joining us. The first ~0 minutes were quite uneventful. The center candle barely moved and the room was quiet (except for the Cinco de

Mayo clean-up crews out on the street). It's not easy to think of questions to ask of the dead. 'How's the weather?" "Do you haunt here often?" Michael warned us not to ask how the ghosts had died because it might upset them since (in true Sixth Sense-speak)"some of these people don't know that they're dead."

In an attempt to broaden our discussion with the spirits I asked, "Did George W. Bush really win the election?" The candle flickered a "yes," but Michael noted, "ghosts can be biased too." Michael's reading of the candle flame fluctuations was far from definitive. He kept asking, "was that a 'yes'?"

Questions then began to get what appeared to be more emphatic answers in the form of noises and movements from the table. First we heard a rapid tapping sound from the middle of the table. It first sounded like creaking wood, but it was too rhythmic and fast. It was like someone tapping out Morse code with pencils. All of our hands were flat atop the table and in clear view, so the night was starting to get interesting. The table antics then got more dramatic. The tapping seemed to travel around the table and we began to see and feel the table vibrating. One woman said it felt "like an earthquake." Several times we could see the corner of the table nearest Michael lift up and fall back with a bang as the leg hit the floor. The light-hearted nature of our seance suddenly got more serious.

Michael reminded us not to get scared and Mrs. Pat Brian, one of the paranormal investigators on hand, commented that this was pretty tame compared with her past experiences. The tapping and shaking continued. Questions were asked of Thomas and Anna Whaley and "Yankee" Jim Robinson who was reportedly hanged at the site before the house was built. Questions about Violet Whaley, who committed suicide as a young woman, brought aggressive responses. The rattling (continued from previous page) was loud and quick, the chandelier in the room, which had been still all night, began to swing.

Having been a witness to the evening's events, I must admit that I don't have a logical explanation for what I heard and saw. The candle flame was unconvincing, but the table noises and movements defied easy explanation. Although the part of the table that raised and dropped was near Michael Kouri, his hands were flat on the table and his legs were not near the corner that lifted.

During a break I looked under the table and sat in Michael's seat. My knee could easily reach the bottom of the table, but I wasn't able to lift the corner like I had witnessed. At different times, there were two non-psychics next to the moving corner and if they were making it move I don't see how. Plus the rapidness of the shaking and tapping would make it near impossible for someone to use their leg without it being obvious.

The spirits apparently wandered off during our intermission because the table rattling didn't resume and the candle remained still. Our night of communicating with the dead was drawing to a close. As Regis might have asked, "Is that your final rattle?" The evening's drama was not exactly an episode of "The X-Files," but it was still a fascinating experience. Michael, Rob, Pat and the others were enthusiastic and seemed genuinely interested in documenting unexplainable phenomena at the Whaley House. Earlier in the evening I had asked Rob how the Old Town landmark compared to the many other haunted sites he'd investigated and written about. "On a scale of 1 to 10, he told me, "this house is probably a 16."

The Whaley House is open to visitors Monday through Sunday from 10:00 to 4:00. Admission is free to SOHO members. The Haunted San Diego Ghosts and Gravestones nighttime tours in partnership with San Diego Historical Society and Old Town Trolley may also be purchased at the Whaley House.

Haunted or not, this place is definitely alive

Volumes of speculations are already written on the explanations of ghosts, angels, and other contacts from the spiritual realms. A high degree of these seems to conflict with each other. However, it is important to realize that numerous possibilities exist simultaneously. Energy thought-forms can be suspended in space to appear once again to the highly sensitive individual. Particularly emotional or traumatic events can produce very dramatic results hundreds of years beyond the time-frame of their original occurrence.

Nannette Morrison, **A Thundering Silence** (1996)

The following story was provided by Jonathan Lamas, founder of FindAGhost.Com Online Magazine. Be sure to check out his Website at: www.findaghost.com

Recently, while visiting two good friends in San Diego, California, I had the wonderful opportunity of stopping by the Whaley House in Old Town. For those of you who are not familiar with The Whaley House, it is believed to be one of the most haunted houses in America. I, being somewhat skeptical when hearing the phrase "most haunted", could not see anything ominous while starring at this 146 year old structure from across the street. The old brick building with green shutters and white wooden railing surrounded by a yard full of large trees and green grass looked rather quaint to me. It wasn't until I entered the building that I realized this structure is anything but quaint.

The history of the Whaley House dates back to 1857 when Thomas Whaley built the house for both residential and business use. Over the years, the house was the location of several deaths. A child playing with the Whaley children ran into a low hanging clothesline in the back yard of the house and crushed her throat. She later died in Mr. Whaley's arms in the kitchen of the house. One of Thomas Whaley's children died at age of 11 in the house. The death was mysterious and was ruled accidental poisoning. Her ghost is said to occasionally play pranks on visitors by playing with the kitchen cleaver.

Later Whaley's daughter Violet committed suicide in the back yard. She was believed to have been distraught over a failed marriage. The Whaleys are said to have heard the shot from inside the house. They ran into the backyard to see if everything was OK, knowing that their daughter had been emotionally disturbed. Mr. Whaley picked his daughter up off of the lawn and brought her into the home where she was pronounced dead of a gunshot wound to the heart. Even more interesting, some historians claim that the land where the Whaley House resides was once used for burial purposes by Native Americans.

When Thomas Whaley designed the house, he envisioned it being used as a general store downstairs with residential quarters on the second floor. The oldest portion of the house, which was originally built as a granary, was used as a Courtroom by the people of Old Town. It has also been reported that the courtroom was used as meeting places, a school, a billiard hall, a church, and even a morgue. Some say that the ghost of a corrupt judge still watches over this room from time to time. Others say they have smelt Mr. Whaley's cigars while sitting in this room. During my visit, the room felt rather void of any anomalies, although I did pick up a very faint orb in one photo. Sunlight lit up the room from outside windows as visitors sat in the room looking through photo albums of orbs and other strange photos taken at the house by previous visitors.

Upstairs Guestroom
(Courtesy of SOHO)

Directly outside of the courtroom is the old general store. Whaley was known to be a shrewd businessman, and sold coffee, utensils, fabrics, candles, oil, lamps, and other similar items here. Up to this point, we had not yet experienced any oddities within the Whaley House. The atmosphere was rather tranquil. As we left the general store made our way into the Dinning room, I felt somewhat of a draft. I asked my two companions to stop while I took a picture. I didn't see anything, but wanted to document the room with my camera. At the time, nothing showed up on my camera as I snapped of my shot. Later, when I arrived home from my trip, I noticed a strange irregularity in the image. There appears to be a discoloration of light that was picked up by my camera.

We briefly glanced over the dinning room before making our way to the most interesting part of the Whaley House. The stairway which leads to the upstairs portion of the house has been the sight of many documented occurrences. Many orbs have been captured in this portion of the house, as well as many other unexplained photo anomalies. Some visitors have even reported encountering cold spots on the stairwell.

Legend has is that years before the Whaley House was built, a man by the name of Jim Robinson, 'A.K.A. Yankee Jim', was hung from a noose in the vicinity of where the existing stairwell resides. At that time, the area was vacant land. His energy is said to still make its presence known in this location. Some people feel a choking sensation when passing step nine on the staircase. During our visit, I recall being totally intrigued by the staircase. As I approached the top portion of the staircase, I took a few photos looking down to the first floor and captured several more orbs on my camera. Another shot in the same location revealed nothing. As time passed, we eventually explored every room in the Whaley House. Although I had felt a draft when entering the dinning room, the only other strange occurrences up to that point had been the orbs I had captured with my camera. Given the fact these orbs could have originated from dust or light glare, I definitely did not feel as though the Whaley House deserved to be called the most haunted house in America.

As the sun slowly began to set outside, we began to wrap up our visit of this historic house. Very few people were present as we made our final walk through the upstairs portion of the home. Earlier in the day we had heard one of the Whaley House employees tell of a strange occurrence that took place in the children's room adjacent to the upstairs theater. Supposedly, several people witnessed two children tossing a ball back and forth inside the room. The people were curious to know how the children had made their way to the closed off portion of the house. When they turned to show the Whaley House employee, the children had vanished.

Thinking that we might see something in this room as well, we stopped for a bit and took several images. As I held my camera up to the room's entrance, I slowly began to notice what appeared to be a black ball shaped object in the rear corner of the room moving from right to left, then left to right. I glanced up in amazement, hoping to see the black ball with my own eyes and saw absolutely nothing. I looked back at the display on my digital camera and saw the black ball shaped object moving again, left to right, right-to-left. I immediately called over a friend, who I hoped would be able to validate what I was seeing. She immediately said,'"What is that moving in the background? It looks like a black ball." We both glanced up, looking into the room, and again saw nothing. We looked into the camera, and witnessed the black object smoothly moving back and forth in the rear corner of the room.

The Parlor
(Courtesy of SOHO)

After standing in shock for about 30 seconds, overcome by a cold chill that ran through my body, I zoomed in on the object and took a picture. When I looked at the display on my camera, I couldn't believe my eyes. The display was completely white. The oddity had not been captured. The two of us looked into the viewfinder and could no longer see the black object in the rear of the room. Whatever it was, it had gone away, leaving us with nothing more than an extremely unsettling feeling in our stomachs.

My friend's wife, who happened to be my witness, could not believe what she had just seen. As a Graduate student currently finishing up her Masters degree in Psychology, she commented that she had never witness anything like what she saw in that room. She was visibly shaken. I was puzzled as well, and could not understand how the object could show up in my camera's viewfinder, but not show up before my own two eyes. As we left the house that evening, we thanked the people there for their time, and walked off into the setting sun. As the door to the Whaley House closed shut behind me, I imagined the things that must go on there after hours. Someday I would like to return with a team of qualified investigators. Haunted or not, this place is definitely alive.

A Whale[y] of a Tale... or two

> It was Henry W. Longfellow who said, "All houses wherein men have lived and died are haunted. Through the open doors the harmless phantoms on their errands glide, with feet that make no sound upon the floors." We can't escape the evidence. Paranormal things are happening. Yes, something is hout there!
>
> Don Farrant, **Ghosts of the Georgian Coast** (2002)

Bonnie Vent is a Spirit Advocate and founder of the San Diego Paranormal Research Project (www.sdparanormal.com). She graciously provided us with a couple of stories for the book pertaining to events that happened to her in the house.

Anna Whaley's Black Dress: Full Circle: Life can be funny sometimes. You start in one place and research your way into a full circle. Because I am a spirit advocate and a researcher, it is very important to me to get as much physical evidence as possible to prove what the spiritualist side of me already knows intuitively. My purpose is to provide evidence that everyone can see, feel, and examine.

Back in 1990, I visited the Whaley House. I had not been there for years. For those who have seen pictures from that time frame, you might remember there used to be some very spooky-looking mannequins in the upstairs bedrooms. I walked past the master bedroom and I heard the voice of Anna Whaley. She explained to me plainly that she did not like HER DRESS on that mannequin and the fact that people were so spooked by the mannequins. She found it disrespectful.

There was a lady sitting sewing upstairs. I went up to this nice looking woman and said "Excuse me, I hope you do not think I am crazy, but Anna told me she doesn't like her black dress on that mannequin." She looked at me, very seriously, and said, "I believe you. Not many things in this house actually belonged to a Whaley family member, but that is indeed Mrs. Whaley's dress." The lady also remarked that she and I were the only ones who knew that fact, so of course she believed me. This lady was June Reading who was instrumental in saving the house. The Whaleys and their house were her life's work and joy.

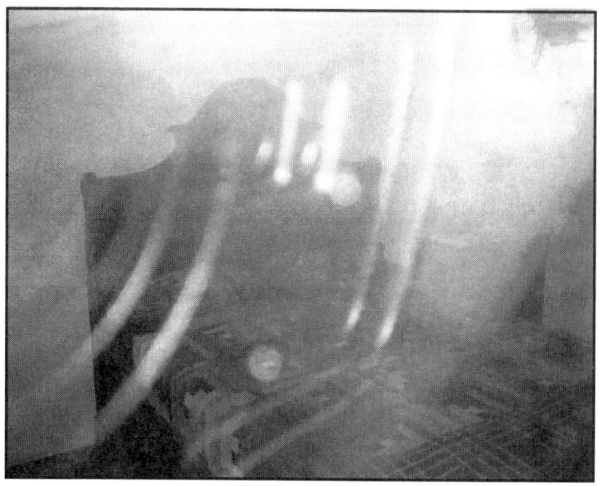

Streaks of light, orbs and mist in upstairs older childrens bedroom
(Courtesy of SOHO)

I came back to the house a few months later and found that all of the mannequins had been removed, and the black dress was now laid out on the bed. As I was standing there, Anna thanked me for delivering her message. Little did I know that in the year 2000 a battle would ensue in court over what was and what was not Whaley property. I told every docent who would listen to save Anna's black dress. To this day, I do not know if it was my insistence or some documentation left by June Reading, but the dress was saved. You cannot even get into this area of the house anymore. There is a theatre stage there now, but if you look at old pictures on the Internet, you will see Anna's black dress laid out on the bed. Up to this point, I only had a spirit voice and the word of June Reading, who passed in 1998, as proof of that being Anna's black dress.

In August of 2003, I was researching through newspapers from the 1887-1888 time frame. In the San Diego Union I found an article about a Gala Ball held at the Hotel Del Coronado in 1888, a few months after it opened. Anna and Miss Lillie are included on the guest list. There is a detailed description of what all the ladies wore. What do I find but the exact description of Anna's black dress! This must have been the occasion that caused her to buy the dress that came all the way from Paris—full circle!

Violet Whaley -Was it murder, suicide or something in between? I spent a lot of time at the Whaley House during the transition from the Historic Shrine Foundation to the Save Our Heritage Organization in 2000 and 2001. One of the big family secrets was Violet Whaley, and how she died. The Whaley family had an agreement with the Historic Shrine Foundation never to talk about Violet. I had never heard anything about her until this one day...

I was standing out by the big tree in the front yard, when I was greeted by a young girl (of the spirit persuasion). She came up and held my hand. My friend Pat, who also has some psychic abilities, saw her too. This little spirit girl turned me around and gave me a firm nudge to follow her to the back yard. As I walked on the path, I felt the impact of a gunshot to my chest. For a minute, I was unable to breathe. I always report these incidents to the docents to see if there is an historic record of what I am experiencing. Well, for some reason the ban had been lifted. I was told the story of how Violet Whaley, while in the backyard privy, died of a gunshot wound to the chest. There has always been controversy over what really happened.

About a month later, the Travel Channel was at the house filming a re-enactment of Violet Whaley's death. Violet was there and was irate. She kept telling me this was all wrong and not what happened at all. I asked Violet for the true story but she refused to talk about it. She did not feel it was anybody's business, even mine, although I was trying to help her.

Strange band of light above docent
(Courtesy of SOHO)

A few weeks later I went to the cemetery to visit the Whaley family plot. I asked Violet one more time if she wanted to tell me the true story. Her comment to me was, "It was an assisted suicide". I went back to the house and told a docent what Violet had said. I gather it makes sense since the gun that killed her belonged to Thomas Whaley and he gave her the key to open the locked box in which it was housed. These statements were made by Thomas Whaley during the inquest that was customarily performed for any suspicious death. The record of the inquest is an historical document. I hope these real stories show the reader that we do live on after crossing and the personality remains intact.

From the files of San Diego Paranormal

Not everyone can see ghosts. Even when a whole roomful of people are witnessing ghastly ghostly goings-on, one stolid person is likely to sit there seeing and hearing nothing whatever of the manifestations. He, of course, thinks everyone else is either crazy or "seeing things." Perhaps, instead, it is the man who can't see ghosts who is having the hallucination—the hallucination that every thing in this world is solid and material and matter-of-fact and routine. Those who have ghostly experiences—and there are a fantastic number of us—know that the world, instead, is filled with curious psychical phenomena which challenge every iota of our intellect and ingenuity to explain. And thus every haunted house is a Pandora's box of potential excitement. Luckily, even if you can't see ghosts, you can read about them. So read now of a great many of the interesting haunted houses of the world. Read—and enjoy!

Susy Smith, **Haunted Houses For The Millions** (1967)

The following stories were published by Bonnie Vent, San Diego Paranormal (www.sdparanormal.com), and permission was granted for their inclusion in our book. Contact Information for San Diego Paranormal Research Project is: E-mail is info@sdparanormal.com and her Website is www.sdparanormal.com. Thanks Bonnie for your fantastic Website and for all those who shared their experiences via your Website.

I wished I had a camera then!

A visitor from Stockton related these experiences while in the backyard of the Whaley House, and also inside.. It was around 3:00 p.m. when this young girl went into the backyard area of the house with her friend. She saw a little girl playing in the backyard, who looked up at the two visitors. The little girl smiled as she played in her "Period" clothing. Everything seemed so real that the guests thought nothing of the child, except she seemed out of place. Within seconds, the girl got up and began running away, until she vanished. At this point one of the girls began to shiver, and suggested that both of them better go inside the house. Once inside, the visitors asked if the little girl that they had just witnessed was part of the tour. The docents looked confused, and responded that there was no little girl dressed up from another time, playing anywhere on the property.

Over the years one of the girls was continually drawn to the house where she spent numerous hours inside, soaking up the ambiance. During that time, she had several experiences with the unknown, including: Witnessing a woman disappear; smelling flowers; chasing a dog that suddenly vanished; witnessing a tall man who glared at here for a second before dematerializing; hearing unexplained noises; watching as furniture moved just before closing time; nothing shadows move on walls; and, hearing ethereal music. Haunted; Yes! But her only regret was that she wished she had a camera then!

Possible mist forming in lower left of the photograph
(Courtesy of SOHO)

A tune for Anna
Dan from San Francisco had his unusual paranormal experience inside the house around lunchtime. According to Dan, "The tour guide let me go into the room with the piano and play on it for a minute; it was the same piano used in the movie, Gone With the Wind. As I was sitting on the bench playing, a exceedingly bright, but soft white light appeared to my right. As I looked over, I saw a nearly full-torso ghost of a woman sitting on the piano bench beside me. There was not much detail in appearance, but clearly, the face of a woman whom the tour guide and I believed was Anna Whaley. The apparition was there for maybe eight or ten seconds (although it felt like an eternity!) before it literally faded away.

Courtroom encounter
According to Lyndsay of Hollister, California, "I was sitting in the courtroom, and while there was no one sitting behind me, or next to me (within

touching distance) something [unseen] kept tapping me on the shoulder. I also experienced the cold spots in the hallway.

The truth about cats and dogs
Amy from Escondido, California had the following encounter in the backyard of the house around midnight, "When I decided to visit house, it was pretty late at night. While in the backyard, I saw a dog and of course, I tried to call it over to me. I chased after it, which is when I spotted a cat that the dog was chasing. At the time, I had no idea that a dog had been spotted in previous cases. It was just really scary, when the dog literally disappeared with the cat by the back of the house, near the stairs."

Halloween orbs
Dana from Coronado, California had an otherworldly experience in the backyard of the Whaley House around 11:00 p.m. one night. According to Dana, after waiting in a long line trying to get tickets with her daughter for the annual Whaley House Halloween event, she was told that the event was sold out. Disappointed, she stayed around the building for a few minutes and began taking digital pictures on the side of the house, knowing that an enormous amount of activity continually occurs in that area. At first she started taking them at ground level, then she distinctly heard a voice tell her, "Hey! look up!, what makes you think we wanna be around all those crazy people down there?"

Clearly visible shoulder of a woman in an upstairs young children's bedroom
(Courtesy of SOHO)

She has always been very respectful of spirits and would talk to them as she would anyone. She communicated to the energy that she would appreciate them showing themselves to her. Within minutes, Dana and her daughter had a large group following them around. Everyone could see "orbs" moving when the camera flash would occur. After shooting numerous pictures in the backyard and even in the middle of the street next to the Whaley House, Dana decided to go down to El Campo Santo, the cemetery down the street. As they arrived, Dana's daughter got the distinct sense that the spirits disliked all that building across the street from the cemetery. With that, Dana began taking more pictures, with quite a few orbs showing up. She and her daughter may have missed the regular Halloween tour, but what they got instead, was a very personal tour of the unknown, by some of the spirits who preferred less crowded conditions.

Girl at the top of the stairs

Nicolette of Canada, touched the unknown during her first visit to the Whaley House. It was early afternoon during her excursion through the house, when she reached the stairs leading to the second floor. As she stared toward the top of the stairs and out of the corner of her eye, she saw a blonde girl, approximately 10 years old, standing on the right side if you were starting to go downstairs. The young girl was wearing an early 1900's style, knee length white dress and had some brown in her hair. At first, Nicolette thought she was a kid who was touring the house, but when she turned away for a second, the young girl had vanished. Nicolette said that the girl was very pretty and a little luminescent.

Halloween at the Whaley House

Bonnie Vent described one Halloween night at the Whaley House, as follows, "The house was lit using the lighting of the Whaley family's day. There were kerosene lanterns in each room of the house and sconces with lit candles on the walls. It satisfied the need of those looking for ghostly events as well as the true historians. I must say the smell of kerosene was quite overwhelming. All of the Whaley House docents were dressed in period costumes. One docent who was wearing a hat with a big feather plume, bent over one of the lanterns to see something a guest was showing her. The big feather caught on fire. No damage done but quite a show for a few minutes. There was also a guest with a camcorder that got a very clear picture of a ghostly lady. He showed it to one of the docents. As she described it to me it sounded very familiar. We are hoping to get a copy of this photo. Pictures in general were hard to take since the setting was so dark. I did get some regular shots that I put into a slide show (see the link at the bottom of the page).

The line was very long, with approximately 800 tickets sold. They had to stop selling tickets at 10:30pm even though the house was open until midnight. One of the reasons for the crowd was a local radio station DJ and guest who spent all night in the house the night before Halloween, and people were excited about what they had heard on the radio show. Most of the information was of the urban legend variety. If you heard the rolling marble story or if you read about it, the fact is it was a gumball rolled across the floor by a radio station producer to scare his guest. The truth of the matter is the Whaley House ghosts snubbed their overnight guests. No one has spent the night in the house since the famous Regis Philbin incident. I guess the Whaley House ghosts have not forgiven the media yet.

Guests on Halloween night were treated to some real ghost stories about the Whaley's and Yankee Jim in the Courthouse portion of the house. I did witness a ghostly event there. While the docent was talking about Yankee Jim's hanging a column of white light enveloped her. Then a black shadowy figure appeared behind her. I asked her after the talk if she was aware of his presence. Her comment was, "nothing ever happens to me." I told her she could no longer make that claim and shared the experience with her. It was also mentioned to me there is a story going around that Halloween night the alarm went off and would not stop. Sorry, not true. The alarm does make a tone sound a few minutes after it is set. Perhaps that is what started this story."

Unusual rectangle of light in doorway of former study (now a guest room)
(Courtesy of the Authors)

Sometimes, Lex is more

This story is from "Lex the great," who described his encounter in the Whaley House as follows: "I went to the Whaley House on the Ghost and Gravestones tour. There were no more than about 10 of us, because aside from us being the last tour of the night, it was also raining heavily. We got the grand tour and actually spent quite a bit of time in the Whaley House. When we got there, a man named Martin was going upstairs and taking pictures with a digital camera then bringing them down and showing us (since nobody is allowed upstairs at night). One of the pictures was a perfect image of a woman holding what looks like a baby in the children's room. That was my first experience with paranormal photographs.

We were all crowded in the dining room as he stood in the doorway by the stairs and was talking to us about what attracts ghosts and such. While listening to him, my arm was suddenly smacked forward, as if somebody had bumped into me; hard. So I turned around and realized that nobody was behind me. Before that could sink in, my skeptic mother grabbed my arm and said, 'Ohmigaaawd, did you feel that?' Then at the same moment Martin said, "there is definately something in this room!" Later, after talking to my mom she said, she felt a warm rush as if someone walked through her."

"After that, we went into the garden, and the tour guide was telling us all those creepy, garden stories. When the tour guide was talking about how some people step into the round part of the garden they can feel a presence, one of the men who was with us seemed kind of skeptical and asked if he could go up there. This guy was well over six-feet tall, and was all shoulders; he was a big guy! After he stepped into the middle, he immediately turned and hightailed it back to us saying, 'Oooooh no, I am getting out of there!' When he was asked what had happened, he wouldnt say anything; he just kept shaking his head. So as everyone headed back to the bus I lagged behind a little bit and headed into the garden. Picturing that big guy running out of the garden got the best of me and a hurried to catch up with the group."

"When we got back to the hotel and I told my dad our stories, he laughed at us and said, 'Your imagination was running wild.' The next day we took him to the Whaley House for a tour. My Mom and I were particular excited because this time we were allowed upstairs. My Mom and I were in the master bedroom watching that curtain in the closet sway back and forth in and out of the closet. We assumed that it was a fan, draft, or something that was causing the motion. We were still trying to freak my dad out, when he came up from behind us. We pointed the curtain out and said, 'There's the ghost, Dad' As he rolled his eyes and huffed, 'yeah,' the curtain suddenly shot up as high as it could go in the opposite direction it was swaying before. All we heard after that, was my Dad's footsteps racing down the stairs."

"That same day, I finally got the courage to go in the garden. Walking around the circle part, I reached the furthest end, when I felt a cold spot, and an overwhelming feeling of sadness rush over me. When I walked out of the garden, I felt fine. Since then, I always make it a point to go to the Whaley House whenever I'm in San Diego. One of the binders in the front room, before entering the court house, has many ghostly pictures, some of which were taken the night I was there. Since then, I bought a digital camera and recorder, and a regular recorder, and I am slowly discovering this whole ghost hunting thing. I can't wait to put it into use next time I'm in San Diego."

September Spirits: A Fall Investigation at the Whaley House

Questions arise in each of our hearts as we recall our favorite stories of ghosts, and haunted locations in our world. What is causing the unexplained seeming presence of spirits in our world? And if these are indeed what we believe that are then who are those spirits that roam to and from in our dimension? Fear tells us they may be demons, negative forces we cannot touch, or control. But our heart tells us they are loved one returning to check on those they departed from in death. Creepy chills run up our arms, and hour hairs tickle our heads as though someone was pulling them upward. At times we are tempting fate, and yet we are attracted to peep once more into that room which good judgment tells us to stay away from. Not all of you have had a chance to see into this other dimension, a place in time and space where something, someone passes. But you have had experiences you could not explain. You just explained them away. Don't let me stop you. I want you to live in your safe world where no one is standing by your bed, or peeping out of the hallway as you read the newspaper. Can I join you there in that safe world of yours?

Carol Gist, **Is it Really Haunted: A Concise Resource for Ghost Enthusiasts** (2002)

The following story was provided, courtesy of gifted Paranormal Investigator, Chad Patterson from Corona, California. You can contact Chad Patterson, at: California Society for Ghost Research, PMB 153, 541 S. Main St. Ste. 104, Corona, California 92880. We recommend you check out his Website at: www.csgr.us.

Since I was a young boy paranormal research has fascinated me, and been part of my life. Through my early teenage years, growing up in Topeka, Kansas, I collected books, articles, and anything else I could find on supposed "true accounts" of paranormal phenomena. I remember staying up into the early morning hours reading, and pondering cases and stories involving ghosts and hauntings. I was intrigued by many of the locations mentioned in these publications.

Orb on the courtroom wall
(Courtesy of SOHO)

I remember reading about the Whaley House in Old Town San Diego. The history behind this location and its inhabitants had sparked my interest for years. I remember reading about known paranormal researchers such as Hans Holzer and Richard Senate investigating and writing about their experiences at this location. I also remember lying awake in bed at night, thinking that perhaps a day would come when I would have my chance to investigate the reported "most haunted house in the Western United States." The Whaley House ghosts as they exist within their environment(s) continue to fascinate me to this day.

On the evening of Saturday September 22, 2001, a group of paranormal researchers, including myself, began an investigation of the Whaley House in Old Town San Diego. This was something we had sought permission to do, and had taken months of preparation.

Our investigation was separated into three essential phases. The first phase was designed for gathering technological data such as EMF and temperature readings. During this period, we also sought video and photographic evidence. We divided the house into three areas of focus and split into small teams. These teams rotated shifts covering the house. Each team had equal periods in all three divided sections of the house. One team would cover the courtroom, located downstairs, and two other small groups would focus on the remaining downstairs and upstairs levels. The second phase was designed to capture Electronic Voice Phenomena (EVP). This is where one attempts to record disembodied voices, and/ or other possible audible sounds associated with a specific haunted location.

EVP, and/ or Instrumental Transcommunication (ITC) can be collected in a number of ways.

Our selected method was for one investigator to walk the house and ask a series of questions in randomly selected rooms. This individual would record while asking these questions. The rest of us during this time would be assigned to room observation, so to speak. During room observation the rest of us would observe, listen, record for EVP, record video, and take still photos. We were instructed to remain as quiet in our assigned areas as possible. This was to ensure that the possible EVP, we might record, would be as free from noise contamination as possible. The third phase was designed for a psychic evaluation of the location. During this time Psychic Investigator, Virginia Marco, would randomly walk the house and attempt to communicate with any earthbound spirits at the location. Also, during this time we would further investigate the house for technical, and photographic evidence to possibly corroborate Virginia's findings. It would be a night I would never forget.

At 10:00 PM members gathered in the courtroom. While some prepared their equipment for the investigation, others listened to one docent tell of his own experiences in the house. Psychic Virginia Marco was not present for these stories. One experience the docent spoke of was the sighting of a phantom dog. The docent said that one night he was giving an evening tour of the museum and he and about thirty other witnesses all heard and saw a phantom dog move through the house. I had previously read about a phantom dog being sited on the premises. He also spoke of a dark figure witnessed in the courtroom. This docent also shared photographs taken by past visitors to the house with different anomalous shapes, or mists in them.

Orbs in the Theater
(Courtesy of SOHO)

During this time, as the docent shared his information, a few of the other investigators noticed orb activity near the jury box, and judge's bench. I also noticed orb activity in these areas. Orbs are often small, and sometimes large, sphere-like energy anomalies believed to be related to paranormal activity. These orbs are usually only captured in still photos or on video. Orbs are also arguably not seen with the naked eye, although I personally witness them from time to time at haunted locations, and did witness glimpses of them during our preparation in the Courtroom. If one has seen true orb activity on video, as I have, they would take notice to the fact that some orbs behave and react with one another as well as the living. True orbs also seem to avoid the direct vision of the living. This may be why they are not often witnessed with the naked eye. One of the female investigators was photographing these orbs with her digital camera, merely to capture and observe their patterns of movement. I would like to add to the record that these were not dust particles we were observing.

At about 10:30 PM we began the initial investigation by taking ten minutes to sit in silence and let the house quiet down. We then split into our assigned groups and the investigation continued. In addition to myself, I led a group of three investigators upstairs where we would begin, while the other two groups would begin downstairs. Upon ascending the staircase, I noticed a thickness or a heaviness increase in the atmosphere of the home. Things seemed a lot heavier upstairs then downstairs. It was dark, but not pitch black. We had flashlights for safety reasons. No one wants to trip over anything. There was also some illumination from streetlights protruding through the windows from the outside. Most of the upstairs was under some sort of renovation, during this time, and was bare. Some rooms, such as the Boys Guest Room where completely empty, while the Girl's Room and Master Bedroom possessed some furniture.

I went from room to room checking for increases and/ or decreases in electromagnetic fields with two different EMF detectors. The EMF Detector I spent most of my time with was the Trifield Natural EMF Detector. During this time there were two others taking still photographs, while a fourth investigator took temperature readings. We were occasional visited by a fifth investigator assigned to slowly roam the house for video. In the Master Bedroom, I did take a few suspicious EMF readings in the far right hand corner of the room that I could find no natural explanation. I also had similar suspicious readings in the Boys Guestroom and one such reading in the Nursery.

While I was in the Nursery testing for questionable readings one of the female investigators came and asked me to follow her. Her eyes had a serious look to them. That kind of look I was familiar with when an individual had had something strange occur and was about to show, or describe it. She brought me back to the Master Bedroom. She quietly informed me she had set her notebook and pen down on a fixture in this room while proceeding to take digital photographs. She explained that she had briefly forgotten about the notebook for several minutes, and had left the room to investigate the other upstairs rooms. Upon her return to retrieve the notebook and pen, she noticed someone had written the word "Hello" in very shaky penmanship. She handed me this notebook and I studied it carefully. There were a few other jotted notes and chicken scratches on the page. She explained to me that the other notes and scratches were her own, but the word "Hello" was not there when she had left the notebook. The penmanship of this word, although I am no expert in hand writing, did not seem to match her own.

These were investigators I had worked with in the past on other cases, and had earned their credibility. I would ask our entire group later if they had retrieved or seen a stray notebook. No one had seemed to remember seeing a notebook lying around. After asking them a few questions, we showed them the notebook. They all stared in amazement at the shaky word. I knew that due to the fact the notebook was left alone, that I could never fully prove to others, outside our group, that it as evidence of the paranormal. To this day in my personal opinion, I believe the word came from a ghostly source.

The Parlor
(Courtesy of SOHO)

As we finished our time upstairs, we caught further orb activity on digital camera. After finishing, we rotated groups and continued phase one of our investigation in the downstairs level of the house. There were numerous cold spots in the living room area, and more orb activity in the Courtroom. I continued about the location taking EMF readings. In comparison with the upstairs, the downstairs would produce fewer questionable EMF readings. Downstairs the only suspicious EMF reading I would get would be in the Courtroom.

Once it was time to begin phase two everyone gathered back in the Courtroom and then went to their assigned locations. Some investigators seemed a little nervous, but I had the plan set up so they were all in view of at least one other person from different angles in the house. All except myself. I went to the Boys Guestroom alone, and upon entering positioned myself in the far left hand corner beside one of the windows and sat. For the next five minutes we would sit, prepare ourselves for observation, let our eyes adjust, and let the house again quiet down.

The male investigator placed in charge of EVP soon began his session. He began downstairs. I could hear his footsteps reverberate through the house. I could tell which rooms he went into as he asked a series of questions. I sat and observed the empty darkness of the Boy's Guestroom as I listened to his questions. I listened for possible audible replies, or sounds. Again it was not pitch black, but it was dark. After sitting for several minutes, I was able to see perfectly. I continued to hear him ask such questions as, "Is anyone here? What year is it? What is your name? Do know you are dead? Etc." This went on for about the next twenty minutes before I heard him ascending the stairway outside my stationed room. As the investigator walked into my room, I continued to observe him and the room around us. He positioned himself in the middle of the room and began his session. He first asked if "anyone was there?" Upon this question, I swore I heard an almost soft whisper saying "Hello." I continued to listen to his questions and had hoped the response had been recorded. Later his tape revealed nothing of the word I had thought I'd heard.

After the male investigator left my stationed room he walked down the hallway and continued asking questions in other rooms. I listened to his footsteps as he entered each room, and heard his questions. Not long after he left the Boy's Guest Room, where I sat, I felt I was no longer alone. Directly across from me, in the far corner of the room, I began to notice a dim oval shape appearing from the darkness. After about a minute it became somewhat more noticeable. It was a dim opaque oval shape. The shape was not cast on the wall like light, but stood out about a foot from the wall. It was also about four to five feet from the floor. I did nothing, but continued to observe. I wasn't one hundred percent sure yet that I was actually witnessing something paranormal. The investigator was still off in other rooms of the upper level asking questions. This oval shape never distinctly manifested into anything such as an apparition, or a face, but was about the size of a head. It continued to remain about another minute before the investigator, asking questions, was on his way back toward the Boy's Guestroom.

As the investigator approached in the outside hallway, I did not take my eyes off the shape. It wasn't until this point that all the little hairs on my arms and body stood on end, because the oval shape turned to its left to the sound of the male investigator's approaching foot steps, like a head turning in response, and then quickly turned its attention back to me. I began snapping a serious of photographs with my Olympus 35 MM camera hoping that I would capture the shape. The flash was very bright and drowned out the dim shape and the darkness of the room. I could see the dim shape between flashes, but not during the flash. After this the dim shape quickly and dimly faded away. I would later come to the disappointment that I had captured nothing during this series of about seven photographs. I wished at the time I had snapped photographs without the flash. Perhaps I would have captured the dim opaque shape on film, although it was not something that came to mind during the time. I also still wonder that if I had waited to take pictures what else I may have witnessed. I also thought that if the investigator, taking EVP, hadn't come down the hallway at that moment if I would have seen the shape become something more distinct. Perhaps I would have witnessed a phantom limb, head, or even an apparition? This is something I will never know. The investigator paused by the doorway and continued recording for EVP as he went back downstairs. Soon after this, our phase two EVP session was complete.

We were not disappointed by the outcome of phase two. We did capture two back-to-back EVP's during this session. This two EVP's where both captured by two recorders downstairs. Keep in mind that during this session the male investigator in charge of EVP asked several questions, but the one question that received a response was "Has anyone here ever been murdered?" This was not a question on the list to ask, but I am glad he asked it. On the recorder almost immediately after he asked the question you can hear a dog yipping, and then a soft female voice replying "I was." One of the other male investigators also picked up what sounded like a woman screaming. To this day I have never heard nor read any documentation that states anyone was murdered in the Whaley House. This would be something that would require further investigation and needed proving to be considered as fact. Records state that Yankee Jim Robinson was hung on the Whaley property before the house was built in 1852. I also had read about the death of a young girl, Annabelle Washburn, who was reportedly died in the Whaley kitchen, but never anyone being murdered. According to Psychic Virginia Marco one woman had died of from mysterious reasons on the Whaley property, and this was something that was kept quiet, so to speak.

During phase three Virginia Marco walked the house and attempted to communicate with the spirits. During this period, several investigators and myself swept the house a second time for EMF readings, temperature readings, and photographic evidence.

While Virginia was conducting her evaluation downstairs in the house, I was upstairs testing for EMF readings. At this point, I noticed questionable readings in the Master Bedroom, and Boys Guestroom that where not in the exact same areas as measured during phase one. Some of the other investigators, also during this time, witnessed moving shadows near the stairway and upstairs of the house. With this in mind, it seemed as though these spirits were very active, and quite mobile. They seemed to react to our presence as we moved about the house by either moving away from us, or perhaps by following us.

During Virginia's psychic evaluation, around 12:15 a.m., she noted several ghosts in the Whaley House. According to Virginia there is a strong male presence in the upstairs of the house. She said his name was Robert. In the nursery, Virginia picked up the name "Lilly." I later told her that one of the Whaley daughters was named Corrine Lillian Whaley. According to Virginia, Lilly is still in the house. She said that Lilly was unhappy with the changes that had been made to the house. Downstairs Virginia described a female entity in the living room as being "very friendly." According To Virginia, this female entity was Ana Whaley. She said Ana was very polite and offered her and the two other female investigators standing beside her tea. Virginia also said there were two young girls in the house. One was very curious as to what we were doing. I would like to note that while I was investigating the living room slightly after 12:45 AM, one of the female investigators said she saw an orb as though it was in a sitting position on the stool near the piano by me. In the courtroom Virginia also stated there was the "spirit of a soldier." She said this "solider was dressed in gray from the late 1800's. He had no hat, and his arm was hurt." She said she could physically see the blood from his wound.

Possible spirit in Guest Bedroom
(Courtesy of SOHO)

Toward the end of Virginia's psychic evaluation, at about 1:00 AM, I took her up to the Boy's Guest Room and asked her if there was anything significant about this room. According to Virginia, there was a young boy with blondish hair in the middle of the room crying, and rocking himself back and forth. I felt my goose bumps slightly return. She then asked the boy telepathically "Why are you crying?" According to Virginia's report the boy replied, "Because he doesn't let me go outside." Virginia said she then asked the boy "who doesn't let you?" According to her report, the boy replied "him", and would not specify whom. I wondered if there was a connection between this boy, and what I had witnessed. After telling her what I had witnessed, she said that it had been the boy, and he was curious as to what I was doing in the room.

At about 1:15 a.m. on September 23, 2001 we gathered back in the downstairs Courtroom to share our information. We all felt very drained. Virginia had mentioned that the spirits were feeding off our energy. She stated that the Whaley House was so haunted that as soon as she stepped in side she was overwhelmed by the immense energy. She stated there was a great deal of both residual and spirit energy present in the house. I would have to say that this was the most drained I had ever felt from an any investigation prior to this. We gathered our gear, and I had many thoughts racing through my mind. Instead of solid answers, I had new questions. After examining my notes, and hearing the experiences of the other investigators that night, I had some leads that raised new questions. Virginia and I both feel there are possible unknown isolated events that once went on behind the closed doors of the Whaley House. Events kept private and not known to the public, as could exist in any case. There are numerous reasons why this house is so haunted, and continues to be one of the most haunted houses I have ever investigated. Reasons known, and perhaps reasons unknown to the public which may forever remain in the past.

The Solstice Investigation

The existence of finer dimensions of reality is not a matter of debate for the learned men of physical science. The related issue that is frequently considered is the possibility of what exactly these delineating dimensions consist of, and what precise manner of altered forms constitute the vast realm of differing vibrational rates. However, such consideration's were no great ponderable dilemma for the wise No-Eyes. Her statement was a clear and as simple as the fact itself. It interpreted as the following: The existence of spirits cannot be stupidly ignored or eradicated by skepticism or atheism, for spirits are not affected by either, but continue to exist in spite of them both.

Mary Summer Rain,**Phantoms Afoot: Helping the Spirits Among Us** (2003)

On the night of the summer solstice, June 21, 2003, a group of psychics and paranormal investigator conducted a closed investigation inside the Whaley House from 10:00 p.m. until 1:00 a.m. The participants included: Robert Wlodarski, author, paranormal investigator and the investigation organizer for the International Paranormal Research Organization (IPRO), and psychics Ginnie McGovern, Deann Burch, Robin Collier, Victoria Gross, and Colin Birch. Alex and Lonnie Sill were scheduled participants, but had to leave during the beginning of the investigation. Three Docents were present from SOHO, including: Casey O'Hanlon, Julie Wolfe and Robin Sweeton. The following is the group summary of the investigation.

Orb on the courtroom wall
(Courtesy of SOHO)

After entering, group members remarked that the energy was intense inside and several members remarked that they had either passed through electrically charged areas or felt as if someone unseen was standing next to them or passing through them. The entrance hallway and room immediately to the left leading to the courtroom, were absolutely intense. One person remarked that it felt like several people were passing right through them. Initially, there was a sense of people other than the Whaley family inside the house. At this point, someone remarked that the change in the way the house was redecorated, painted and modified, had shifted the energy to being uncomfortable, rather than having a homey feel. It's as if the house now embodied the energy of all the people who formerly occupied the house rather than just the Whaley family, as was felt a year or so ago. Were the Whaley spirits unhappy with or confused about the changes that were occurring, or confused and trying to adapt to them?

There was a consensus that the once dominant Whaley spirits, had given way to a mixed energy indicative of numerous occupants from different time periods. In the past, the spirits of Thomas, Anna, Frank, Violet and the children, were the first sensory experience felt by most "sensitive" individuals upon entering the building. The once, "homey" feel was now replaced by a more transient energy, like a train station terminal, where energy was constantly moving and shifting.

The people in the group were feeling hot and cold upon entering the house, as these energy spots seemed to be everywhere. The EMF meter malfunctioned and the Gaussmeter was turned off because it simply "spiked" all the time. The meter became useless as a means of identifying potential energy locations, since there was just too much energy throughout the house to isolate specific locations using anomalous readings from the EMF or Gauss meters as a guide. There were also several instances where white or yellow orbs of light floated through various rooms in the house. Several photographs were taken which produced unexplained mists, beams of light or other anomalies. After entering, the group split up and wandered throughout the house. After roughly two-and-a-half hours, we all met in the courtroom for the following summary in the words of the participants:

Ginnie McGovern
First when I walked in, this entry and hallway felt like a freeway, there was so much going on. One lady walked right by me, or kind of through me, and she had on a long, maroon dress with like a black, lace trim around it (door slams in the background). First I went upstairs, and going up the stairs felt kind of strange, because I wasn't really sure what happened on the staircase. We got up to the top of the stairs and we started to walk into the theater room, and as I turned around, I saw a woman come up behind us on the stairs, and she stopped at the top of the stairs for just a minute or two, looked at us all and then she continued around and went right out through the glass doors at the back of the hallway (low moaning on tape)

In the theater room itself, I plugged into a big, burly, gruff man. Then I noticed that there was also a younger man that was up on the stage area, and I think I got a name Andrew or Andre Wooley, or something like that. He was explaining to me that he was a kind of orator and used to do things like debate, when they had historical readings, and he would do that there.

I then went into the far bedroom at the end of the hall, and there was a lot of activity in there. There was a young girl, maybe about 6-7 years old that was in the corner by the single bed, near the window. Then there was a gentleman standing between the wall and the door, probably around 30-to-early-40s. Then, an older woman walked by and through the room.

She was rather bent over. Then I went back into the theater room and I saw a couple of orbs in there.

Then, we went into the master bedroom, and there was movement in the chandelier up there. I also felt that there had been a cat in the room. There was also in the far corner where there was a wooden chair, I was seeing, in my head, a completely different chair and a different set-up in that corner. But, there was a man sitting in the chair, but it wasn't really that chair, it was the old chair, and he was kind of balding. again with a moustache, and he was smoking I think a pipe which I could smell. Then when I came out of there, I went back into the other bedroom where the little girl had been before, and she was still there. The gentleman that was standing in the corner before, had moved between the chair and the bed, and he had one foot up on the chair and he was lacing up his boot. Just after I noticed him, I noticed the big gentleman from the theater come into the room kind if through the wall area, and I did not like that feeling at all of him coming in there, so I stepped out of that room.

The children's room was funny. I just think I didn't like it because I didn't like that little baby carriage, doll carriage thing that was in the front. It rather looked a like a little hearse thing to me. Then I came back downstairs, and we went through the kitchen area. The kitchen to me, in the far right corner where there's a little winder there right now, it felt to me like someone had died in that corner. We were debating back and forth whether a dead body had been laid out, and I didn't get that feeling. I felt more that it was someone who had actually died in that room, in that corner area. Then I came around, I went into that far bedroom in the back there, the one that's adjacent to the living room area, and it was a very masculine feeling. I could smell a pipe smoke, but it was a different type of thing then upstairs. There was just a lot of activity, a lot of things going on and lots of people walking by, and all this kind of stuff. There were a lot of cold spots and hot spots in that room. We felt like something had passed through us, coming out of that room, and then as I was walking back up the hall I felt like there was a man behind me. I was feeling that energy very strongly.

In the living room, there was a woman sitting in a rocking chair, and I got a name like Amanda, or Adelle; I got a couple of different names. I think she was actually talking about these people, because usually I get a name pretty specifically, but I was getting a couple of different names. Then I came back into the living room through the other door, and I was going to step over the rail, because they said we could, and I felt that I would be really intruding, so I didn't do that. Then I came into this little room (the general store), and I felt at one point that there had been meat, that had been butchered or something in this corner, by the front of the house, and I asked what the room was, and Casey said it was a general store, and there was a possibility that it did happen. I don't know if it was really likely or not. In the court room, we all concurred that there was a gentleman in the seat that Robin picked up [far corner of the room where the jury chairs were - northwesternmost chair), and that was about it.

Strange light effect in foreground as a group of psychics discuss the spirited clientele in the courtroom
(Courtesy of the International Paranormal Research Organization)

Robin Collier
When we first entered and were in the hallway, my stomach was in knots and I felt nauseated. Then we came into the courtroom and I really sensed a man in the far right corner, in the last seat in the jury box. When we went through into the kitchen, That felt heavy in there, I really don't like that little door, and I didn't want to touch it. So, I moved through there really quickly. We were going up the stairs next, but I really didn't want to go first. It really felt like there was something at the top of the stairs kind of looking and watching as we started to come up. It was almost as if they were saying don't come up here. I didn't get much in the theater room, but I did get the word, orator. I did sense a woman come up, swish through and then go down the hallway and through the window door at the end of the hallway on the second floor.

When everyone was standing and looking in the first bedroom, and I was on the outside of it, just as I moved to put my arm around behind Ginnie, because I have this real sense of needing to protect her. She turned at the same time and said Robin come in here and look. In that little corner off to my right shoulder, there was something right there that I didn't want to identify. Then, in the kids bedroom, I really didn't get much in there. In the master bedroom, I did smell some kind of smoke, but I didn't want to go in there with the rest of the people, so I stayed outside and when the two ladies moved away from there, I went back into the theater and waited for them to walk back around, because I wasn't going to stand in that place by myself.

Going down the stairs to the bottom, and looking in that first room in front of the stairs (at that moment, everyone in the room felt as if someone unseen had just entered. RC said that this person had been slowly been creeping in while she was talking) it felt real cold down there, and the cold blew right through us. While I stood there looking in that little room, I saw a red flash of light go right passed me. In fact, I came right out to see if someone had a red laser light that they were pointing with, like a pointer light. When I looked up the stairs, I saw little white balls of light, orbs. The hair on my body all over has just been standing on end since I've walked in (a low rumbling or moaning sound can be heard on the tape at this point), and even before I came through the door. There's just a lot going on in here.

GM - There's a real strong masculine presence behind us right now; not a big guy, but an average size man, and his energy is really powerful, a really strong guy. I think this is the guy Colin drew a picture of. This person is not that tall, just average size.
RW - I suspect that it is [Thomas Whaley] (a small click is followed by a loud bang on the tape which we didn't hear during the discussion).
GM- There he is, right behind us, and it's really cold (several people chime in that they felt a presence standing in the back of the room at this time).
RC - I was getting stuff across my back. It's interesting, because the first encounter I had was walking up that sidewalk along the back of the house.
GM - Yes, there were quite a few things outside.
DB - I didn't see this guy. I'm disappointed.

<u>Deann Burch</u>
Usually I'm quite the writer on these things, but I didn't tonight. I just have a couple of things. In the hallway, it just felt immediately like there is conflict, and there is an energy that lends itself to confusion or misunderstandings in here in general. I came in here (courtroom) and my left side, internally, I felt jittery, almost like an appendicitis attack. I felt something clinching inside. Then I sat down and I had the image of a black feather crossing my face. Then later, I felt like a black hat being pulled across my face, tipping the hat a little. My back hurt horribly in here. I wasn't sure if it was kidneys, or lower back, and the I almost felt like I was hit across my back, in the lower back like with a two-by-four.

In another portion of the courtroom, I could almost picture like a gate there, and I was not allowed passed that point. I sensed a woman there with her head down, and I could almost see her do this motion like she was shocked at what was said, and then tears. She was in a dark, long dress. In the room outside the courtroom, near where you [GM] was feeling the butchering area, I was walking, and then all of a sudden I was only using my right foot. I had no left foot to walk. At first I thought it was like I stumbled, life from alcohol, but then I thought, no, I don't have a left foot, or left leg from the knee down. So I felt like there was an amputation or something from the knee down [one of the docents chimed in that someone in the family had a severe leg injury on the left side].

In the kitchen area, I just felt like "Wow," this place lends itself to sitting around, holding hands and greeting all the spirits in there. It's very heavy, heavy energy. But I felt in the one corner when you first walked in, the corner with the little passageway, I felt just sickness, it felt like a stomach cancer, or someone very ill and dying there. It was a long illness, very sad, very weakening illness. Going up the stairs, I was the last one in our group, and I felt a constriction in my throat. A very deep constriction, and very unstable, just my walking wasn't stable. This was in the middle of the stairs, about the 7th or 8th stairs where I felt very unstable.

When I walked into the theater room and I just felt the need to walk right toward the window that's across from the door, and I started pacing. I felt myself take on this man's energy. He was a big, burly, angry energy. I got a name with a "J" like Joseph or John, it was a "J" a hard "J" sound, and I just kept pacing. Victoria placed herself between me and the window, and did that twice. She didn't want me near that window. Once I got talking, he was saying that, he was waiting for his wife. She's betrayed me, she's betrayed me. So, at first I thought. love affair situation, but then later I went back and felt that it was a monetary betrayal. That she had given money to a brother, and I'm not sure if it was his brother or her brother, but money to a brother, or someone he had specifically said, no!. He felt this betrayal by her, and he was so angry. It was just this horrible anger. Then, I was also aware of this younger man on the stage, and I got a name more like Alister the, and I also picked up an orator feeling about him.

In the master bedroom, I could smell the sweetness of smoke, and it felt more like pipe. I was very drawn to the chandelier above the bed. It felt like it would twist or move. I also got a sense of stumbling, but more alcohol. I could almost smell the alcohol in there. Then I went down to that one room, off the hallway, the one that's dark, and I could see a little girl totally oblivious to everything, playing near window, not playing, but standing near the window. She was there, but it was like she was unaware of anything going on around her. I walked away because I really didn't want to be near there, but then I walked back in and I could, where you walk in and off to the right, there was just something in that corner, and the same as Robin said, I didn't want to identify it; I didn't want to see it. It was very heavy and very masculine. That was a very uncomfortable feeling right there. Then, when I pulled out of there, I saw an orb go by; just one single orb.

Then, I came down the stairs and again, at that same mid-way point, I just felt very unsteady (a single knock can be heard on the tape) and very constricted. At the base of the stairs, I felt like my clothes were uncomfortable and I almost felt like I had sores from my clothes. They were very uncomfortable on me. I felt like a woman in a long dress, but it was very uncomfortable. I felt not constriction, but I just felt like the collar was very uncomfortable around the neck There were cold spots in that area. In the second little study room, I also had a woman in that rocking chair, just sort of observing everything. Then in the living room, I was overcome by a strong sensation of vertigo and I felt the energy swirling in a clockwise direction.

Unusual ball of light in front of two guests
(Courtesy of SOHO)

Victoria Gross
I just going to comment on a couple of things. Much of this is the same as what has been said before. Earlier when I was in here, the courtroom, where I'm sitting now, I felt someone walk through me. That is very interesting, because later on, Colin was sitting in the same area, and he was drawing someone.

The main thing was, in the theater room, between Deann and the window, to protect Deann, then, when she left the area, I saw someone hit their head against the window. It wasn't Deann, it was an impression of somebody. I do not like the stairs. I did see someone who either fell over the banister or down the stairs, so the stairs really scared me. I think that's about it. There's more, but a lot has been covered already.

Drawing of a spirit by Colin Birch

<u>Colin Birch</u>
The first impression as soon as I walked in, was the vibration, the actual power within the building was very, very high. But I felt as though I was being pushed out. That's what I was getting and I think that's what everyone was getting. It was as if we were intruding and that we shouldn't be here. My intention was when I joined the group, to do my thing, which was to stay away from all of you. What I did, I always protect myself, then I sat in the corner of the courtroom. Then I took a slow walk around the building, and I was hitting various hot spots and cold spots all the way through the building.

Specifically, at the top of the stairs, as you walk into the theater, there was a show or something going on the right hand side of the stage. There were children and there were other people, but this guy who I drew on the paper here, you call him Thomas, is that right, he was with me all the way, he was following me all the way, and I was asking him questions, but he wouldn't answer me. So I said, you can stay with me because you are not doing me any harm. So, as I came down the stairs, again, there was a lady, who lady I drew first, she was at the bottom, and she actually held her hand out to me. So I took her hand. Then I moved into the corner room [former study], and it felt like a refrigerator, because it was really, really cold. She seemed to walk back into that room and faded away.

I continue on and sat down in various places, and I put myself in a semi-trance upstairs, and there were absolutely hundreds of things going on in that room. It was as though shows were being flashed in front of me over a period of time. And there were hundreds and hundreds from the spirit world coming in, going out, and coming in. All walks of life and all different types of dress. It was unbelievable and very colorful. I see in color while a lot of people see in black and white. I came back down here [courtroom] and started to do some drawings, and basically that was it.

Drawing of a spirit by Colin Birch

As the summary ended you could hear seven distinct "clicks" on the tape. The tape rolled as the group continued talking among themselves. Several photographs were taken in the courtroom during the summary session, four of which had distinct anomalies including a while rod of light that hovered above one of the docents which she was sitting in a jury chair off to the right of the judge's bench. This was the very chair that all of the psychics remarked that the spirit of a man was sitting in. While outside, some psychics picked up on the presence of Violet Whaley and animal energy.

Other photographs had orbs, sunspot like orb in front of one of the psychics, and red streaks of light. The were four more clicks a few minutes after the initial seven clicks, as the people were still talking. There is a "frog-like sound, whispering sounds, more noticeable clicking sounds (three clicks once, nine times, nine times, ten times, ten times, seven times, and nine times).

The Whaley House of Spirits

While researching, I have encountered both the inexplicable and the mundane. When something out of the ordinary is occurring, the first conclusion by some is that the phenomenon is ghostly in nature. In other words, a ghost is responsible. This may of may not be the case. There are so many logical explanations that must be examined and ruled out before the [possibility] of paranormal phenomena can be seriously considered, Electrical wires, nearby televisions, birds, water pipes, noisy refrigerators, wind, and even the antics of household pets are a few things that have been perceived as ghostly, until investigations proved otherwise.

Janice Oberding, **Ghosthunters Guide to Virginia City** (2003)

This wonderful article was submitted by Alexander Sill, a friend and future paranormal investigator from West Hills, California.

Possible mist above bed in upstairs master bedroom
(Courtesy of Alexander Sill, West Hills, California)

My name is Alexander Sill and I am 10 years old. I love history, and helping people. Someday, I want to become a parapsychologist. This is my story about my favorite Ghost Hunting place. I think it was about two days after we got back from San Diego with Rob Wlodarski and his group of professional psychics and paranormal investigators, when I had this dream about the Whaley House. I totally forgot about the dream until I began writing this chapter. I dreamt that the Whaley House was turned into something other then a museum. I became sad in my dream and started crying. So I went inside the house and found that the original piano from the old parlor was still there, as was the old piano stool. I saw something sitting on the stool so I moved towards it to see what it was. There was a note saying, "We are still here!" In my opinion, the dream meant that even though the house was changed into a whole new building the spirits were telling me they would never leave.

It was mid July 2002, when my family and I went to San Diego and took the Ghost and Gravestones tour which included a trip to the Whaley House at night. For some reason I was very attracted to the Whaley House and desperately wanted to go back. I finally convinced my Uncle Joel to take me back to Old Town San Diego. I remember it was a cold and rainy day, on November 9th 2002 when my uncle, my dad, my sister and I walked into the Whaley House, where we were greeted by a docent named Robin. She told us about the curtains that moved a lot by themselves upstairs in the master bedroom.

First, we walked through the downstairs portion of the house. After that, we went upstairs to the master bedroom and saw the curtains moving around without human assistance. There was no ventilation in the house, nor any open windows to create drafts that would cause the curtains to move at all. Next, I felt that someone was on the bed, so I told my dad to take a picture. We had a digital camera and noticed that the picture we took had a very strange orange and white colored cloud floating over the bed with two noticeable orbs beneath it.

We came back later that day for a few minutes and witnessed quite a bit of activity. As we walked upstairs, all of a sudden I smelled perfume. As I smelled the perfume, I heard another tourist say, "The light bulb just blew out!" Robin, the docent, told us that she had replaced that very same light, several times that month! I went upstairs to tell my uncle Joel and noticed that it seemed much colder then in the downstairs area. Later that evening, we came back on the Ghost and Gravestones Tour and although we witnessed no activity, we did get some pretty strange pictures.

On March 29, 2003, I again convinced my Mom and Dad to visit San Diego. We arrived at the Whaley House around 11:00 a.m., and I walked directly into the parlor with my Mom. I began to talk openly about Violet Whaley (Thomas Whaley's daughter) and immediately one piece of the chandelier above us began to move rapidly for no apparent reason. Perhaps it was because I said the name Violet that caused the unexplained movement.

Then we proceeded to the upstairs portion of the house, and I immediately smelled the unmistakable essence of lilac perfume around the staircase area. We stayed upstairs for a little while and then went back down after no unusual occurrences had taken place. My Dad noticed that the curtains in the kitchen were moving in a very strange non-uniform motion, and caught the action on tape. There were absolutely no widows open or drafts coming from anywhere in the house. My Dad then went into the kitchen with our digital camera and took a photo of the wall. The picture had an unusual figure that looked like a woman standing next to a chair.

We were invited to come back at the end of the day by the docents Robin and Casey. We came back at around 4:30 and walked directly upstairs when I smelled the lilac perfume again but this time it I also smelled like cigar smoke. The scent followed me up the stairs, then vanished into thin air. I recalled that Thomas Whaley used to smoke cigars, and it sent chills up my spine! We enjoyed walking around the house when it was quiet with no other visitors to disturb us. As soon as we reached the courtroom, we noticed the barrier chains began to move back and forth on their own for at least a minute or so. There were no open windows or drafts what so ever, to have caused the chains to move back and forth like that. We captured some of this activity on videotape! I was excited about our visit and couldn't wait to tell my friends about it!

Mist above bed in upstairs Guest bedroom
(Courtesy of Alexander Sill, West Hills, California)

June 21, 2003 (Summer Solstice), would be a day that I would never forget. I went to the Whaley House with Rob Wlodarski, my Dad, and a group of talented, professional psychics. We had planned a nighttime investigation of the Whaley House. Upon arriving in Old Town, we drove directly to the Whaley House, and prepared our research equipment in preparation for later that night, as well as for visiting a few other haunted places in Old Town. We wandered through the Whaley House for a little while, and proceeded up the stairs when all of a sudden we all smelled cigar smoke. The aroma of perfume soon followed the smell of cigars. Nothing logical or within reason could account for this. We proceeded to the theatre, where we felt a very warm spot in one area, and at the same time my Dad felt a tingling sensation on his left arm. He explained that it felt as if someone unseen had lightly touched his arm.

Just as we were about to leave, Rob's dowsing rods indicated significant activity when he asked if a there was little girl and a dog following me. We had just heard a true story from a historian researching the Whaley House, about a little girl named Marianne Reynolds who had accidentally ingested some poison in the house and died inside.

Rob sensed that it might have been her. There was another story about a little girl named Annabelle Washburn who broke her neck on a close line and choked to death from a broken trachea in the backyard. One of the docents verified the Marianne Reynolds story, but said the Annabelle Washburn story was completely false. The dog that was said to be following me was supposedly Thomas Whaley's dog named Dolly Varden.

We came back to the house around 10:00 p.m., for the full investigation. As I began walking up the stairs to the Whaley House, I began feeling sick to my stomach and very dizzy. Every time I tried to go into the house I began feeling sick again. It was like someone was trying to keep me out of the house.

Rob felt that the little girl Marianne Reynolds and the dog Dolly Varden were protecting me from possible psychic harm inside. Although I did not complete the investigation, I was still happy to have had the rare opportunity to be a part of a fascinating paranormal investigation with such distinguished professionals.

Mist above bed in upstairs Guest Bedroom
(Courtesy of Alexander Sill, West Hills, California)

A Psychic Greets the Ghosts

> Perhaps spirits are our own psyches, thoughts, and emotions, projected externally. Maybe they are the archetypes: the lost child, the hanged man of the Tarot deck, the weeping woman, the soul in torment, the stuff of folklore. Perhaps they are what we fear to believe—the spirits of departed souls, battering against the window that separates them from the living pleading, "Remember m, Remember me..." I have met the wandering, lonely ghost, lost and caught in some private Limbo. I've seen the suicide, horrified by his own actions, afraid to stay and afraid to go. I have encountered the "memory ghost," nothing more than a shadow of a life. But I can prove nothing. Many people claim to have the answers. I continue to have questions.
>
> Chris Woodyard, **Haunted Ohio V** (2003)

This is a record of an interesting sojourn to the Whaley House by internationally gifted psychic, Alma Carey (818-972-2953 or www.almacarey.com), who had never visited the house before. On October 25, 2003, Meteorologist, Dave Scott of KUSI, Channel 9 News in San Diego and his cameraman followed Carey and Rob Wlodarski as they undertook a paranormal investigation in the house. A tape recorder was used by Carey to document the event. KUSI TV, Channel 9 also videotaped portions of the investigation during the evening.

The investigation actually began in the Derby-Pendleton House, adjacent and in back of the Whaley House. This is where Save Our Heritage Organization (SOHO) allowed us to store our equipment and a change of clothing while conducting our research. We began on the side of the Derby Pendleton House, which essentially represents the back yard of the Whaley House. Here, around 4:00 p.m., Alma Carey began her walk-through of the grounds, obtaining the following impressions:

There's a tree on the left-hand side of the house, as you look out from the house or to the right hand side of the house as you face toward it. There's a long, thick branch jutting out from the tree, and one of the first things I saw, was some man hanging from the tree. I get the name Peters or Peter, and I also get the name, Petersburg. I do see people standing around down below looking at the body hanging from the tree. That's the first thing I'm seeing, but I'm also sensing a lot of other things in this area from different time periods.

We then entered the Derby-Pendleton House (the building is currently used as an office for SOHO), the impression thing I get is that I don't like it in here, at all. I wouldn't want to be working in here and I would like to leave it. I'm in the center room where they do have some computers. The feeling that I get in this room is that it's not a healthy room to be in. I'm getting images. I feel as if I'm picking up somebody else's thoughts in this room and I just don't like it right now.

Back into the living room here. This is the larger room that apparently has a front door out onto the street. It appears that this building has two front doors or is actually two separate buildings, each with its own entryway. I heard Rob say or use the name, Captain Fitch or something. Now, back at home in Burbank, when I first put my attention here [there is a definite sound of a child screaming on tape over Alma's words], I was getting the word, Captain, like someone was calling somebody, "Captain!" I am also picking up something about a boat; so, Captain, and a boat, and I don't know what the name of the boat is right now, but the word Captain seems to fit in this house somehow. Perhaps someone who once lived inside was a Captain or related to the sea?

Okay, I am going upstairs now. I'm in the upstairs landing, and I get the name Mary or Maria for some reason. I'm in the front bedroom. It has a door and three windows, and it has a door that opens to a little closet. I feel pressure on my body in the room with the three windows. The room faces the street or something, it may be a side street, but it's definitely facing a street. I am getting the name Mary very strongly, and something that's like Cohol, that could be short for alcohol? I'm definitely getting an intense pressure while standing near the closet. The light is very bright, very beautiful, and there's just something about the place that's highly uncomfortable for me. I really do not want to be in here at all. Something unpleasant happened inside this building.

I'm upstairs in the upper landing, and one of the first things I'm getting clearly, is somebody's emotion and it feels like a young man. The emotion is, that if he doesn't leave this place, he's just going to die here. So the feeling is, that he just wants to get out of here, and a desire to change his life. He's got to get out; he's got to go and do something with his life. The young man is about 5'10", slim, brunette, narrow face, and kind of a narrow build and wiry, and I think he would be in his 20s, but he has an older look. I don't think that he's a teenager, but he might be. Perhaps the old feeling may be coming from the time he is in... before the turn-of-the-century?

There are women sitting in the room that has the fireplace, and they are busy discussing social situations and gossiping. They are talking about their husbands and they are conversing about upcoming social events and goings in town. In the little room that's next to the room with the fireplace with the windows opposite each other, and a doorway leading outside, I am getting pressure in the upper part of the chest, pressure in the throat, and its hard to breathe, in this room. This may be where someone had a heart attack or health issues.

I'm now on the outside of the house where there is a plaque dedicating the house to Lt. George Derby. I'm walking towards the front porch, and I sense that nothing that that is here on the outside now, was here when the Whaley House was here. In front of the house I'm getting sea captain, boats, there's something about boats for sure. It's something to do with the social conditions of the day or something legal, social, and a lot of discussion, and people discussing the events of the day; social awareness and social conditions. I see men and women out here on the porch.

I'm now out in the back of the Whaley House between it and the Derby-Pendleton House, in the back a little bit. Boy is this place busy. My, there are quite a few people around here. This was an area where I sense that numerous parties and festivities took place. It is also a place where I sense that there was a tragedy involving a jilted woman and a man who did not love her. There is an overwhelming feeling of loss here mixed in with all the partying and all the playful energy. Near the water trough, and under the big oak tree — this is where I sense the sorrow, the longing and the feeling of loss and despair the most involving a young girl.

Dining room doorway tleading o the backyard
(Courtesy of SOHO)

I'm now inside the Whaley House, and I'm in the room to the left of the entrance. They've tuned it into something that looks like a little shop. Out by the large two windows that face the street, standing to the left side of the window, there's a feeling of fear. Someone is standing there looking out the window and feeling fear. At first, I thought it was a male, then I sensed a female — now I'm pretty sure that it's a female. There's just a sense of fear connected to it, and great apprehension. For some reason, I get a boat connected to that feeling in some way. Maybe it's just because we are so close to the ocean that I'm getting that impression.

Now I'm in the room with the dining table and the little pot-bellied stove close to the floor. I'm just getting some flickering images of men and women sitting around the table and talking while they eat. I definitely get children in this room. I am getting the strongest sense of people sitting at the table or sitting in this room — it's very social in nature and family oriented. It feels okay; it doesn't feel bad. There are people from all walks of life gathered here as well as one family in particular.

I'm standing at the base of the staircase that leads up to the second floor. The first thing that I am getting is somebody standing at the top of the stairs. I also sense people on the staircase including a woman in a long, light-colored dress with stripes that go up and down; She's a grown up and, she's not moving. I guess I'm going to have to walk through her to get up the stairs. My heart was pounding as I went through her. It's a physical sensation that is like walking through something thick and cool.

I'm looking at the bedroom that's immediately to the left of the upper floor landing, separated by a glass doorway [the nursery]. I sense children here as a woman who tended to the children when they were very young. There is some loss in this area of the house as if a child died in this room. I'm now going to the back of the house in a little nook that allows me into the second bedroom where they have two beds. There is a double bed and a single bed in this room. This place is chock full of people. Okay, I just saw somebody sit on the narrow bed. I get a strong sense of a woman in this room. She considers this her room.

I'm existing again and I'm going to the front where there's a little porch outside and a doorway. A glass-fronted doorway with a curtain on it that leads to the porch. I guess the porch is actually to the side of the house, and leads to a back wooden stairway. Interestingly enough, I see people up and down that staircase too. One of the things I saw fleetingly, were a woman and a young man. It was one of the females here I believe, meeting a young man briefly; very light and nothing too heavy. This was an easy entrance and access.

I'm in the room here that has a little theater and stage, and I like it. There are numerous what are called Captain's chairs, the wooden chairs with the arms that curve around, with the little spikes around the back, so that you sit and it kind of curves around your back. I feel that people would come in the past and they would sit and watch little theater productions take place. I see a beautiful little piano or maybe an organ to the left of the stage. The keys are covered so I'm not sure what kind of a piano it is, but there it is.

Okay, something's going down my throat. Words are being caught in my mouth. I'm getting some sensations and feelings about the theater. I have the urge to get on that stage and perform. It's a wonderful little room. I'm getting political speeches, acting, memorized words, great hilarity and laughter to the front right of the audience. I'm seeing some burly men, robust men in the audience. There are all kinds of emotions in this particular room where the stage is; it's fun. I think the political speeches are the ones that you get that horrible feeling when you're hearing something or knowing something, or finding out something you don't want to hear, and people are going, "Oh, please, no!" There is that feeling of resistance to hearing bad news about something in this room. This room had several uses and may also have served as several rooms that people occupied or rented as well as a family bedroom. I see the room is several different forms, with different doors, windows, window coverings and furniture. I am sure that this was not always used as a stage, but had many uses over time.

Orbs in the upstairs older children bedroom
(Courtesy of the International Paranormal Research Organization)

Across the hallway, alongside the staircase, there is a back wall of the bedroom that runs alongside the staircase. This room is decorated as a man's bedroom. What I'm basically getting in this particular room, is gloominess and sadness — it maybe because the lighting creates a kind of melancholy mood. There's cool light that comes into this room, and the lighting is creepy — this room does not produce happy emotions. There is also a feeling of some kind of pathos or something traumatic that occurred here. This would actually be a very hard room for people to live in. There is a constant cool breeze that is blowing throughout this building. I see the curtain blowing in and out and back and forth. One minute I feel a breeze and the next minute I don't. The curtain leads from the bedroom towards the back of the stage in the other room. The curtain is definitely blowing at times, and I can't figure out what is causing this because there are no windows open, and it comes and goes and if people are walking back and forth, creating the breeze.

I'm now standing at the top of the stairs, and I'm looking for that breeze. I don't feel a breeze at the top of the steps. Okay, here's the breeze. I'm back in the theater and I'm looking for the source, but now there's no breeze. There ought to be a breeze blowing, but no breeze. [A docent named Athena enters the room].

AC - I have question for you. You know the curtains that are blowing in the little closet over there? Docent, "Yes!"

AC - Where is the cross breeze there?

Docent - That's when the window in the front of the house is open, and in the back there's the walk through closet behind the white curtain, and on this doorway there's a heavier velvet curtain.

AC- So that's why these are not blowing and that's why that white cotton one's blowing so easily? Because it's more easily moveable in the breeze that was there when the window was open?

Docent - It could be. You know, I've seen it move when all the windows in the house were closed.

A very pretty girl in a lovely, wine-colored Victorian dress. Okay, very interesting. Yeah, I can't find the breeze as I physically walk around, and the thing was just blowing away. So, the curtain moves when nobody's here, and there's no breeze! She mentioned that the window had been open. I'm going to hunt it down again because there are people in there right now. So, I'm just walking around looking for that breeze. Okay, I'm standing at the top of the staircase now, looking for that breeze that I can't find anymore. I'm stepping into that little bedroom and I'm looking for that breeze. I'm stepping in; okay, the curtain is moving very subtly. Actually, it stopped. Oh, here we go again, it's picking up. Now, there is a possibility that breeze is blowing from underneath bottom floor, up through the floorboards. So, that's a possibility, but now it very, very low and it had been blowing rather heavily before. How interesting, and I had definitely felt a breeze before, but now everything seems to have stopped moving. Okay, may I interview you, my name is Alma, what did you say before?

Docent [Sunshine] - Well, it's moving now, and it wasn't a minute ago. She just said she went downstairs and shut all the windows.

AC- There it goes again. Okay, I'm going to go downstairs and see if there's a draft. So, this has been observed as a phenomenon; the movement of the library curtains. Although the girl Athena, said that possibly the other ones weren't moving that easily because they were heavy weight velvet. I'm downstairs looking for the breeze. I'm stepping into the bedroom, where's there's a little nook that you can step into the room, and this feels occupied as well. I'm trying to find [the source of] the breeze. Okay, I'm standing here and I'm looking for that breeze; no breeze.

I'm in where the kitchen is, and I'm feeling a breeze, but they did open the front door just now, and I'm standing downstairs. Okay, that stopped. So I'm theoretically standing right below where those white, cotton curtains would be up above. I'm looking up to see if there is a way that wind could have blown up, and there is no way. I thought that maybe there would be cracks in the ceiling, down here that would allow a breeze to come and blow up through the place, and it's pristinely plastered, and no way for a breeze to blow. Okay.

Mist to the right of the bed in upstairs Guest Bedroom
(Courtesy of SOHO)

I'm now in the courtroom actually, which is a nice, big size room... oh, I felt a breeze, although the girl just walked by with her skirt and is closing the shades. I'm still having the feeling that the floor is dipped or sagging, although looking at the floor with my eyes, I can't perceive that dip. I'm walking forward and it looks like a bench, a judge's bench, court bench up front facing the room, where its a heavy wooden bench, and then there's a rather large table with four chairs facing it, and there's a court reporter with a table and chair sitting right in front of the judge's bench. I'm coming up to the left hand side of it. This guy handed down some kind of verdict, which was really, very unpopular — highly unpopular. I'm looking and hunting down that darn breeze, and no breeze. There are three very long, beautiful looking benches that have, I guess you call it ladder-back chairs, but its sideways, whatever you call that, spindles I think you call it, and the jury to the side over here. There are certainly some, cool breezy spots here that I keep running into.

Okay, I'm exiting this room. What went on in this room? I was just pulled back in. Someone's in great protest over a particular finding on the part of the judge or jury. A great protest in this room. That emotion of "No, no, that can't be," is not good; absolutely not. Okay, I'm existing this room, and I'm coming into the lobby right now.

I'm going into the kitchen area in the back of the house. My goodness, these people really are all over the place, walking around. This place will just about come alive for you, and act out everything that went on it. It's very, very full of people, everywhere.

I'm in the back of the house and there's a little door with a white, wooden overhang, and what I'm basically getting from the little double door that's in the back, is someone that is sort of being brought out; almost like a prisoner, it almost seems that way, like a prisoner that is being brought out by two people. I don't know if he's manacled, but it almost seems like that. He's being brought on to the back porch to just in front of the little bricked rose garden.

I'm to the side now where's there's earth, and the side street. To the left of me is a brick path, and underneath is the earth under my feet. I'm walking along now, and upstairs, I can see on that side of the building, there's like a little closed window. it looks like a little door in the side of the wall up high on the second story. There's something in that room; I know that there's something in that room, but I don't know what. However, there's an energy that comes from that room, that's unusual. As I walk along the front porch and face the window to the general store, I still sense that there is a lot of activity inside, and that there are a lot of spirits gathered inside. This is not surprising since the house has been called the most haunted house in America.

Later that evening, prior to entering the Whaley House for the Channel 9 broadcast, Alma and Rob Wlodarski sat in the kitchen area of the Derby-Pendleton House, where numerous paranormal events have been reported over the year. Here, the two of us, while on camera, made contact with a Chinese cook and Violet Whaley. With the dowsing rods, we were able to determine that the cook is responsible for making people feel uncomfortable in the kitchen and and adjoining rooms, as he considers the area his domain. He will move things and actually try and force people to leave if he doesn't like them. Violet did say that she was aware of how she passed away, and that she does talk to her father on occasion in the afterlife. She was not a happy person in life and being jilted by her husband sent her into a deep depression from which she never recovered. She seemed to say that the lack of support from her family also contributed toward her taking her life. She fought with the idea of suicide for a long time, and had tried several times to end it all. She seemed genuinely sorry for causing her mother so much grief, but that was the only way out of her desperate situation she could think of. She is still tied to the house and is aware of many other spirits who are in the house. There was a sense that she spends as much time in the backyard area as she does in the house she grew up in. She is still sad and lonely and seems confined to this physical setting for some time to come.

A Docent's Encounters with the Unknown

The existence of ghosts is not important. Some people will believe and others will not; it has never been my intention to change people's beliefs — I prefer to leave that aspect up to the individual and the ghost. Ghosts have taken the country by storm over the past several years with multiple ghost tours popping up in every major city and ghosts dominating the movies, print media and cable networks across the nation. Their stories are waiting to be told and more continue to unfold, as we collectively become more receptive. A favorite question of mine when interviewing potential tour guides for Key West's Original Ghost Tour is, "Do you believe in Ghosts?" Some do, some don't, and most fall somewhere in between. After a month or two of touring they are all believers.

David L. Sloan, **Haunted key West** (2003)

The Dining Room
(Courtesy of SOHO)

The following information was provided by docent and friend, Robin M. Sweeton. Working at the Whaley House has provided Robin with a unique opportunity to tour the house with guests and alone... we'll maybe not alone. As you will see, the stories she is sharing below for the first time, represent a unique perspective from someone who knows that there is a very thin line between this world and the next — it's a line she has crossed several times during her our of duty at America's most haunted house. We decided to have Robin tell the stories in her own words.

My most recent event took place about a week ago, on a Monday evening. Another docent, named Jokie Tolentino, stayed in the house after hours so that Jokie could take some photographs in the house. It was about 9:00 p.m. We pulled the shades in the lower rooms to eliminate lights and reflections off the street. While in the Courtroom, I began to pull down the shade next to the Judge's bench. The entire roller shade apparatus flew off the top of the window, hitting me on the head. I was of course a little startled, but not hurt. I stood there looking at the shade on the floor, thinking, "Now I'm going to have to go find a ladder somewhere and fix this darn shade." During this thought process, I felt a hand pass over my forehead, or what felt like a hand. It was very fleeting, yet comforting, as though "someone" had witnessed my accident and was concerned that I'd been hurt.

After Jokie and I got the shade back up, we went into the parlor to begin taking the photographs. It was Jokie's camera, and she had just replaced the camera batteries, as well as the batteries for the flash. She didn't know where to start shooting, so I suggested sitting on the floor for a weird angle. Jokie thought this was creepy and I really had to talk her into it. She did NOT like being down there. I had to sit on the floor with her. She aimed the camera at the portrait of Rachel & Harriet Whaley on the mantle. While she was trying to focus, the camera took a picture. She cried out, "I swear I didn't do that!" and she put the camera down quickly and scooted away. I urged her to calm down and try again. When she touched the camera, the flash went off.

We sat there trying to determine if her camera was malfunctioning, or if something ELSE was going on. I said, "Whaley Family are you doing this?" The camera advanced another picture. This entire time the camera is sitting on the floor, about two feet away from us. Jokie was VERY nervous...I was really enjoying the event. I spoke to the Whaley's again: "Are you playing with us?" The camera took another photo.

I asked, "Is this Anna? Is this Thomas?" Nothing. "I think I know who this is! Is this Frank?" The camera took three pictures in rapid succession. I then asked, "Francis, is it really you? Tell me." AnOther photo was spontaneously taken. Needless to say, Jokie had 19 exposures left on her roll of film when we began this "photo shoot". By the time we decided we ought to leave, the camera had taken 15 photos of it's own accord. I would have to say that the just described event was by far the most enjoyable "paranormal" experience I have ever witnessed.

Mist and orbs in upstairs master bedroom
(Courtesy of Alexander Sill, West Hills, California)

Some of the more mundane and general experiences I have had are as follows:

- I heard heavy footsteps on the 2nd floor while alone.
- On one occasion when I came into the house, I heard fleeting piano music. It was very light, happy, sparkling music. I only heard this one time and it lasted for a few moments.
- I heard the sound of a man loudly clearing his throat in the master bedroom, while I changed clothes in the adjacent closet, which we use as a dressing room. I was alone in the house. Another docent, Athena Jaharis has had this same experience under the same circumstances.
- I smelled heavy, sugary sweet lavender perfume on three occasions. Once in the Parlor, and twice in the downstairs hallway.
- I have heard a "woman" walk down the lower hallway. This was at night, while we were waiting for a Ghost & Gravestones tour to come through. I heard quick, short steps, followed by the rustle of skirts and then I felt a breeze as these sounds passed me in the hallway. The sounds began at the parlor door and traveled down the hallway to the back stairs, on into the dining room, where the floor actually creaked. I had this experience only once.
- I have had something "fly" past my face in the courtroom. It was very

fast, and very startling. The sensation had a "wind" to it, and was formless, gray in color...really a grayish blur. This occurred right in my face and that is the only thing that has really frightened me.

- I have smelled the tobacco. What I always smell is a sweet pipe smoke... never a cigar.
- I have had the honor of smelling the pipe smoke more times than I can count. This occurred almost immediately after I began working at the Whaley House. The aroma is always at my immediate left. I thought this was odd, until I started describing these experiences to an older person, who said, "My dear, don't you know that in the old days, a gentleman always stood to the left of a lady, keeping her on his right!" It is nice to know that Mr. Whaley is a gentleman!
- I usually smell the tobacco when I am talking about Mr. Whaley, or giving a talk to a group in the house, or when I'm doing something "new" in the house. I get the sense that he is just letting me know that he knows what I am doing. Mr. Whaley, the micro-manager!
- I have been tickled, on my feet; I have been tweaked on my elbow: I have stood in the closet under the stairs with the door closed, on the phone (so I wouldn't disturb a Ghost & Gravestone tour) and felt three successive "blows" (breath) on the back of my neck. This was not cold, but room temperature.
- I have heard my name called out, while alone on the property. I was in the courtroom, the soft male voice seemed to come from the general store, which is in the adjoining room. More recently, I heard the same, soft male voice while inside the janitor closet. This time the voice said, in a plaintive, pleading voice, "Why are you doing this? I know what this is about, I think. In March the Whaley House began a new program, held on Sunday evenings... Our Haunted History Tour. This is a two-hour tour, from 7:00 p.m. to 9:00 p.m. Our quests have a guided tour of the downstairs and come upstairs into the theater for a special presentation about the spirits, the house, and the tragedies. I smelled the tobacco when I was rehearsing for this. I am sure that the spirits are not happy about this new development and are trying to make me aware of this.
- We have, as you no doubt are aware, many people with psychic abilities come to the house. I always listen politely to whatever they have to say. Sometimes they are really good! On one occasion, a woman told me that a "young woman" had come up to us that she had died young, and was "disturbed". I said, "Well, that's most likely Violet. Say, while you have her there with you, could you find out if she likes or dislikes me? I always like to find these things out!" The woman paused for a moment and said, "Well, she says that she's not mad at you or anything, but she wants you to give back the thing you took from her". I of course "defended" myself, for indeed I have never taken anything of Violets. The woman said that Violet was insisting

that I indeed "had" taken something, a small handkerchief that was a gift from her Grandmother. The woman, of course didn't believe that I'd done this, she just was conveying what she was told. I found this event very interesting. For about a year before this, a woman had come to see the house. She was, as it turned out, a psychic. She did not mention this to anyone. She simply had taken a paper out of her purse and began to write he her "observations" about the house and those who were present. She then handed this paper to the docent upon her departure. I wish we knew who this woman was, as I sure would love to talk with her myself. Anyway, one of the things she noticed was a young woman, who liked to stay on the second floor. She wanders around up there, she seeks a treasure lost, something small, that was her Grandmothers. We had been wondering what the "treasure" was. Now I'm pretty sure I know! A while after this event, I sat up in the theater, sewing by the window. I suddenly felt a cold presence, just behind me, on my right side. It stayed there for quite awhile. I thought it odd, as I have sat up there and sewed on almost every Sunday afternoon. I had never felt a presence with me there before. So, I wondered who it might be, and why they would be suddenly curious about what I was doing. Then I noticed that the white ladies housecap I was sewing lace onto looked a lot like a white handkerchief… So I guess it was Violet!

The Courtroom
(Courtesy of SOHO)

- I have been sharing stories about Violet lately in the theater. Now, I often feel that same cold presence next to me. I have also been feeling something messing about my face, hair and neck...tickling sensations that just keep going. It feels like I have a bug crawling around on my head, or as though I've just walked through a spiderweb. I never let people know when this is happening. I like to keep it to myself.
- Recently, in April 2004, I encountered a tall, black form in the hallway, just to the left of the parlor door. A Ghost & Gravestones tour had arrived on the front porch, and I walked into the hallway from the general store to let them in. This is when I noticed the black form. I kept on my way to the front door, not wanting to look at it again. I called out the docent standing on the stairs, "Julie, I know I didn't see what I just saw!" I opened the front door, letting the tour inside. The first person in the house made a beeline for the parlor doorway, and began to take photos of the room. I don't think she even took the time to look at the room with her own eyes. She just immediately began to take pictures. She then looked at her camera screen and announced, "Oh my gosh, there's a big black thing in my picture!" Apparently, the dark form moved directly from outside the parlor door inside to the parlor as I let the tour group into the house!
- I have seen a brown blur about a foot off the ground on two occasions. Both times, it went past so fast that there was, no way I could discern what it was. The first time I saw it in my peripheral vision while seated in the hallway. It shot from the door of the general store, through the hall into the parlor. The second time I witnessed this, I was sweeping the dining room. I began to sweep under the table, when to my surprise, directly in my line of vision, the same brown blur shot out from underneath the table, went through the dining chair and directly into the sideboard. A distance of about 2Ω feet. Both of these events occurred in the daytime. I guess that was Dolly!
- Another Docent, Julie Wolfe, was there with her then husband, whom I shall refer to as "the other docent". They were standing in the front hallway on either side of the doorway to the general store. It was during an evening Ghost & Gravestone tour. The tour group was being given a talk in the courtroom. As Julie and the other docent were standing on either side of the store doorway, they both saw the apparitions of, first, a dog running through the store doorway, through the hallway and disappear into the parlor. The visage of the dog was followed immediately by a very tall man who seemed to be chasing the dog. He too ran through the store doorway, through the hall and into the parlor. What was interesting about this (beyond the fact that it even happened!) was that the man ducked through both of the doorways. Couldn't he feasibly just go through them?!! His habits in life seem to have followed him to the other side! Julie described both

images as being opaque, solid looking, but completely gray in color, no features. Just a gray dog and a gray man.
- Julie has also seen who she feels is Anna Whaley standing in the courtroom, wearing a black dress. Julie also often feels Anna's presence with her as she stands on the ninth step, during the Ghost & Graveyard tours. She describes it as a comforting feeling, sometimes she feels a hand on her shoulder.
- I enjoy working in the Whaley House very much, and I feel very much at home and safe there. I think that some things I might do or say can be upsetting to the spirits who remain there, but regardless, I feel that they are very protective of all of us, and as tolerant as they can be, given that we are, quite frankly, uninvited guests invading their privacy. I have only on one or two occasions felt something unsettling there, and I don't feel that they had anything whatsoever to do with the family spirits.

Possible hand coming from Grant's photograph
(Courtesy of SOHO)

Visitors and Employees Speak Their Peace

> Even when a building earns a reputation for being haunted, manifestations do not occur all the time. In some instances, certain individuals may set off the phenomenon, afterlife is an emotional empathy between it and them. Perhaps during times of inactivity at haunted places, the phenomenon is there but dormant. Such places may lie at a point where the "veil" between our world and the next is finer, allowing easier access for spirits and demons. These places could be conceived as gateway. Unconsciously, perhaps, psychically gifted people have the ability to open these gates, allowing entry from the other side.
>
> Jenny Randles and Peter Hough, **The Afterlife** (1993)

One of the more enjoyable aspects of writing books comes not necessarily from the results of dealing with paranormal investigators, psychics and ghosthunters, people trained in dealing with ghosts, but in finding accounts of unexplainable phenomena attributed to the average person who visits a purported haunt, or from interviewing the non-investigative person. like our prior book on the Haunted Queen Mary, the Whaley House offers numerous accounts from those who worked at the Whaley House or visited the haunted structure since it opened as a historic landmark. It is their recorded impressions of unexplainable events that provides potential evidence far the existence of ghosts and such. Their impressions and accounts have been gleaned from records provided by Whaley House personnel as well as interviews from a number of people who have been fortunate enough to penetrate the veil to the unknown. This brief tidbit in the Journal of San Diego History (Zink, 1969:5) is attributed to Anna Whaley— Miss Whaley stated that she encouraged the Mexican children to believe that the Whaley House was haunted. She told them, "Hay espantos aqui con ojos grandes." A rough translation of this is, "There are ghosts here, with big eyes." This was all that was necessary to induce them to "skedaddle."

According to the **San Diego Union** (July 7, 1968), "A lady in gingham, a gentleman in a frock coat, a little girl, 13, and a spotted dog. A family maybe out of a 19th century daguerreotype. No, says parapsychologist Hans Holzer, they're the resident ghosts of Whaley House, the ones who are mysteriously opening the windows, causing the furniture to levitate, making the soft footfalls on the floor above and playing the eerie music on the old building's organ. A New Yorker, Holzer has compiled all the accounts of occult happenings at the House and made them the first chapter of his new book, Ghosts of the Golden West. Some of the accounts, he relates, come from witnesses who have seen the apparitions with sufficient clarity to provide a description.

A Mrs. Kirbey, the wife of a physician, was visiting the house in October of 1960. Holzer writes, "As she walked about she felt pressures against her, had the distinct feeling someone was standing behind her." Suddenly, she told a companion: "I see a small figure of a woman who has a swarthy complexion. She is wearing a long full skirt, reaching to the floor. The skirt appears to *be a calico or gingham, small print. She has a kind of cap on her head, dark hair and eyes and she is wearing gold hoops in her pierced ears. She seems to stay in this room. Lives here. I gather and I get the impression we are sort of invading her privacy."

Three years later, a Mrs. Grace Bourquin was in the house in December. On the upper landing she told others she saw an apparition - the figure of a man clad in a frock coat and pantaloons. The face was turned away from her so she could not make it out. It faded away. In December, a year later, J. Milton Keller saw the apparition of a woman dressed in a green plaid gingham dress. She had long dark hair coiled in a bun and was seated on a settee in a bedroom. On this same occasion, Holzer said, "he saw a spotted dog, like a fox terrier, that ran with his flapping down the hall and into the dining room."

The Authors

Although we had read a little about the history of hauntings at the Whaley House, primarily through the books of Dr. hans Holzer, we had visited other reportedly haunted houses after reading their history with negligible results—in other words, we did not let the prior haunted history no our imaginations get the better of us once we were in the house. Nor, did we feel predisposed to see something just because we read that strange things often occurred to those who visited the Whaley House. We were open to the possibilities of seeing something out of the ordinary, without raising our expectations to the point of hallucinating or imagining a paranormal/ event just to satisfy a need to "see a ghost."

With this in mind, we took our video camera and open-minds on a tour of what was reputed to be "The most Haunted House in America." The one-half hour tour with our friends was not without results. In fact on two occasions "strange" things happened which we could not explain. Within the first ten minutes, while walking through the courthouse, we noticed that although everything was still when we entered, a heavy chain which blocked the entrance to the remainder of the courthouse (employees only beyond this point) began swinging back and forth on its own. We were the only ones in there at the time; in fact outside of our friends exploring another part of the house, there were no other tourists. After watching in awe as the chain dance for a full minute, it came to rest—as if an unseen hand had started the motion, then moved on, allowing the chain to stop an its own. Unfortunately, we did not have the video camera going at the time since we had just arrived and we were trying to get a feel for the place, and once the event started, we were so mesmerized by the phenomenon that we Simply forget to tape it. Before leaving the room, a quick glance toward the far end of the room on the right hand side of the judge's bench where several chairs were lined up, produced a strange, mist-like figure of a man who appeared to be sitting down and facing the bench. Although no features could be discerned, the man did appear to be wearing a long, dark, coat—this scene also disappeared or evaporated within seconds after appearing.

After walking through the lower part of the house without incident, other than "feeling' as if we were being watched the entire time, we headed upstairs, this time the video focused and ready for anything out of the ordinary. While videotaping the upstairs bedrooms, we had our back to the glass partition on the left as reach the top of the stairs, and while looking into the bedroom to the right. After a couple of minutes, a distinctive "tapping" sound from inside the glass partition, began, and for several seconds a series of distinctive taps, like someone tapping a coin against glass, rang out in the quiet corridor. Turning abruptly thinking that someone was inside the partition, perhaps a caretaker, or docent, we focused our attention on the place where the sound emanated—there wasn't a living soul around. It was as if someone was; trying to get our attention—and did. No other incidents occurred while we toured the historic building, but when we went home to play the tape, the "tapping" sounds could be distinctly heard on tape. Maybe a spirit of the Whaley House spirit was saying high or playing a little trick to try and unnerve us—even spirits enjoy playing pranks to liven up their day.

orbs on the headboard and unusal light with a small halo above the lamp in upstairs older children's bedroom
(Courtesy of H. Parson of New Zealand)

Mrs. Kirbey of Canada

Mrs. Kirbey and her husband visited the house after it opened to the public, and at once became interested in an exhibit in one of the display cases. Mrs. Kirbey was familiar with Victorian Period antiques and artifacts and wanted a closer look at the exhibit. While her husband remained downstairs talking with June Reading, Mrs. Kirbey breezed through the house to her hearts content. The curiosity exhibited by Mrs. Kirbey apparently attracted the attention of a ghostly house guest. After a short time, Mrs. Kirbey returned to greet her husband and June Reading who were discussing professional topics. She asked in a rather tentative manner if Reading had ever encountered anything strange in the upstairs area. Upon further inquiry, Mrs. Kirbey blurted out that when she walked upstairs, she felt a cool breeze above her head, and although she was unaware of anything visible, felt a pressure against her, that prevented her from making the easy trip upstairs. Furthermore, when she made it to the top of the stairs and began browsing in each of the bedrooms, she had the distinct feeling that someone was standing directly behind her. This feeling was to strong that she continually turned around, expecting to see someone each time she looked. The presence was so close to her, which she felt that a tap on the shoulder would follow shortly. Nothing ever manifested and after a short unnerving tour of the upstairs, she came back down to ask whether this was a common occurrence.

The strangeness of the visit to the house continued for Mrs. Kirbey as she entered the courtroom. Again, she asked Reading if could see the person standing by the bailiffs table: apparently, Mrs. Kirbey was the only person who could see the ghostly visitor in the courtroom. Ask to describe the presence, Mrs. Kirbey said that it was a woman of slight stature with a dark-skinned complexion, and wearing a long full, skirt which reached to the floor. Incredibly, the description included the fact that the skirt appeared to be of calico or gingham, small print, and that the phantom lady wore a cap on her head, had dark hair and dark eyes, and gold hoops in her pierced ears. Mrs. Kirbey's impression was that the woman liked to stay in the courthouse room, and that she didn't like when people invaded her privacy. Reading confirmed that none of the Whaley family were swarthy, as Mrs. Kirbey described, and as far as Reading knew, Mrs. Kirbey was the only person who brought up that fact in connection with the courtroom.

Although, a number of visitors have commented upon the almost "oppressive" atmosphere in this room, and that staff have found it difficult to concentrate while working in the room, no one had ever seen that particular female manifestation before. Mrs. Kirbey got much more than she bargained while enjoying ambiance of the Victorian Period within the haunted Whaley House.

Trick or Treat

This event took place during Halloween. During one of the final Halloween tours that are held annually by Save Our Heritage Organization, the courtroom was packed. As is normal during the tour, a docent prepares the group by telling the history and ghost stories. On this particular tour, the docent summoned a middle-aged woman to tell her ghost story to the anxious group. She stated that while visiting from out of state, she had heard all the stories and rumors about spirits who called the Whaley House home. This was her first trip and she was excited to finally see America's most haunted house. As she was sitting in the court room, she observed an odd-looking man, who was dressed in a military uniform, approach the curator as he spoke to the group. She immediately thought that the man was a volunteer who was part of the presentation. To her surprise, the soldier approached the curator and then vanished before her eyes. An even stranger twist occurred when she asked those around if they had witnessed the spectral soldier. Apparently she was the only one in the crowded room allowed to view this otherworldly visitor; a rare experience for a first time visitor.

Look closely at the center of the photograph and you might see the faint of someone standing near the carriage in the nursery.
(Courtesy of John and Arlene Cascio)

J.P. got his Money's Worth

Several years ago, J.P. visited the Whaley House. After entering the house, he began exploring the upstairs and downstairs area, including the courtroom. His initial walk through produced no ghosts, and disappointment was setting in. However, shortly before he was about to leave a mother and small child were standing in front of him when all of a sudden, the child blurted out to the Mother, "Look, mama!" The child was pointing in the direction of J.P. Both turned around and faced the direction that the child was pointing. To their amazement, the door to the garden, already partially open, slowly began opening wider, as if assisted by some unseen force that the child was able to connect with. There was no breeze to speak of, so there was nothing physically that would account for what was happening. As the door stopped moving, the Mother, child and J.P quickly left the premises; they all got their money's worth, that day.

The late June Reading's spirited encounter
During February 1996, Reading arrived to open the house with a volunteer. As Reading entered, she inspected the hallway and then poked her head into the parlor, but there was nothing unusual to report. It was only after entering the dining room across the hallway from the parlor room, that she witnessed an amazing site. There in front of her stood a Native American, as clear as day and as real as you or I; except for the fact that a quick scan of the intruder revealed that he had no feet—as if he was floating above the carpet. Reading couldn't take her eyes off the man, and quickly realized that he was not looking at her, but rather through her; this person was an apparition. She tried to remember as much about the spirit as she could within the few seconds that she was confronted by the ghost.

She clearly saw the statuesque form of a tall, husky, brown-skinned man a few steps away. He wore black trousers and a green plaid shirt with full sleeves. The shirt had a deep yolk, no button collar. Resting on top of his long, black hair, was a black hat with a straight, deep rim. The hat looked like it came directly from the days of the Wild West with a high crown and uncreased, broad rim. Gathering her senses, she walked out of the room, called to the volunteer to come have a look and both women returned to the dining room. Unfortunately, the phantom Native American had taken his leave. Reading had never before witnessed a ghost of a Native American in the Whaley House, but was not surprised at the fact that one might co-inhabit the house with other members of the Whaley family. According to Reading, there used to be an Indian Rancheria in back of the house, and Thomas Whaley used to sell goods from his store to Native Americans—in fact, several of them used to work for the Whaleys, including those who helped Anna Whaley with everyday chores. Maybe this particular phantom decided that it was about time to show his face—after all, it only been a hundred and fifty years since the Native Americans worked for the Whaleys and bought his goods.

P.H. While visiting the Whaley House
I took a tour of the Whaley House with my family. The tour guide led us to each room, then took us upstairs. I remember looking in Mr. & Mrs. Whaley's bedroom. There was a gate to keep visitors from entering the room. I was standing right outside the gate. I saw a man and woman sitting on the bed. The man had his back to me with his feet on the floor. The woman had her feet on the floor and was facing me. The woman had a large, opened Bible (or what looked like a Bible) in her lap. She looked up at me. As she did so, the man rose from the bed, walked around the

foot of the bed and started toward me. I wondered at the time why there were people inside the room. I knew they weren't supposed to be there. I looked around and realized the rest of the tour had gone back downstairs and I was alone. I got scared and ran back down the stairs. I did not tell anyone of this experience at the time. Seven years later, I was living in Washington State, when I told my older sister about the experience. I described the man and woman in detail to her. She looked at me strangely, went to her dresser and pulled out an old newspaper clipping that she had kept, but not shown me, of a picture of Mr. and Mrs. Whaley. The man and woman I had described were the same as the couple in the picture. I have been a true believer since that day.

William H. Richardson: This former docent had an otherworldly experience while working in the house part-time, giving tours. One morning, before the house was open to the public, he was one of several employees who were seated in the music room downstairs when they all heard the distinct sound of heavy boots walking across the upstairs floor. Everyone jumped up to investigate, thinking someone had broken in. All they found were locked and shuttered windows, and no one "human" anywhere to be seen—this event piqued his interest in the paranormal.

Numerous orbs floating around the trees in the backyard of the Whaley House
(Courtesy of SOHO)

Grace Borquin
Her two experiences with the unknown involved the upper part of the house. The first occurrence in January when Borquin was seated in the hall downstairs having lunch. Hearing the sound of footsteps, she went to look for the cause and found nothing. less than a month later, on a cold,

winter day, she heard footsteps once again. This time, however, the footsteps would result in an apparitional encounter she would long remember. As Borquin walked down the hall to investigate the strange sounds, she glanced up the staircase. On the upper landing she saw the figure of a man, clad in a frock coat and wearing pantaloons. As she stood and stared in awe, the face turned away from her, so she could not make it out. Within a few seconds, the phantom form vanished in front of her disbelieving eyes. The encounter could never be explained away—it was yet another visit from the veiled inhabitants of the Whaley House.

Guest
While I was at the Whaley House with my Father and Brother, we listened to the introduction, at which time, no one felt anything unusual of out of the ordinary. This changed, however, when we all made our way upstairs. As we climbed the stairs, slowly making our way to the upper landing, a very creepy feeling began to engulf me. With each step, the feeling intensified until we reached the upper landing. When reached the top, I proceeded to the first bedroom on the right. As I stood there for a few moments, the air began to feel very heavy, as if something was pressing in on me. This was followed by a strong sense of being watched. A feeling of oppression began to grow especially when I was staring at the bed. After a few minutes of this, the feeling became so strong, that I ran down the stairs and refused to go back up there. This all happened in the space of a few minutes. Although no one saw anything, the feeling of someone watching me was so pervasive, that it made me uncomfortable enough to want to leave the area; which I did, immediately.

One Docent's Perspective
One night before closing the house and locking up, I began to hear footsteps coming from the upstairs area. The floorboards were creaking so loudly, another docent and I thought that a visitor was upstairs. I walked toward the stairs, and was about to call up to them when I met the visitor and a fellow docent at the bottom of the staircase. They informed me that there was no one upstairs. I told them what I had just heard, but they assured me that everyone else had left the building. I could only conclude that it must have been Yankee Jim stalking his characteristic spot.

People are frequently able to obtain pictures with orbs in the house, and we have one good picture that shows the manifestation of a little girl. Then there's the dining room, where the spirit of Anna Whaley is often captured on film. On one occasion, a person with a digital camera captured what appeared to be an silhouette of Thomas Whaley in one of the corners of the dining room, accompanied by a noticeable cold spot. There have been numerous reports of people smelling tobacco smoke and perfume throughout the house.

Visitor from San Diego
One frequent visitor stated, "Every time I've gone to the Whaley House, it is absolutely haunted." The individual was skeptical at first about the house being haunted, but that changed. As a youngster, he was part of a school tour that went into the house as part of a historical San Diego program. As the boy entered the house, some girls were frightened and holding on to him for protection. His first impressions were, that there were plenty of ghosts inside. Nothing actually happened out of the ordinary that year, other than the pervasive sense of spirits being present; however the next year he visited the Whaley House with his family.

After he and his family had dinner nearby, they decided to go in to the house for fun. While upstairs, nothing unusual happened. Then, as the rest of the family went downstairs into the courthouse, he stayed alone upstairs just looking at the bed in the master bedroom. As the boy stood in silence, he noticed that there was an impression forming in the bed as if someone unseen was sitting down as he looked on. Frightened, he left the area and began moving his way toward the stairs when he became engulfed in a cold breeze. Just then, something caught his attention out of the corner of his eyes. While about to head downstairs, he clearly saw a little girl in the adjacent room to the right of the stairs. The girl wasn't there for long, as she seemed to walk right behind the wall out of his sight. Curiosity got the better of him and he went up to the window blocking access to the room and looked around the wall to see where the girl had gone to. Of course, there was no one there. Running downstairs, the boy told his family what had just transpired, but they didn't seem to believe him. It didn't really matter, because he knew what he had just seen and that the Whaley House was a very haunted place where visitors are almost guaranteed to witness something unexplained when they go in.

Julie, Docent
She has been employed for over three years as a docent in the Whaley House, and works primarily at night when the Ghosts and Gravestone tours come through. According to Julie, one of the more common events that occur at night, is that she feels an intense cold sensation on the right side of her body after clearing the house of visitors. This sensation does not happen every night, but it is something that she is frequently aware of late at night. One night, a little boy was standing at the bottom of the stairs with his camera, as Julie stood on the 9th step of the stairs. He asked her why she was standing on the 9th step of the stairs, and Julie replied that Mrs. Whaley has been frequently sighted on this step. She then instructed the boy to take a picture, which he did. On the picture that he took, there was a misty presence next to Julie that was captured on film. Julie also felt as if a hand was touching her while this event was taking place.

Julie had another close encounter on the stairs. Late one night, she witnessed a little dog run from the back bedroom down the hallway and then vanish. It was a small terrier. She has also felt a presence inside the courtroom, almost as if she is being watched or followed when she's in there alone. It's a common feeling quite a few people get when they visit the room. Upstairs, she has witnessed the curtain suddenly move as if someone unseen is walking through the area. During those moments she does not feel comfortable, and usually walks away because she doesn't want to have anything to do with the energy. Other times, Julie has had to change in the upstairs bedroom to the right as you reach the top of the stairs. It's called the haunted bedroom, but then again, the whole place is considered haunted. She never feels real comfortable in that room, and on one particular occasion, while changing into her Victorian costume for the tours, she sensed a man standing near her, looking at her. It's in the area where the curtain often billows on its own.

Too much of a ghostly thing
Another visitor to the house related this story. It was a cool evening until he entered the dinning room. As the visitor and his group of friends were standing around the table in the downstairs dining room, everyone heard a child laughing out loud. The trouble was, that there was no child in the house at the time; at least that could be seen. As the laughter resonated through the room, the people backed away from the table as if they had triggered some paranormal laugh box. At that moment, another member of the group began laughing out loud, and repeating that someone unseen was tickling her. With that, the entourage left the room and began making their way upstairs. It was on the 9th step that another member remarked that she could not make it another step because someone had a hold of her foot. Of course, there was no one there, but that is the step where many people have felt pressure, or have experienced strange phenomena. Finally, everyone freed themselves of the spirited shackles and reached the nursery. Once again, the group began hearing laughter from some unseen person, and they all moved away and entered the master bedroom. The paranormal followed them as a faint whiff of cigar smoke permeated the room. As if to collectively say, what else could happen, several members of the group watched in stunned silence as the bed sheets began to move as if they were being straightened out by some ethereal maid; or perhaps Anna Whaley herself.. That was enough for one member of the group who ran down the stairs and left the house, vowing never to return.

M.G.
A couple of friends and I visited the Whaley House around 11:30pm, I guess we were trespassing a little too much. We were all around the house, we were in the back yard, going upstairs the back yard stairs, and

looking inside the windows of course we were not inside the actual house. My friends were peeking inside the windows, trying to open each door they could find, and just trying so hard to get in the house. Finally we just sat outside up the stairs were the master bedroom is at "I GUEES" so we were just talking and then we heard noises inside the house. We all stood quite, and got close to the door, we put our ear on the door, and we clearly heard conversations inside the house. Fist we heard a man and a woman's voice talking, we could exactly heard what they were speaking about, but we were 100% sure they were talking. After a little while they went away, my friends and I were all shocked, and freaked out because we knew that no one could possibly be inside the house. Even one of my friends went to the front of the house to check if someone was inside. After that the voices stopped, and then we began to hear noises inside. Like objects moving, like if someone was setting something on a table, or placing things on different spots. Then the weird noises went away, so we decided to leave after a while, as we got down the stairs, we then again heard noises in the yard, like if someone was running and hitting the bushes, but no one was there, it was pretty crazy. I couldn't believe it was really happening. After my experience last Friday I just wanted to learn a little more about the Whaley's and that's why I ended up writing up on this Website, I was searching for information about the house, it's just my curiosity on it.

Unusual band of light on the back balcony
(Courtesy of SOHO)

Jule Milton Keller

Keller was giving a tour of the house during the fall months. This particular tour was different from others he had given. During the tour, while the group was standing at the balustrade in the parlor, the crystal drops hanging from a lamp which rested on the parlor table began to swing back and forth. Keller and guests watched in amazement as the crystal lamp drops swayed back and forth for almost two full minutes—the strange thing was, only the drops on one side of the lamp moved, while the others were perfectly still—no logical explanation could be found and the tour continue.

On another occasion, in December, Keller was in the process of closing down the house far the day with other volunteers, usually a very simple and uneventful procedure. This time, however, after one of the volunteers returned from securing one of the restrooms, he was handed the security key while partially inside the hall closet attempting to reach for the master switch which turns off all the lights in the house. After switching off the lights and before turning to take the key, a voice told him not to move or he would step on the dog. The other person put his hands out, gesturing for Keller not to move just yet. In that instant of turning to see what all the concern was about, a bright light went off between the two men. Within seconds, Keller saw what appeared to be the back of a dog scurrying down the hallway and head into the dining room. He kidded the volunteer about trying to scare him, although the volunteer denied doing any such thing.

Ectoplasmic mist and orbs outside the Whaley House
(Courtesy of SOHO)

Since other volunteers were waiting for them at the front door, Keller naturally assumed that they had also witnessed the dog trot by—none had, and the person giving him the key swore that he never said anything about watching out for a dog. After describing the animal as spotted, like a fox terrier that ran down the hall with its ears flapping, it didn't take the group long to realize that Keller had witnessed an apparition—a dog from another dimension that he avoided stepping on thanks to a kindly voice from beyond.

In May, while escorting visitors through the upstairs portion of the house, Keller called down in an urgent tone to June Reading, the director, insisting she come upstairs at once. Rushing upstairs, Reading, Keller and the astonished tour group watched as the black rocking chair, moved back and forth as if occupied by a person. It had started moving on its own as the tour was being conducted and lasted about three minutes—while the tour guests were watching the haunted chair move—someone unseen, was kicking back to watch the tour group's response. No doubt, everyone enjoyed the action from their respective positions.

Another foray into the unknown happened to Keller during December. Prior to closing, he was interrupted by the apparition of a woman, seated on a settee in the upstairs bedroom, dressed in a green plaid gingham dress, she had long dark hair, coiled up in a bun at the neck, and remained for a few moments before vanishing. A February encounter involved two elderly ladies. As Keller was involved with a tour downstairs, the two ladies called down and asked him to come upstairs, to the door of the nursery. Leaving the tour downstairs, he rushed up as quickly as he could to see what all the fuss was. Upon reaching the nursery, her heard, along with the elderly visitors, a sound like that of a baby crying. Within seconds, the sound was hushed and the three onlookers shook their heads and left.

A final episode took place in early spring when Keller was in the house with another volunteer entertaining his parents. While delivering his spiel, his attention was diverted for a few moments to the foot of the staircase where he heard the sound of someone whistling upstairs. There were no visitors up there at the time and this occurrence, and the whistling was never explained. The appearance of a woman; a child crying: and a strange whistling sound from the invisible side of the Whaley House are a few of the manifestations which oftentimes greets visitors and volunteer alike—apparently, the ghosts are not selective on who they haunt.

School daze, school haze
School children are always a good source of stories about the Whaley House spirits. There have been countless times, when visiting school children will blurt out statements, whenever they see or hear anything out of the ordinary. There have been sightings of phantom children, chains that will begin swinging back and forth by themselves, spectral animals, smells of perfume or cigar smoke, and even sightings of Whaley family members when the descriptions given by the children are matched against historical evidence. Children, according to most researchers, seem to trigger quite a bit of paranormal activity, and their numerous stories attest to that fact.

On one occasion, a group of twenty children were in the courtroom listening to the historical lecture with only one thing on their minds, to see the ghost photographs and hear stories about the haunted Whaley house. As the Docent was delivering her rehearsed lines, a gasp filled the room. The children were pointing behind the startled docent. Turning toward the south side of the room where a chain separated the judge's bench from visitor seating, the chain was swinging wildly back and forth as if someone unseen was playing with it.

Funnel-like mists in the Parlor
(Courtesy of SOHO)

Anita Kirwin

As a former Whaley House volunteer, Kirwin reported that prior to working at the Whaley House, she worked on the grounds at the adjacent spice and tea shop. She knew nothing about the huanted history of the Whaley House at that time. When June Reading called Kirwin to see if she would come to work part time at the Whaley House, Kirwin accepted and became a guide. According to her, she had no preconceived notions about the spirit population inside.

Her brush with the paranormal, however, did not begin with her association with the Whaley House, but rather, when she worked at the spice and tea shop, called the Spice of Life. The building was a gunsmith shop dating to around 1838. One afternoon she heard footsteps on the outside porch. The sounds were distinctly those of a heavy-set man who was walking around outside her shop. After a minute or so, no one came in the shop, so she walked outside to see who the visitor might be. Opening the door and looking around, she saw no one remotely close to the building, so she dismissed the incident. Over her years of service as the shop, she witnessed a gentlemen in the yard who would stand near the ferns along the backyard walkway. He wore a frock coat, and a black top hat as he stood in backyard and just stared into the shop.

Because the little shop and the adjacent Whaley House were part of a major, local tourist attraction, Kirwin assumed the man was an eccentric tourist or someone from the theater (a small theater is located near the Whaley House) who enjoyed the ambiance of the quaint little shop and adjoining grounds. The odd-looking man would be there one minute, then gone the next— as though he vanished into thin air. Kerwin never actually saw him walking, he just stood there, looking over at the house.

When Kirwin began working at the Whaley House, she learned the history of Old Town and the Whaleys. Her job was to take groups through the house. Her first tour with several of the people. After a few minutes, Kirwin noticed that members of the group were smiling at her. It was unnerving and she thought that she might be doing something wrong. Later, a member of the tour group told June Reading that she saw a man standing next to Kirwin who description fit that of Yankee Jim—several people saw this apparition. Asking Reading if the tour group mentioned the man wearing a black, top hat, she no, but that the top hat belonged to Mr. Whaley.

Unexplained image on the wall to the left of the boy
(Courtesy of SOHO)

Several times after Kirwin gave talks in the courtroom, people would come up to Kirwin or Reading and say that they saw a man standing next to Kirwin—the description fit that of Yankee Jim Robinson, the man who was reportedly hanged on the spot where the Whaley House now stood. On another occasion while Kirwin was talking to a young girl about her collection of cigar boxes, both women began smelling a faint scent of cigar smoke drift by them. Soon it became almost overpowering—there is no smoking allowed in the house, neither of the women smoked, and there was no one around who could have carried the scent on their clothing.

Searching the house, they found no carrier of the tobacco smoked. As they continued talking, they heard a door slam. It sounded as if it was an interior door that might be located between the front and back doors off the main corridor. There is no such door at the present time. Mrs. Reading located some old records and diagrams of the house made by Lillian Whaley which showed that there had once been a door in the area where the noise had been heard—it had long since been removed.

E for Extraordinary

E. was a teen-ager when she first visited the Whaley House. She knew a little about the haunted nature of the building, but had never been inside, until this day. After entering, E. took the tour with a few other eager visitors. The upstairs tour proved uneventful, and after heading downstairs, the thought of encountering anything out of the ordinary, was becoming less likely; that is, until she entered the courtroom. That's when the usual taped history of the building was played for all of the visitors. It was during the presentation, that E. suddenly had an urge to get up and wander alone upstairs. Something was pulling her up the flight of stairs to the top of the landing. She then felt compelled to look into the nursery. At that moment, the female mannequin that had faced the outside window a few minutes earlier, was now facing E. with it's rigid finger pointing directly at E! That was too much to comprehend, and as fast as her feet could propel her, E stated down the stairs. Within seconds, she was engulfed in a wall of perfumed which seemed to follow her to the first floor. As she reached the bottom landing, a disembodied voice called out to her as she quickly exited the Whaley House. It was her first encounter with the spirits of the house; one that turned an ordinary day into an extraordinary journey into the unknown.

Oh, the tangled web[site] we weave of paranormal ponderings

According to several Websites devoted to the Whaley House spirits, summaries of phenomena reported inside include: cigar smoke; flowery perfume; moving a meat cleaver, silverware or other implements and items; orbs of light that have been captured on film; misty forms appearing out of thin air; the disembodied sounds of laughing, crying, discussing, arguing, or singing; the sound of music playing or singing; keys on the piano playing by themselves; the glass droplets on the chandeliers moving on their own; footsteps; impressions of people materializing on the beds or couches; curtains moving upstairs when there is no breeze; certain rocking chairs moving back and forth on their own; phantom animals brushing by startled visitors; feelings of being watched or followed; sudden equipment failure;

being touched by someone unseen; smells of food cooking; lights dimming; shadows on the walls; courtroom chains swinging unassisted; moving cold spots; and, feelings of having their throat constricted on the stairs—particularly around the 9th step. Every room in the house has had some form of unexplained event take place over the years.

Sightings of spirits have included: Anna Whaley who has been spotted as a young, petite, beautiful woman is the most frequently sighted energy in the house. She is reportedly responsible for piano music playing, the sudden smell of sweet perfume, and for appearing in period clothing upstairs and downstairs. Numerous psychics have come in contact with her over the years, and is considered the caretaker of the Whaley House; Thomas Whaley in a frock-coat in the downstairs den and courtroom and upstairs master bedroom, now the theater. Although his spirit is rarely sighted, his trademark is the smell of cigar smoke he leaves behind; "Yankee Jim" Robinson who was reportedly hanged on the spot where the Whaley House is built (unjustly as most researchers believe), is often sensed but rarely sighted inside.

Three photographs showing a mist forming into a possible figure on the downstairs Dining Room wall
(Courtesy of SOHO)

Some individuals say that the gallows would have been near the front porch, while others say they would have been in the area between the parlor and music room, or near the present-day stairs. Tightness in the throat, feelings of uneasiness, and unexplained footsteps are often blamed on Jim's restless spirit; Violet Whaley is another spirit who frequents the building as well as the area behind the house. Her troubled energy has been felt in the courtroom during a seance, in the Derby-Pendleton House, in the kitchen and upstairs guestroom adjacent to the nursery.

Violet may be responsible for the crying people have heard in the house and feelings of depression visitors have felt throughout the house; The spirit of a little girl, mistakenly called the Washburn girl has been most frequently sighted and felt in the hallway and kitchen/dining area. According to historical information and young girl accidentally ingested poison, and died in the house. Some say she has red hair and is responsible for moving items, playing with the chandelier, laughing, footsteps and tugging at people's hair or clothing; Dolly Varden, the Whaley's dog has been frequently sighted downstairs in the hallway, faintly barking, panting, or brushing up against people; a black, ghost cat is often seen scampering through the downstairs area, and in the backyard behind the house; a Native American spirit was spotted in the downstairs area near the courtroom; a civil war soldier has been sighted in the courtroom; a young woman in a calico dress, with hoop earrings, has been spotted resting in a courtroom chair; two men have been frequently sighted in the jury box in the courtroom as misty forms.

The spirits have also appeared as orbs and funnels of light above certain people who sit in their respective chairs; the chair in the corner of the jury box, and the third chair in from the right in the first row; and at least ten other visiting energies that have been picked up by psychics who say that they are not trapped in the house, but come to visit. These include friends of the Whaleys, a few of their children, a cook, a member of the Tanner Troupe, and some of the past renters who lived in the house. There has been a recent sighting of Corrine Lillian Whaley in the downstairs living room.

Millicent Brabant
As a former Whaley House employee who worked there for nine years, Brabant remembers hearing the sounds of heavy footsteps upstairs that many say belong to Yankee Jim. She has also encountered what sounds like a large meeting of men in the courtroom. The sounds include feet shuffling and furniture being moved around—the chairs don't actually move said Brabant, it just sounds like they are. Then there are the voices coming from the vicinity of the study which was Mr. Whaley's office. On occasion, voices can also be heard in the back of the house as well as sounds of furniture being moved, as if a group of people is preparing for a meeting.

While arriving at the Whaley House to open up, she has been greeted by the sound of mandolins playing. As she would turn to close the door, the music would stop. She has also heard the music box play as well as other instruments, including the piano playing.

Lawrence Riveroll
Riveroll was alone and seated in the front hallway one January afternoon, when the distinctive sounds of music and singing began filtering softly through the Whaley House. Listening intently, L.R. was able to discern the song as "Home Again,"—it was being sung by a woman. The entire event lasted less than a minute and as quickly as the melody began, the house once again became quiet. Upon inspection of the room where the music had come from, no one had entered the house—at least no one that could be seen by Riveroll.

Materializing figure in the Master Bedroom
(Courtesy of SOHO)

On another occasion in January, while Riveroll accompanied several visitors upstairs, the sound of organ music could be heard coming from the courthouse downstairs, since the Jenny Lind piano was in another room. The sound of a piano playing was a much more common occurrence than that of the organ, so he went down to see if someone was fooling around with the instrument. Reaching the courthouse and looking over at the organ, he was startled to see that the organ cover was closed and there was no one in the room—the person playing the organ was playing with a lot of spirit. Twelve days later, when the museum was closed to the public, Riveroll had another encounter. While closing the downstairs shutters, he heard the sound of footsteps upstairs. He made his way upstairs to see if someone had broken in, or possibly, a workman had come for repairs without his knowledge—there was no one to be found anywhere.

A final episode occurred in September at dusk. While closing up the house with another worker after the daily round of tourists had all gone home, Riveroll went to inspect the music room on his rounds. To his surprise, the piano began playing on its own. To make matters worse, as the piano played, he felt pressure being applied to his hands as if an unseen guest was there with him. Turning to face the front hallway in the direction of the desk, hoping to get the attention of the other volunteer, an astonished Riveroll was greeted by the free-floating vaporous apparition of a slightly built woman dressed in a hoop skirt. In the dim light he was unable to clearly discern her features. As suddenly the figure appeared, it vanished along with the pressure on his hands- The ghostly piano music also ceased—was a ghostly woman attempting to serenade Riveroll while another ghostly presence held him to ensure he had to listen?

Four from Texas
While visiting the Whaley House two women and two children encountered the restless spirits several years ago. After the group of ghost enthusiasts, arrived, just after the house opened to the public, the four had the place to themselves, or so they thought. They listened to the history and stories of the paranormal, and gazed at the myriad photographs of unexplained phenomena that people had taken inside over the years. While exploring the historic building, the group became a little discouraged that nothing unusual was happening to them. They didn't see anything, nor did they feel cold spots. However, as they were wondering whether the house was really haunted, the two children said they were each hearing the sounds of children laughing on the stairs to the second floor. The adults heard nothing unusual, but the children were emphatic about what the sounds they heard. As they were about to leave the house, the adults had all but given up on having anything unusual happen, when both suddenly picked up a strong lavender smell. The sensation was quick, but intense, and occurred several times within the span of a few minutes. The entire group was able to leave with a sense of being touched by the spirits of the house. But that's not all. Upon returning to the Lone Star State, and having the pictures developed, several of the pictures contained anomalies including: An odd blue light glowing near the upstairs mannequin; wisps of mist emanating from a lamp on a piano in the parlor; and, a partial form of a woman in a period dress reflecting in a mirror, next to one of the people having their picture taken. A trip to America's most haunted house would never be forgotten.

Charles, Docent
I really haven't seen anything since I've been working in the house, but I do feel things sometimes. There are times when I have a sensation of not being alone in a room, or there are times when I feel a lot of charged air in a particular room. There are other times when I get cold or fell a chilly draft blow right through me, although it's a stifling hot day. There was an occasion when the chandelier moved on its own in the courtroom, but I'm not sure what caused that; maybe a draft or something.

Suzanne Pere
Her encounter took place during the spring while she was engaged in typing a manuscript in the courtroom. Busily typing, Pere was suddenly interrupted by a loud noise coming from upstairs. She called out to June Reading who was working with her that day, and both of the women went to investigate. As it was near closing time, and finding no one there, they decided to secure the windows. As they did, Pere kept feeling a chilly breeze at the back of her head, accompanied by the distinct sensation that someone, though invisible, was following her from one window to another. This feeling continued until she left the house—someone wanted her out post haste, and she readily obliged.

Streaks and bands of light in the General Store
(Courtesy of SOHO)

Over a year later, on the 14th and 21st of October and November 18th, Pere became aware of a sudden sensory exposure to smoke as well as a heavy-scented perfume or cologne—she was once again working with June Reading, and both women noticed the strong odors. The women traced the scents to three locations in the house: the front parlor, upstairs hallway, and an upstairs bedroom. The perfume scents were of a light floral odor, similar to wisteria, and other like a heavy concentrated perfume which was very musky, like that of an import—although she was sure nothing on the market today duplicated the smell. Additionally, in the girls bedroom, Pere smelled something resembling dusting powder coming from the room—emanating odors were the ghostly fare for those three days.

On another occasion, while Pere was performing her duties, she saw apparitions in the study. She reported observing a group of men dressed in frock coats, some with plain vests, others with patterns on them. One of the men in this group sported a large gold watch chain across his vest. The entire atmosphere seemed to her like a kind of gentlemen's meeting or gathering, since all of the figures were animated; some pacing the floor while others were carrying on conversations. They all appeared to be serious and agitated, but oblivious to her. One man in the group seemed to be an official or a person of prominence who stood off by himself. She was able to describe this person as being was of medium stocky build, light brown hair, and mustache which was quite full and long. He had very piercing light blue eyes, penetrating gaze. Pere was exhausted by her experience, and her pulse was racing, yet she was curious about the man with the penetrating gaze. She asked Ms. Reading if she knew of anyone answering this description, because it remained with her for some time—the strange man with the powerful gaze has yet to be identified.

This time, in early October, Pere reported hearing unaccountable sounds from kitchen area, as if someone were hard at work preparing food. The same day, she also reported the distinct smell of something baking, like pumpkin pie. This was followed in late November, early in the morning after opening, by a distinct noise coming from the kitchen, as though something had dropped to the floor—possibly a utensil. Ms. Reading was also present when this occurred. Pere called to Ms. Reading asking what she was doing in the kitchen. Pere assumed that Ms. Reading had been rearranging the kitchen exhibit. However, she was busily at work in courtroom. Both women reached the kitchen at the same time, and stood staring at the floor as one of the utensils on the shelf rack had managed to disengage itself, and striking a copper boiler directly below on its way to the floor. No one else was in the house at the time, and both women were at a loss to explain the event—perhaps a ghostly hand dislodged it while trying to cook up a spirited meal.

Mrs. Allen

A volunteer for three years, Allen had several unexplainable events occur during her tenure in the building. The first event took place in early January when she heard organ music issue from courtroom. Like Lawrence Riveroll who was also there, she thought a child was playing with the organ. Upon reaching the courthouse, expecting to find someone at the organ, she too was shocked to see the cover to the organ closed and no one besides her and Riveroll in the courtroom.

Another encounter took place at closing time in mid-September. It was on the same day Lawrence Riveroll, while playing the piano, witnessed an apparition of a lady wearing a hoop skirt. As Ms. Allen was making her way upstairs to close the windows, she felt a distinct breeze come over her head. Once she reached the landing, she opened the balustrade and walked toward the front windows. Suddenly she heard a sound behind her, as though something had dropped to the floor. She turned to look, saw nothing, but again experienced the feeling of having an invisible something hover near her—a feeling of fear gripped her, a feeling of being watched but not knowing who was watching or from what direction it was coming from. She completed her task as quickly as possible, and hurried to leave the house with Mr. Riveroll once June Reading returned to lock up. A final episode occurred one afternoon in May when Ms. Allen was seated downstairs in the hall when the silence was broken by the sound of someone walking between the parlor and the music room.

A bright orb on the tree in the backyard of the Whaley House
(Courtesy of SOHO)

Kay Sterner

Sterner, the President of The California Parapsychology Foundation at the time, was asked to visit the Whaley House when strange and unusual activities were continually being reported by June Reading and her staff. Sterner, a known clairvoyant, who had no prior knowledge of the history of the Whaley House or its prior occupants, visited the Whaley House on a number of occasions, with the following results.

On her first visit, Sterner was content to remain outside the brick structure in order to get a feel for the surroundings. As she rounded the corner to the house she was confronted by a vision from the past. She witnessed a scaffold, a long since disappeared coach house, and a wagon with two horses pulling away in the confines of the backyard area—could this scene have been related to the death of Yankee Jim Robinson? Sterner left the backyard, entered the house and immediately climbed the stairs. As she reached the second floor, she peered into one of the bedrooms, and was startled to see a woman in a theatrical costume gazing out of the window—could this have been the spirit of one of the members of the Tanner Troupe who leased space in the Whaley House? Her tour continued in another of the upstairs rooms where she stumbled on yet another apparition, this time of a young woman sporting a mauve dress and standing in front of another window. She later remarked that the dress that she witnessed the ghostly woman wearing, was the same dress worn by one of the mannequins—the hand made dress was worn by Whaley's daughters, who were excellent dressmakers.

On another occasion Sterner entered what she felt was an emotionally charged courtroom. As she stood in the empty courtroom (empty for those non-psychics) she saw a group of rowdy sailors, prostitutes and what looked like, bandits going before a judge—the house obviously is not adverse to providing replays of high charged and emotional events which took place over one hundred years ago. Sterner also witnessed a stocky man wearing boots and carrying what appeared to be a log book. She felt that the man was upset about a legal case he had adjudicated. The man appeared to be very scrupulous, and suffered what she felt was a leg injury. June Reading provided an answer to this riddle, when she told Sterner that her description matched that of a man known as Squire A.R. Ensworth, who had been Thomas Whaley's lawyer and business manager, as well as a magistrate—Reading showed Sterner letters indicating great concern on Ensworth's part as to whether he had made the right decision in a specific case involving Whaley, a fact no one else would have been privy to. The topper came when Reading told Sterner that Ensworth had fallen into a hole on the property and broke his leg—it had never been properly set, causing the man pain and shackling him with a noticeable limp.

Even more dramatic was the reenactment before the medium's very eyes of a brutal murder. The phenomenon began with loud, agonizing screams. Then she saw a Mexican woman with long flowing dark hair, a bright blouse and long ruffled skirt run shrieking down the hall. She was pursued by a man of dark complexion who accused her of being unfaithful. There was a violent quarrel and Sterner watched in helpless terror as the man drew a knife and slashed his errant love to death. Later she learned from Reading that a heated quarrel between a Mexican couple had ended with the wife's stabbing. The tragedy had occurred in the upstairs bedroom as the medium had seen it.

Sterner's visits always seemed to produce a new array of psychic phenomena. While visiting the house on another occasion, she spent a good portion of the night in the upstairs area. She remained intent on discovering more about the spiritual side of the house while other members of the San Diego Parapsychology Foundations remained downstairs with director June Reading. Sterner became aware of a large, rugged man in dark clothing and dusty boots in one of the rooms. It was later confirmed that her description fit that of the owner, Thomas Whaley. Sterner then observed a young woman sauntering toward her carrying whalebone handled razor. Similar to the other apparitions, this image too, faded into the ether. Sterner also had a strong mindfulness that a woman in the house had contemplated suicide—Sterner was told that a young woman had attempted to kill herself while she stayed at the house.

On yet another occasion, Sterner had an eerie and frightening experience, which left her weak and trembling. On this night, a particularly dark and gloomy one, Sterner had to feel her way up the staircase. When she reached the top, she began hearing agonizing screams. It was at that

Unexplained mist in the Master Bedroom
(Courtesy of SOHO)

moment that she clearly viewed a Mexican couple having a violent argument. The focus of the heated rumpus was the woman's infidelity and took place in an upstairs bedroom. To Sterner's horror, she watched helplessly as the man took a knife and stabbed his wife to death in a fit of rage—he disemboweled her—Sterner learned that the couple had been tenants of the house and that a brutal murder had occurred. She also witnessed the tragic death of a small child in one of the upstairs bedrooms, the same bedroom according to historic records where the Whaleys son of seventeen months passed away. Finally, Sterner saw the apparition of a woman wearing a cap and nightgown making her rounds through the house. The phantom woman was going from room to room to make sure that the Whaley children were safely tucked in as well as ensuring that the windows were fastened and doors bolted—could this have been the spectral form of Anna Whaley still watching over her brood.

Canadian Visitor

A Canadian woman reported to the Whaley House staff, of feeling a noticeable pressure as she went upstairs—as if someone, or something, didn't want her to go up there. She also experienced cool breezes swirling over her head and a strong sensation of someone standing behind her. In the courthouse section, she saw a petite, dark woman, with hoop earrings and wearing a long, calico dress. Her immediate impression was that the she was intruding on the ghostly woman's privacy. Her report of the events barely made an impact on the staff that day—reports like that were fairly common at the haunted Whaley House.

Present-day staff, as well as visitors continues to report seeing and hearing things on a regular basis. The range of phenomena include: smells of cigar smoke and perfume; sightings of spectral forms in the parlor, courtroom, study, hallway, stairs and kitchen areas of the house; hearing footsteps, people talking, children's laughter, doors opening and shutting on their own, a game of billiards being played, rockers moving back and forth without a soul in them, rumpled linens on the beds as if invisible forms were sleeping on the beds, lamps and chandeliers swaying; and the common feelings of being watched, cold spots and sensations of pressure and of being touched—all an integral part of spending time in the most haunted house in America.

Although it may appear that "strange events" happen every day, the truth is, some periods are more active than others, and some people, especially children appear to bring out the psychic energy of the house, more than other individuals. There are no guarantees upon entering that you will have an experience or brush with the paranormal, however, in the Whaley House, you stand a better chance then almost anywhere else in the United States—at least that what the stories tell us. So, take a trip to San Diego, and take your chances while slowly wandering through the house. Let the feel of the house filter through your senses, approach the subject with an open mind and show some respect and you too may one day be a footnote in a future edition of the Haunted Whaley House book.

Illinois Meets the Whaley Spirits

J. and A Cascio came all the way from Bloomingdale, Illinois to visit the Whaley House. They heard all about the restless spirits in the house before visiting, so they were prepared for just about anything upon entering... or so they thought. The following story is presented by Mrs. Cascio.

My husband and I visited the Whaley House on Monday, March 27, 2000 at 10:30 a.m. After we paid our admittance, I noticed a boy in the courtroom taking photos. I verified with the gentleman at the door that photos could indeed be taken, so I sent my husband back to our room (three blocks away at the Heritage Inn) to get our camera. In the meantime, the boy left and went to the backyard.

Possible ghost image of a man in General Store
Photograph by Stephen Savlack (Courtesy of SOHO)

I could see and hear from the back windows that there was a small group of young children in the backyard getting a tour lecture. I returned to the hallway, where I stood facing the courtroom (I could see into the courtroom from where I was standing in the hallway door) and was talking with the gentleman at the desk when I heard a moan; like a Nooooo, and then heard something heavy drop to the floor (it sounded like a metal box or something metal hitting the floor with a loud clank) coming from the courtroom. I didn't respond immediately because I couldn't believe what I just heard and wasn't sure anyone else heard it. The gentleman at the front desk looked at me and asked me, "Did you hear that?" I admitted I did. The other docent was at her desk in front of us the entire time as well. She admitted that she heard it too. I went toward the room and found that it was empty. In my mind, I already knew it was empty because we were among the first five individuals touring inside, and I had seen the boy and an elderly couple who were there earlier, go out the back door when my husband left to go get our camera. No one else had entered either door (front or back) since my husband left, or I would have seen them.

After my husband returned with our camera, I took several photographs downstairs. While I was initially alone taking the first photo upstairs, I felt a warm "presence." I wasn't frightened, but actually felt comforted or welcomed and even talked aloud to myself, remarking about how beautiful the house is and how nice the furniture was. My husband joined me upstairs and stood near me as I took the second photograph that was of the nursery. I was anxious to get the photos back, because I was certain that they would prove or reveal the "presence" I felt.

Of the 48 photos on two rolls taken while in California, eight were taken in the Whaley House. Of the eight photographs taken inside, only the three taken upstairs of the bedrooms came out; they all had "hazy" areas within the photograph. My husband said the "haze" in the photo of the nursery must be his or my reflection in the glass barrier. However, the clear photographs taken downstairs, clearly show that he was wearing a dark blue sweatshirt over a short-sleeve beige shirt. I was standing near the open door, and he was behind me to my right as I took the photo of the nursery. I was wearing a fitted long-sleeve black wool blazer over a v-neck green stretch, fitted top. In one of the photographs, you can see the outline of someone wearing a white puffy top or dress with puffy "sleeves" The first photograph I took of the adult's bedroom with the rocking chair is almost a blur. That's where I was originally alone before my husband joined me upstairs and where I felt the initial "presence." [we have included two of the photographs in our ghost gallery in the back of the book – have a look at the nursery photo showing a possible female phantom].

New Zealander Finds a Ghost
Hillena, a part time sales assistant, came to the Whaley House while visiting from New Zealand with her mother. The two came to the house around 10:15 a.m. just after it had opened and it was their first encounter with the house after reading so much about its haunted history. They were taking their time while absorbing the ambiance of the building when they finally made their way upstairs. Hillena recounted that when she and her mother approached the nursery, her heart began racing. This was followed in short order by a strange sensation of feeling very uncomfortable, which she related to her mother. There was something about the upstairs area that hit Hillena hard, a sense of foreboding that began as soon as she

reached the top of the stairs. Quite honestly, she felt "spooked" a sensation even her mother felt.

They both stood quietly in front of the paned nursery window, as the air felt thick and almost electrically charged. She noted the double bed, a doll in a stroller, dresser, and table and chair in the room. The two women had little desire to remain upstairs given their level of unease. Before departing, Hillena's mother took two photographs of the nursery with her 35mm camera using 200 ASA film, then they quickly existed the house. When they had the film developed, there was an outline of someone standing between the bed and next to the doll and stroller on one of the two photographs [to us it looks like a woman wearing a long white dress with long sleeves. It a faint misty outline of something, and the seam of the dress is visible on the floor near the bed] We've included the photograph in our ghost gallery section at the back of the book. According to Hillena, there was a black spot on the negative between the two photographs that puzzled the Kodak staff who called it'"very unusual." You be the judge when you see the result of Hillena's encounter with the unknown.

A large black shape blots out a portion of the courtroom
(Courtesy of the International Paranormal Research Organization)

Epilogue

As long as this house stands as a testament to the Whaley's, an early pioneering family in San Diego, there will be spirits who will greet visitors. Although by our frame of time which is our construct in the physical dimension, it's been over 140 years since the house was built for the Whaleys, it's only a wink of an eye for them, and those who followed in their footsteps. Although the spirits lack form, they do not lack hospitality, or in this case, hauntspitality. They continue to greet people in every way imaginable from beyond a very thin veil that separates their world from ours. They are very protective of this building, and nighttime is their time. We have found out on several occasions, that the spirits seem to become very possessive of house the later it gets. It's as if they respectfully allow us to visit with them in daylight, but as night descends, they prefer their solitude, to be with their own kind. All too often people have reported feeling as if they have overstayed their welcome in the house, as they conduct investigations.

And so, we will continue to meet them in the light of day, or the dead of night, as a whiff or perfume, a disembodied footstep, whispered conversation, a child's playful laugh, an orb of light, a glimpse out of the corner of ones eye, or for a few lucky ones, a full frontal manifestation. That's the Whaley House 1861 to the present— still very much alive and well, and one of the most haunted places in the world.

At the time of this second printing, stories of daily visitations from otherworldly guests continue to reach us. Even as this book goes to press, you can bet that the ghostly footsteps in the upstairs rooms, the phantom smells of perfume and cigar smoke, the brief glimpses of the former occupants, courtroom chains swinging, ethereal music playing, and the feeling of being watched, continue to greet visitors of the Haunted Whaley House on a daily basis.

Remember when visiting the most haunted house in America, be respectful, be as quiet as possible, and keep your senses about you at all times. If you keep an open mind, you just might catch a glimpse of Thomas, Anna, the children, or a number of other spirits who keep things extremely lively at this dwelling.

Good Luck with your journey into the unknown, and keep in touch—although we can't guarantee you won't BE TOUCHED!

Happy Haunting!

Haunted Whaley House References

Ghostwatching is exciting; it can also be psychically exhausting and mentally challenging. For 90 per cent of the time the main requirement of a ghostwatcher is patience, because nothing is happening. But the other 10 per cent—when the action starts—can be extremely rewarding.

John Spencer & Tony Wells, Ghost Watching (1994)

The following references dealing solely with the Whaley House have been compiled by the authors. Some information was gleaned from researchers, Thomas & Amiee Logue, (E-mail: whaleyhouse@geocities.com).

San Diego Union, "18,000 Whaley Letters Found", December 27, 1957.

San Diego Union, "Study of Whaley Letters Gets 'O.K.'", March 14, 1958.

San Diego Tribune, "Antiques Sought for Whaley House", Friday, January 30, 1959.

San Diego Tribune, "Whaley House Seen As Tourist Magnet", March 24, 1959.

San Diego Tribune, "County Weighs Whaley House Plans", Weds, June 3, 1959.

San Diego Union, "Whaley's Letter Talk From History", Sunday, June 14, 1959.

San Diego Historical Society Quarterly, Vol VI, No. 2: "The Whaley House", April 1960.

San Diego Tribune, "Whaley House Slated For Opening May 25th", Wednesday, May 11, 1960.

San Diego Tribune: "Reincarnation of Past Begin Life", May 11, 1960.

San Diego Tribune, "Time Stands Still In Whaley House", September 27, 1960.

Hans Holzer, "The Whaley House Ghosts," in, Great American Ghost Stories (1963), pp. 341-376.

Suzy Smith, "The Whaley House, The House on Hanging Ground," in, Prominent American Ghosts (1967), pp. 51-60.

San Diego Tribune: "Ghosts At Whaley House Too Spirited To Play Dead", Thursday, April 23, 1970.

The Independent: "Whaley House Ghosts Star In New Book", Wednesday, January 26, 1972.

Antoinette May, "The Thomas Whaley House," in, Haunted Houses and Wandering Ghosts of California (1977), pp. 12-19.

Patricia Schaelchlin, The Whaley House, San Diego, Home & Garden Magazine, November 1979.

Richard Winer and Nancy Osborn, "Whaley House," in, Haunted Houses (1979), pp. 70-71.

Joan Bingham and Dolores Riccio, "The Whaley House," (1980), in Haunted Houses USA, pp. 20-28.

Michael Marinacci, "Whaley House," Mysterious California by (1988), pp. 131-134.

Diane Hill, "Ghosts of the Whaley House", FEDCO Reporter, October 1990.

Antoinette May, "The Thomas Whaley House," Haunted Houses of California (1990, rev. 1993), pp. 199-211.

Arthur Myers, "Thomas Whaley Is Still Very Much in Possession of His Own Home," The Ghostly Gazetteer: America's Most Fascinating Haunted Landmarks (1990), pp. 64-72.

Raymond Buckland, editor, "The Whaley House Ghosts," Ghosts, Hauntings and Possessions:The Best of Hans Holzer Book 1, (1991), pp. 135-179.

Phyllis Raybin Emert, "The Whaley House," Strange Unsolved Mysteries: Ghosts, Hauntings and Mysterious Happenings (1992), pp. 1-5.

Hans Holzer, "The Most Haunted House in America," True Ghost Stories - (1992), pp. 473-498.

Gail White, "The Whaley House, You Can Hang a Good Man, But He'll Still Hang Around," Haunted San Diego: A Historic Guide to San Diego's Favorite Haunts (1992): pp. 3-16.

Hans Holzer, "Mr. Whaley Wants His Day In Court," America's Restless Ghosts (1993), pp. 172-174

Readers Digest, "The Whaley House," Quest For The Unknown: Ghosts and Hauntings (1993), p. 61.

Richard Senate, "California's Most Haunted House," The Haunted Southland (1994), pp. 4-7.

Hans Holzer, "The Whaley House California," Where the Ghosts Are;" The Ultimate Guide to Haunted Houses (1995): pp. 29-31.

Hans Holzer, "The Whaley House Ghosts," in, Ghosts: True Encounters With The World Beyond (1997), Black Dog & Leventhal Publishers, New York, pp. 296-308.

Michael Norman and Beth Scott, "Yankee Jim's Legacy," Historic Haunted America (1995): pp. 46-55.

John J. Lamb, "America's Most Famous Haunted Place: The Whaley House," in, San Diego Specters (1999), Sunbelt Publications, San Diego, California, pp. 31-46.

Barbara Smith, "The Whaley House," in, Ghost Stories of California (2000), Lone Pine Publishing, Canada, pp. 24-29.

Troy Taylor, "Yankee Jim and Others: The Hauntings of The Whaley House," in, The Haunting of America (2001), Whitechapel Productions Press, Alton, Illinois, pp. 203-211.

Dennis William Hauck, The National Directory: Haunted Places, Ghostly Abodes, Sacred Sites, UFO Landings and Other Supernatural Locations (revised and updated, 2002), pp. 69.

Additional Paranormal Reading

(This is not an exhaustive list of books on ghosts and the paranormal, but merely a taste what's out there. We recommend that you check out www.prairieghosts.com for available ghost titles):

Olyve Hallmark Abbott, Ghosts in the Graveyard: Texas Cemetery Tales, Republic of Texas Press, Plano, Texas
Charles J. Adams III, Cape May Ghost Stories, Book 2 (1997) Exeter House Books, Reading, Pennsylvania
Charles J. Adams III, Ghost Stories of Berks County (1982), Exeter House Books, Reading, Pennsylvania
Charles J. Adams III, Ghost Stories of Berks County, Book Two (1984), Exeter House Books, Reading, Pennsylvania
Charles J. Adams III, Pennsylvania Dutch Country Ghosts Legends and Lore (1994), Exeter House Books, Reading, Pennsylvania
Charles J. Adams III, Berks The Bizarre (1995), Exeter House Books, Reading, Pennsylvania
Charles Adams III, New York City Ghost Stories (1996), Exeter House Books, Pennsylvania
Charles Adams III, Philadelphia Ghost Stories (1998), Exeter House Books, Pennsylvania
Charles J. Adams III, Bucks County Ghost Stories (1999), Exeter House Books, Reading, Pennsylvania
Charles J. Adams III, and Gary Lee Clothier, Ghost Stories of Berks County, Book 3 (1988), Exeter House Books, Reading, Pennsylvania
Charles Adams III, and David J. Seibold, Ghost Stories of the Lehigh Valley (1993), Exeter House Books, Pennsylvania
Charles J. Adams III, and David Seibold, Pocono Ghosts, Legends, and Lore, Book Two, (1995), Exeter House Books, Reading, Pennsylvania
John Alexander, Ghosts: Washington's Most Famous Ghost Stories (1988), The Washington Book Trading Company, Arlington, Virginia
John Alexander, Ghosts: Washington Revisited (1998), Schiffer Publishing, Atglen, Pennsylvania
Jean Anderson, The Haunting of America (1973), Houghton Mifflin Company, Boston, Massachusetts
Melissa Arnold, The Hauntings of Ellicott Mills (1998), Inch-by-Inch Enterprises, Ellicott City, Maryland
Dan Asfar, Ghost Stories of Michigan (2002), Ghost House Publishing, Edmonton, Canada
Dan Asfar, Ghost Stories of Pennsylvania (2002), Ghost House Publishing, Edmonton, Canada
Dan Asfar, Haunted Highways (2003), Ghost House Books, Edmonton, Canada.
Dan Asfar, Ghost Stories of the Old West (2003), Ghost House Books, Edmonton, Canada.
Dan Asfar and Eric Thay, Ghost Stories of America (2001), Ghost House Books, Edmonton, Canada.
Dan Asfar and Eric Thay, Ghost Stories of The Civil War (2003), Ghost House Books, Edmonton, Canada
LoydAuerback, ESP, Hauntings and Poltergeists (1986), Warner Books, Inc. N.Y.
Blue Balliett, The Ghosts of Nantucket (1984), Down East Books, Camden, Maine
Blue Balliett, Nantucket Hauntings (1990), Down East Books, Camden, Maine
Daniel W. Barefoot, Piedmont Phantoms (2002), John F. Blair, Publisher, Winston-Salem, North Carolina
Daniel W. Barefoot, Seaside Spectres (2002), John F. Blair, Publisher, Winston-Salem, North Carolina
Ellen Baumler, Spirit Trails: Ghost Tails from Virginia City, Butte, and Helena (2002), Montana Historical Society Press
Jackie Behrend, Ghosts of America's East Coast (2001), Crane Hills Publishers, Canada
Ursula Bielski, Chicago Haunts (1997), Lake Claremont Press, Chicago, Illinois
Ursula Bielski, More Chicago Haunts (2000), Lake Claremont Press, Chicago, Illinois
Joan Bingham and Dolores Riccio, Haunted Houses USA (1989), Pocket Books, New York, New York
Joan Bingham and Dolores Riccio, More Haunted Houses (1991), Pocket Books. N.Y.
Hugh E. Bishop, Haunted Lake Superior: Ghostly Tales and Legends from the Mystical Inland Sea (2003), Laake Superior Port Cities Inc., Duluth, Minnesota
W. Haden Blackman, The Field Guide to North American Hauntings (1998). Three Rivers Press, New York
John Blair Publisher, Boogers and Boo-Daddies (2004), Winston-Salem, North Carolina.
Blue & Gray Magazine, Guide to Haunted Places of the Civil War (1996), Blue & Gray Enterprises, Columbus, Ohio
Jack Bochar and Bob Wasel, Haunted Gettysburg (1996), published by Donny Bayne
Jack Bochar and Bob Wasel, More Haunted Gettysburg (1997), published by Donny Bayne
Dennis Boyer, Northern Frights (1998), Prairie Oak Press, Madison, Wisconsin
Dwight Boyer, Ghost Ships of the Great Lakes (1968), Freshwater Press, Cleveland
Ginnie Siena Bivona, Dorothy McConachie and Mitchel Whittington (editors) , Haunted Encounters: Real Life Stories of Supernatural Experiences (2003), Atriad Press, Dallas, Texas
Nancy Bradley, The Incredible World of Gold Rush Ghosts (1998), Morris Publishing, Kearney, Nebrasks
Nancy Bradley and Vincent Gaddis, Gold Rush Ghosts (1990), Borderland Sciences, Garberville, California

Nancy Bradley and Robert Reppert, The Incredible World of Gold Rush Ghosts (2002), Morris Publishing, Kearney, Nebraska
Trent Brandon, The Ghost Hunters Bible (2000), www.zerotime.com
Alan Brown, Shadows and Cypress: Southern Ghost Stories (2002), University Press of Mississippi, Jackson
Alan Brown, Haunted Places in the American South (2002), University Press of Mississippi, Jackson
James V. Burchill, Linda J. Crider and Peggy Kendrick, The Cold, Cold Hand (1997), Rutledge Hill Press, Nashville, Tennessee
James V. Burchill, Linda J. Crider, Peggy Kendrick and Marcia Wright Bonner, Ghosts and Haunts from the Appalachian Foothills (1993), Rutledge Hill Press, Nashville, Tennessee
Claudine Burnett, Haunted Long Beach (1996). Historical Society of Long Beach, Long Beach, California.
Julie Burtinshaw, Julie (2003), Romantic Ghost Stories, Ghost House Books, Edmonton, Canada.
Robert Ellis Cahill, New England's Ghostly Haunts (1983), Chandler-Smith Publishing House, Inc.
Robert Ellis Cahill, Haunted Happenings (1992), Old Saltbox Publishing House, Inc. Salem, Massachusetts
Robert Ellis Cahill, Lighthouse Mysteries of the North Atlantic (1998), Old Saltbox Publishing House, Salem, Massachusetts
Martin Caidin, Ghosts of the Air (1996), Galde Press, Lakeville, Minnesota
Suzy Cain and Dianne Thompson Jacoby, A Ghostly Experience: Tales of Saint Augustine Florida (1997), Tour Saint Augustine, St. Augustine, Florida
Burt Calloway and Jennifer Fitzsimons, Triad Hauntings (1990), Bandit Books, Winston-Salem, North Carolina
Matthew Sean Casey, Strange Key West (2003), Phantom Press, Key West, Florida
Bruce Carlson, The Best of the Mississippi River Ghosts (1997), Quixote Press
Richard Carrico, San Diego's Spirits: Ghosts and Hauntings in America's Southwest Corner (1991), Recuerdos Press, San Diego, California.
Connie Cartmell, Ghosts of Marietta (1996), The River Press, Marietta, Ohio
Cam Cavanaugh, In Lights and Shadows (1986), The Joint Free Public Library, Morristown, New Jersey
Joseph Citro, The Vermont Ghost Guide (2000), UNiversity Press of New England
Dylan Clearfield, Chicagoland Ghosts (1997), Thunder Bay Press, Grand Rapids, Michigan
Chas S. Clifton, Ghost Tales of Cripple Creek (1983), Little London Press, Colorado Springs, Colorado
Al Cobb, Danny's Bed (2000), Whitaker Street Press, Savannah, Georgia
Al Cobb, Savannah's Ghosts (2001) Whitaker Street Press, Savannah, Georgia
Al Cobb, Savannah's Ghosts II (2003) Whitaker Street Press, Savannah, Georgia
Daniel, Cohen, Real Ghosts (1977), Pocket Books, New York
Daniel, Cohen, The Restless Dead (1984), Pocket Books, New York
Daniel, Cohen, The Encyclopedia of Ghosts (1984), Dodd, Mead and Co. New York
Christopher K. Coleman, Ghosts and Haunts of the Civil War (1999), Rutledge Hill Press, Nashville, Tennessee
Christopher K. Coleman, Dixie Spirits (2002), Cumberland House, Nashville, Tennessee
Elaine Coleman, Texas Haunted Forts (2001), Republic of Texas Press, Plano, Texas
Jerry D. Coleman, Strange Highways (2003), Whitechapel Productions Press, Alton, Illinois
Loren Coleman, Mysterious America (2001), Paraview Press, New York
Matt Connor, Watering Hole: The Colorful History of Booze, Sex and Death at the New Jersey Tavern (2003), 1st Books Library
Kim Cool, Ghost Stories of Venice (2002), Historic Venice Press, Venice, Florida
Robbi Courtaway, Spirits of Saint Louis (1999), Virginia Publishing Company, St. Louis, Missouri
Robbi Courtaway, Spirits of Saint Louis (2002), Virginia Publishing Company, St. Louis, Missouri
Jo-Anne Christensen, Ghost Stories of Illinois (2000), Lone Pine Publishing, Edmonton, Canada
Jo-Anne Christensen, Ghost Stories of Texas (2001), Lone Pine Publishing, Edmonton, Canada
Jo-Anne Christensen, Haunted Hotels (2002), Ghost House Publishing, Edmonton, Canada
Susan Crites, Union Ghosts (1993), Butternut Publications, Martinsburg, West Virginia
Susan Crites, Confederate Ghosts (1993), Butternut Publications, Martinsburg, West Virginia
Susan Crites, More Civil War Ghosts (1994), Butternut Publications, Martinsburg, West Virginia
Susan Crites, The Littlest Ghosts (1995), Butternut Publications, Martinsburg, West Virginia
Susan Crites, Lively Ghosts Along The Potomac (1997), Butternut Publications, Martinsburg, West Virginia
Richard T. Crowe, Chicago's Street Guide to the Supernatural (2000), Carolanda Press, Inc., Oak Park, Illinois
Margaret Wayt DeBolt, Savannah Specters and Other Strange Tales (1984), The Donning Company Publishers, Norfolk, Virginia Beach.
Dennis Deitz, The Greenbrier Ghost (1990), Mountain Memories Books, South Charleston, West Virginia
Karen Hoisington Donaldson, Haunted Houses of Michigan (1998), Whitechapel Productions Press, Alton, Illinois
Discover Travel Adventures, Haunted Holidays (1990). Discovery Communications, Inc. Insight Guides, Langenscheidt Publishers, Inc., Maspeth, New York

Linda Dunning, *Specters In Doorways, The Haunted Utah Series: Book 1 (2003)*, Whitechapel Productions Press, Alton, Illinois
Norma Elizabeth and Bruce Roberts, *Lighthouse Ghosts (1999)*, Crane Hill Publishers, Birmingham, Alabama
Lori Erickson, *Ghosts of the Amana Colonies (1988)*, Quixote Press, Sioux City, Iowa
Lawrence Everett *(2002) Ghosts, Spirits and Legends of Southeastern Ohio*, Infinity Publishing Co., Haverford, Pennsylvania.
Hans J. Eysenck, and Carl Sargent *(1982) Explaining the Unexplained*, Weidenfeld and Nicolson, London.
Don Farrant, *Ghosts of the Georgia Coast (2002)*, Pineapple Press, Sarasota, Florida
Lisa Farwell, *Haunted Texas Vacations (2000)*, Westcliffe Publishers, Englewood, Colorado
Dorothy Burtz Fiedel, *True Ghost Stories (1995)*. Science Press, Ephrata, Pennsylvania
Dorothy Burtz Fiedel, *Living With Ghosts (1999)*. Science Press, Ephrata, Pennsylvania
Blanche W. Floyd, *Tales Along The King's Highway of South Carolina (1999)*, Bandit Books, Winston-Salem, North Carolina
E. Randall Floyd, *In the Realm of Ghosts and Hauntings (2002)*, Harbor House, Augusta, Georgia
Dixie Franklin, *Haunts of the Upper Great Lakes (1997)*, Thunder Bay Press, Michigan
Trish Gallagher, *Ghosts and Haunted Houses of Maryland (1988)*, Tidewater Publishers, Centreville, Maryland
Antonio Garcez, *Adobe Angels: The Ghosts of Albuquerque. (1994)*, Red Rabbit Press, Truth or Consequences, New Mexico
Antonio Garcez, *Adobe Angels: The Ghosts of Santa Fe and Taos. (1995)*, Red Rabbit Press, Truth or Consequences, New Mexico
Antonio Garcez, *Adobe Angels: The Ghosts of Las Cruces and Southern New Mexico. (1996)*, Red Rabbit Press, Truth or Consequences, New Mexico
Antonio Garcez, *Adobe Angels: Arizona Ghost Stories. (1998)*, Red Rabbit Press, Truth or Consequences, New Mexico
Antonio Garcez, *Adobe Angels: Ghost Stories of O'Keeffe Country. (1998)*, Red Rabbit Press, Truth or Consequences, New Mexico
Antonio Garcez, *American Indian Ghost Stories of the Southwest. (2000)*, Red Rabbit Press, Truth or Consequences, New Mexico
Antonio Garcez, *Arizona Ghost Stories. (2003)*, Red Rabbit Press, Hanover, New Mexico
Antonio Garcez, *New Mexico Ghost Stories. (2003)*, Red Rabbit Press, Hanover, New Mexico
Walter Gavenda, and Michael T. Shoemaker, *A Guide to Haunted West Virginia (2001)*, Peter's Creek Publishing, Glen Ferris, West Virginia
Sharon Gill and David Oester, *Twilight Visitors, Vol. One (1995)*, StarWest Images, St. Helens, Oregon
Sharon Gill and David Oester, *The Haunted Reality (1996)*, StarWest Images, St. Helens, Oregon
Joan Gilbert, *Missouri Ghosts (1997)*, Pebble Publishing
Joan Gilbert, *More Missouri Ghosts (2000)*, Mogho Books LLC, Hallsville, Missouri
Carol Gist, *Is It Really Haunted: A Concise Resource For Ghost Encounters*, Writers Club Press, iUniverse, Inc., Lincoln, Nebraska
David Goodwin, *Ghosts of Jefferson Barracks (2001)*, Whitechapel Productions Press, Alton, Illinois
Glen Grant, *Obake Files (1996)*, Mutual Publishing, Honolulu, Hawaii
Jim Graczyk, *A Field Guide to Chicago Hauntings (2001)*, Whitechapel Productions Press, Alton, Illinois
Suzanne Gruber and Bob Wasel, *Haunts of the Cashtown Inn (1998)*, Published by Bob Wasel, Pennsylvania
Rosemary Guiley, *The Encyclopedia of Ghosts and Spirits (1992)*, Facts on File, New York
Karen Harvey, *Oldest Ghosts: St. Augustine Haunts (2000)*, Pineapple Press, Sarasota, Florida
Dennis William Hauck, *The National Directory: Haunted Places (1996)*, Penguin Books, New York
Ruth Hein, *Ghostly Tales of Southwest Minnesota (1989)*, North Star Press of St. Cloud, Inc., Minnesota
Ruth Hein, *Ghostly Tales of Minnesota (1992)*, North Star Press of St. Cloud, Inc., Minnesota
Ruth Hein, *More Ghostly Tales from Minnesota (1996)*, Quixote Press, Soiux City, Iowa
Ruth Hein, *Ghostly Tales of the Black Hills and Badlands (2000)*, North Star Press of St. Cloud, Inc., Minnesota
Ruth D. Hein & Vicky Hinsenbrock, *Ghostly Tales of Northeast Iowa (1988)*, Quixote Press, Soiux City, Iowa
Ruth D. Hein & Vicky Hinsenbrock, *Ghostly Tales of Iowa (1996)*, Iowa State University Press, Ames
Lisa Hefner Heitz, *Haunted Kansas (1997)*, University Press of Kansas, Lawrence
Robert R. Hiatt, *The Ghost of Fort Sill (1989)*, Hiatt Custom Card Company, Lawton, Oklahoma
Hans Holzer, *Ghost's I've Met (1965)*, Bobbs-Merrill Co., Indianapolis, Indiana
Hans Holzer, *Ghosts of the Golden West (1968)*, The Bobbs-Merrill Co. N.Y./also Ace Books
Hans Holzer, *The Phantoms of Dixie (1971)*, Bobbs-Merrill Company, Indiana
Hans Holzer, *Haunted Hollywood (1974)*, The Bobbs-Merril Co. N.Y.
Hans Holzer, *True Ghost Stories (1983)*, Prentice Hall, Englewood Cliffs. N.J.
Hans Holzer, *Great American Ghost Stories (1990)*, Dorset Press, New York
Hans Holzer, *Haunted Houses Album (1992)*, Dorset Press, New York, New York

Hans Holzer, Where The Ghosts Are (1995), A Citadel Press Book, New York
Hans Holzer, Ghosts: True Encounters With The World Beyond (1997), Black Dog & Leventhal Publishers, New York.
Hans Holzer, The Supernatural: Explaining The Unexplained (2003) The Career Press, Franklin Lakes, New Jersey
Elizabeth Hoffman, Here a Ghost, There a Ghost (1978), Simon & Schuster, New York, New York
Elizabeth P. Hoffman, Haunted Places in the Delaware Valley (1992), Camino Books, Philadelphia
Sylvia Booth Hubbard, Ghosts! Personal Accounts of Modern Mississippi Hauntings (1992), QRP Books, Brandon, Mississippi
Matt Hucke and Ursula Bielski, Graveyards of Chicago (1999), Lake Claremont Press, Chicago, Illinois
Elizabeth Robertson Huntsinger, Ghosts of Georgetown (1995), John F. Blair, North Carolina
Duane Hutchinson, A Storyteller's Ghost Stories, Book 2 (1984), Foundation Books, Lincoln, Nebraska
Barb Huyser, Small Town Ghosts: A Ghost Hunter's Casebook of Paranormal Theories and Investigations (2003), Whitechapel Productions Press, Alton, Illinois
Brian Inglis, The Paranormal (1985), Granada Publishing, London
Mary Lee Irby, Ghosts of Macon (1998), Vestige Publishing Company, Inc., Macon, Georgia
Laurie Jacobson and Marc Wanamaker, Hollywood Haunted (1999 - Updated and Revised Edition), Angel City Press, Santa Monica, California
Mark Jager, Mystic Michigan, Part Four (2000), Zosma Publications, Cadillac, Michigan
Sharon Jarvis, True Tales of the Unknown (1985), Bantam Books. New York
Sharon Jarvis, Dead Zones (1992), Warner Books, Inc. New York
Mark Jasper, Haunted Inns of New England (2000), Covered Bridge Press, N. Attleborough, Maine
Adi-Kent Thomas Jeffrey, Ghosts in the Valley (1971), Hampton Publishing Co., Warminster, Pennsylvania
Adi-Kent Thomas Jeffrey, Ghost to Ghost (1975), Hampton Publishing Co., Warminster, Pennsylvania
Mary Ann Johnson, Ghosts Along the Erie (1995), North Country Books, Utica, New York
Sandra Johnson and Leora Sutton, Ghosts, Legends and Folklore of Old Pensacola (1990), Pensacola Historical Society
Vickie Lee Johnson, Lights Out: A Collection of Ghost Stories and Personal Experiences with the Paranormal (2002), 1st Books Library, www.1stbooks.com
Shirley Jonas, Ghosts of the Klondike (1993), Lynn Canal Publishing.
James Gay Jones, A Wayfaring Sin-Eater (1983), McClain Printing Company, Parsons, West Virginia
Charles Jordan, Tales Told in the Shadows of the White Mountains (2003), University Press of New England, Lebanon, New Hampshire.
Dale Kaczmarek, National Register of Haunted Locations. Ghost Research Society, P.O. Box 205, Oak Lawn, Illinois
Dale Kaczmarek, Windy City Ghosts (2000), Whitechapel Productions Press, Alton, Illinois
Dale Kaczmarek, Windy City Ghosts II (2001), Whitechapel Productions Press, Alton, Illinois
John, Keel, Our Haunted Planet (1971), Fawcett Gold Medal Books, Greenwich, Connecticut
Frances Kermeen, Ghostly Encounters: True Stories of America's Haunted Inns and Hotels (2002), Warner Books, New York
Victor C. Klein, New Orleans Ghosts (1993), Professional Press, Chapel Hill, North Carolina
Victor C. Klein, New Orleans Ghosts II (1999), Lycanthrope Press, Metairie, Louisiana
Michael Kouri, The Most Haunted Places in Azusa (2000), Tapestry Autum Press, Burbank, California
Michael Kouri, Haunted Houses Within the Azusa Township (2000), Tapestry Autum Press, Burbank, California
Michael Kouri, Haunted Houses of Pasadena (2002), Tapestry Autum Press, Burbank, California
Sue Kovach, Hidden Files (1997), Contemporary Books, Chicago, Illinois
Marion Kuclo, Michigan Haunts and Hauntings (1997), Thunder Bay Press, Lansing, Michigan
Jack Kutz, Mysteries and Miracles of New Mexico (1988), Rhombus Publishing Company, Corrales, New Mexico
Jack Kutz, Mysteries and Miracles of Arizona (1992), Rhombus Publishing Company, Corrales, New Mexico
Jack Kutz, Mysteries and Miracles of Colorado (1993), Rhombus Publishing Company, Corrales, New Mexico
Jack Kutz, Mysteries and Miracles of Texas (1994), Rhombus Publishing Company, Corrales, New Mexico
Jack Kutz, Mysteries and Miracles of California (1996), Rhombus Publishing Company, Corrales, New Mexico
Bob L'Aloge, Ghosts and Mysteries of the Old West (1991), Yucca Tree Press, Las Cruces, New Mexico
John J. Lamb, San Diego Specters (1999). Sunbelt Publications, San Diego, California
David Lapham, Ghosts of St. Augustine (1997), Pineapple Press, Inc., Sarasota, Florida
Marguerite DuPont Lee, Virginia Ghosts (1966), Virginia Book Company, Berryville, Virginia
Madeline Levatino, Past Masters: The History and Hauntings of Destrehen Plantation (1991), Levatino & Barraco, Destrehan, Louisiana
Megan Long, Ghosts of the Great Lakes (2003), Thunder Bay Press, Holt, Michigan
Jim Longo, Haynted Odyssey: Ghostly Tales of the Mississippi Valley (1986), Ste. Anne's Press, St. Louis, Missouri
Jim Longo, Ghosts Along the Mississippi, Haunted Odyssey II (1993), Ste. Anne's Press, St. Louis, Missouri
Jim Longo, Ghosts Along the Mississippi, Haunted Odyssey III (2000), Ste. Anne's Press, St. Louis, Missouri

Margaret Read MacDonald, Ghost Stories From The Pacific Northwest (1995), August House Publishers, Little Rock, Arkansas
Lynda Lee Macken, Haunted Salem and Beyond (2001), Black Cat Press, Forked River, New Jersey
Lynda Lee Macken, Ghosts of the Garden State (2001), Black Cat Press, Forked River, New Jersey
Lynda Lee Macken, Haunted History of Staten Island (2000), Black Cat Press, Forked River, New Jersey
Edward B. Macy and Julian R. Buxton III, The Ghosts of Charleston (2001), Beaufort Books, New York
Mark Marimen, Haunted Indiana (1997), Thunder Bay Press, Lansing, Michigan
Mark Marimen, School Spirits (1998), Thunder Bay Press, Lansing, Michigan
Mark Marimen, Haunted Indiana 2 (1999), Thunder Bay Press, Lansing, Michigan
Mark Marimen, Haunted Indiana 3 (2001), Thunder Bay Press, Lansing, Michigan
Mike Marinacci, Mysterious California (1988), Panpipes Press, Los Angeles
Margaret Rhett Martin, Charleston Ghosts (1963), University of South Carolina Press, Columbia, South Carolina
MaryJoy Martin, Twilight Dwellers (1985), Pruett Publishing, Boulder, Colorado
Antoinette May, Haunted Houses and Wandering Ghosts of California (1977), The San Francisco Examiner, San Francisco, California
Antoinette May, Haunted Houses of California (1993). Wide World Publishing/Tetra
Robin Mead, Haunted Hotels (1995), Rutledge Hill Press, Nashville, Tennessee
Susan Michaels, Sightings (1996), A Fireside Book, Simon & Schuster
Jim Miles, Weird Georgia (2000), Cumberland House Publishing, Nashville, Tennessee
William Lynwood Montell, Ghosts Along the Cumberland (1975), The University of Tennessee Press, Knoxville
William Lynwood Montell, Kentucky Ghosts (1994), The University Press of Kentucky, Lexington
William Lynwood Montell, Ghosts Across Kentucky (2000), The University Press of Kentucky, Lexington
William Lynwood Montell, Haunted Houses and Family Ghosts of Kentucky (2001), The University of Tennessee Press, Knoxville
Larry Montz and Daena Smoller, ISPR Investigates The Ghosts of New Orleans (2000), Whitford Press, Atglen, Pennsylvania
Joyce Elson Moore, Haunt Hunter's Guide to Florida (1998), Pineapple Press, Inc., Sarasota, Florida
Mark Alan Morris, The Ghost Next Door (2003), Lincoln, Nebraska
A.S. Mott, Ghost Stories of America, Volume II (2003), Ghost House Books, Edmonton, Canada.
A.S. Mott, Haunted Schools (2003), Ghost House Books, Edmonton, Canada.
A.S. Mott, Fireside Ghost Stories (2003), Ghost House Books, Edmonton, Canada.
A.S. Mott, Urban Legends: Strange Stories Behind Modern Myths (2004), Ghost House Books, Edmonton, Canada.
Debra D. Munn, Ghosts on the Range (1989), Pruett Publishing Company, Boulder, Colorado
Debra Munn, Big Sky Ghosts (1994) Pruett Publishing, Boulder, Colorado
Debra Munn, Big Sky Ghosts, Volume II (2002), Pruett Publishing, Boulder, Colorado
Michael Munn, X-rated: The Paranormal Experience of the Movie Star Greats (1996), Robson, London, England
Earl Murray, Ghosts of the Old West (1988), Barnes & Noble Books, New York
Earl Murray, Midnight Sun (2000), A Tom Doherty Associates Book, New York
Arthur Myers, The Ghostly Register (1986). Contemporary Books. Chicago
Arthur Myers, The Ghostly Gazetteer (1990), Contemporary Books, Chicago, Illinois
Arthur Myers, A Ghosthunter's Guide (1993), Contemporary Book, Chicago, Illinois
Holly Mascott Nadler, Haunted Island (1994), Down East Books, Camden, Maine
Holly Mascott Nadler, Ghosts of Boston Town (2002), Down East Books, Camden, Maine
Mark Nesbitt, Ghosts of Gettysburg (1991). Thomas Publications, Gettysburg, Pennsylvania
Mark Nesbitt, More Ghosts of Gettysburg (1992). Thomas Publications, Gettysburg, Pennsylvania
Mark Nesbitt, Ghosts of Gettysburg III (1995), Thomas Publications, P.O. Box 3031, Gettysburg, Pennsylvania
Mark Nesbitt, Ghosts of Gettysburg IV (1998), Thomas Publications, P.O. Box 3031, Gettysburg, Pennsylvania
Mark Nesbitt, Ghosts of Gettysburg V (2000), Thomas Publications, P.O. Box 3031, Gettysburg, Pennsylvania
Leon Netardus, Ghosts of Gonzales (n.d.), Reese's Print Shop, Gonzales, Texas
Janice Oberding, Haunted Nevada (2001), Universal Publishers, uPUPLISH.com
Janice Oberding, Ghosthunting Guide to Virgina City (2003), Thunder Mountain Productions Press, Reno, Nevada.
Janice Oberding, Haunted Gold and Silver (2003), Thunder Mountain Productions Press, Reno, Nevada.
Tom Ogden, The Complete Idiot's Guide to Ghosts and Hauntings (1999), Alpha Books, Indianapolis, Indiana
Ed Okonowicz, Pulling Back the Curtain, Volume I (1994), Myst and Lace Publishers, Elkton, Maryland
Ed Okonowicz, Opening the Door, Volume II (1995), Myst and Lace Publishers, Elkton, Maryland

Ed Okonowicz, Crying in the Kitchen, Volume VI (1998), Myst and Lace Publishers, Elkton, Maryland
Ed Okonowicz, Possessed Possessions (1998), Myst and Lace Publishers, Elkton, Maryland
Ed Okonowicz, Up the Back Stairway, Volume VII (1999), Myst and Lace Publishers, Elkton, Maryland
Ed Okonowicz, Horror in the Hallway, Volume VIII (1999), Myst and Lace Publishers, Elkton, Maryland
Ed Okonowicz, Phantom in the Bedchamber, Volume IX (2000), Myst and Lace Publishers, Elkton, Maryland
Ed Okonowicz, Terrifying Tales of the Beaches and Bays, (2001), Myst and Lace Publishers, Elkton, Maryland
Ed Okonowicz, Ghosts, (2001), Myst and Lace Publishers, Elkton, Maryland
Ed Okonowicz, Terrifying Tales 2 of the Beaches and Bays, (2001), Myst and Lace Publishers, Elkton, Maryland.
Wes Oleszewski, Ghost Ships, Gales & Forgotten Tales (1995), Avery Color Studios, Gwinn, Michigan
Wes Oleszewski, Lighthouse Adventures (1999), Avery Color Studios, Gwinn, Michigan
Colleen O'Connor Olson and Charles Hanion, Scary Stories of Mammoth Cave (2002), Cave Books Publishing, St. Louis, Missouri.
Frank Oppel, Tales of the New England Coast (1985) Castle, Secaucus, N.J
Natalie Osborne-Thomason (2002) Psychic Espisodes From the Life of a Ghost Hunter, Temple Lodge Publishing, Forest Row, East Sussex
Anne Oscard, Tristate Terrors (1996) Hermit Publications, Dayton, Ohio
Elizabeth Parker, Mobile Ghosts: Alabama's Haunted Port City (2000) Apparition Publishing, Spanish Fort, Alabama
David J. Pitkin, Saratoga County Ghosts (1998), Aurora Publications, Ballston Salem, New York
David J. Pitkin, Ghosts of the Northeast (2002), Aurora Publications, Ballston Salem, New York
Jerome Pohlen, Oddball Colorado (2002), Chicago Review Press, Chicago, Illinos.
Jerome Pohlen, Oddball Indiana (2002), Chicago Review Press, Chicago, Illinos.
Jerome Pohlen, Oddball Colorado (2003), Chicago Review Press, Chicago, Illinos.
Jerome Pohlen, Oddball Florida (2004), Chicago Review Press, Chicago, Illinos.
Jerome Pohlen, Oddball Ohio (2004), Chicago Review Press, Chicago, Illinos.
Jane Keane Polonsky and Joan McFarland Drum, The Ghosts of Fort Monroe (1972), Polyndrum Publications, Fredericksburg, Virginia
Jane Keane Polonsky and Joan McFarland Drum, Hampton's Haunted Houses (1998), Polyndrum Publications, Fredericksburg, Virginia
Jack Powell, Haunting Sunshine (2001), Pineapple Press, Sarasota, Florida
Charles Edwin Price, More Haunted Tennessee (1999), The Overmountain Press, Johnson City, Tennessee
Mary Summer Rain, Phantoms Afoot: Helping the Spirits Among Us (2003), Hampton Roads Publishing Company, Charlottesville, Virginia.
Katherine Ramsland, Cemetery Stories (2001), HarperCollins Publishers, New York
Jenny Randles and Peter Hough, The Afterlife (1993), Berkley Books, New York
John Reichley, The Haunted Houses of Fort Leavenworth (1995), Fort Leavenworth Historical Society
Randall, Reinstedt, Ghostly Tales and Mysterious Happennings of Old Monterey (1977), Ghost Town Publications, Carmel, California.
Randall, Reinstedt, Incredible Ghosts of Old Monterey's Hotel Del Monte (1980), Ghost Town Publications, Carmel, California
Tony Reevy, Ghost Train (1998), TLC Publishing, Lynchburg, Virginia
Donna Reis, Seeking Ghosts in the Warwick Valley (2002), Schiffer Publishing Ltd, Atglen, Pennsylvania.
Cheri Revai Haunted Northern New York, (2002) Northern Countrry Books, Utica, New York
Nancy Rhyne, More Tales of the South Carolina Low Country (1995), John F. Blair, Winston-Salem, North Carolina
Geri Rider, Ghosts of Door County, Wisconsin (1992), Quixote Press, Sioux City, Iowa
Rob Riggs, In the Big Thicket (2001), ParaView Press, New York
Nancy Roberts, North Carolina Ghosts and Legends (1967), University of South Carolina Press
Nancy Roberts, America's Most Haunted Places (1974), Sandlapper Publishing Company, South Carolina
Nancy Roberts, Southern Ghosts (1979), Sandlapper Publishing Company, South Carolina
Nancy Roberts, South Carolina Ghosts (1983), University of South Carolina Press
Nancy Roberts, Ghosts and Specters of the Old South (1984), Sandlapper Publishing Company, South Carolina
Nancy Roberts, Haunted Houses: Tales From 30 American Homes (1988), Globe Pequot Press, Chester, Connecticut
Nancy Roberts, Ghosts of the Southern Mountains and Appalachia (1988), University of South Carolina Press
Nancy Roberts, Civil War Ghost Stories and Legends (1992), University of South Carolina Press
Nancy Roberts, Civil War Ghost and Legends (1992), Barnes & Noble Books, New York
Nancy Roberts, Ghosts of the Carolinas (1992), University of South Carolina Press
Nancy Roberts, This Haunted Southland (1992), University of South Carolina Press
Nancy Roberts, Ghosts of the Southern Mountains and Appalachia (1993), University of South Carolina Press
Nancy Roberts, Haunted Houses: Chilling Tales From Nineteen American Homes (1995), The Globe Pequot Press, Old Saybrook, Connecticut

Nancy Roberts, Haunted Houses: Chilling Tales From 24 American Homes (1998), The Globe Pequot Press, Old Saybrook, Connecticut
Charles Turek Robinson, The New England Ghost Files (1994) Covered Bridge Press, Maryland.
Ellen Robson and Diane Halicki, Haunted Highway, The Spirits of Route 66 (1999). Golden West Publishers, Phoenix, Arizona
Ellen Robson, Haunted Arizona, Ghosts of the Grand Canyon State (2002). Golden West Publishers, Phoenix, Arizona
Scott Rogo, An Experience of Phantoms (1974), Taplinger, New York
Scott Rogo, Parapsychology: A Century of Inquiry (1977), Dutton, New York
Randy Russell and Janet Barnett, The Granny Curse (1999), John F. Blair, Winston-Salem, North, Carolina
Randy Russell and Janet Barnett, Ghost Dogs of the South (2003), John F. Blair, Winston-Salem, North, Carolina
Therese Lanigan-Schmidt, Ghostly Beacons: Haunted Lighthouses of North America (2000), Whitford Press, Atglen, Pennsylvania.
Carol Olivieri Schulte, Ghosts on the Coast of Maine, (1989), Quixote Press, Iowa
Maurice Schwalm, Mo-Kan Ghosts (1999), Belfry Books, Laceyville, Pennsylvania
Beth Scott and Michael Norman, Haunted Heartland (1985), Barnes & Noble Books, New York.
Beth Scott and Michael Norman, Haunted America (1994), A Tom Doherty Associates Book, New York
Beth Scott and Michael Norman, Historic Haunted America (1995), A Tom Doherty Associates Book, New York
Beth Scott and Michael Norman, Haunted Heritage (2002), A Tom Doherty Associates Book, New York
Eric Segal, Alexandria Ghosts (1975), The Alexandria Bicentennial Youth Commission
David Seibold, and Charles Adams III, Legends of Long Beach Island (1985), Exeter House Books, Reading, Pennsylvania
David Seibold, and Charles Adams III, Cape May Ghost Stories (1988), Exeter House Books, Reading, Pennsylvania
David J. Seibold, and Charles J. Adams, Pocono Ghosts, Legends, and Lore (1991), Exeter House Books, Reading, Pennsylvania
David Seibold and Charles Adams III, Ghost Stories of the Delaware Coast (1990), Exeter House Books, Reading, Pennsylvania.
Richard L. Senate, Ghosts of the Haunted Coast (1986), Pathfinder Publishing, Ventura, California
Richard L. Senate, Haunted Ventura (1992), Charon Press, Ventura, California
Richard L. Senate, The Haunted Southland (1993), Charon Press, Ventura, California
Richard L. Senate, Ghost Stalker's Guide to Haunted California (1998), Charon Press, Ventura, California
Richard L. Senate, Ghosts of the Ojai (1998), Charon Press, Ventura, California
Richard L.Senate, Ghosts of the Camino Real (2003), Del Sol Publications, Ventura, California.
Richard L.Senate, Hollywood's Ghosts (2003), Del Sol Publications, Ventura, California
Richard L. Senate and Debbie Senate, Psychic Solution: The Lizzie Borden Case (n.d.), Phantom Bookshop, 451 East Main Street, Ventura, California (www.phantoms. com)
Eleyne Austen Sharp, Haunted Newport (1996), Austen Sharp Publishing, P.O. Box 12, Newport, Rhode Island.
Jay Sharp, Texas Unexplained (1999), University of Texas Press, Austin
Susan Sheppard, Cry of the Banshee: History and Hauntings of West Virginia and the Ohio Valley (2004)), Whitechapel Productions Press, Alton, Illinois
Barbara Sillery, The Haunting of Louisiana (2001),Pelican Publishing Company, Gretna, Louisiana.
David L. Sloan, Ghosts of Key West (1998), Phantom Press, Key West, Florida
David L. Sloan, Haunted Key West (2003), Phantom Press, Key West, Florida
Susan Smitten, Ghost Stories of Oregon (2001), Ghost House Books, Edmonton, Canada
Susan Smitten, Ghost Stories of New England (2003), Ghost House Books, Edmonton, Canada
Barbara Smith, Ghost Stories of The Rocky Mountains (1999), Lone Pine Publishing, Edmonton, Canada
Barbara Smith, Ghost Stories of Hollywood (2000), Lone Pine Publishing, Edmonton, Canada
Barbara Smith, Ghost Stories of California (2000), Lone Pine Publishing, Edmonton, Canada
Barbara Smith, Ghost Stories of Washington (2000), Lone Pine Publishing, Edmonton, Canada
Barbara Smith, Haunted Theaters (2002), Ghost House Books, Edmonton, Canada
Barbara Smith, Ghost Stories of The Rocky Mountains, Volume II (2003), Ghost House Books, Edmonton, Canada
Katherine Smith, Haunted History Tours Presents: Journey Into Darkness... Ghost and Vampires of New Orleans (1998), De Simonin Publications, New Orleans, Louisiana
Robin Smith, Columbus Ghosts: Historical Haunts of Ohio's Capital (2002), Emuses, Worthington, Ohio
Robin Smith, Columbus Ghosts II: More Central Ohio Haunts (2003), Emuses, Worthington, Ohio
Susy Smith, Prominent American Ghosts (1967), World Publishing, Cleveland, Ohio
Frank Spaeth (ed), Phantom Army of the Civil War (1997), Llewellyn Publications, St. Paul, Minnesota
Jennifer Spees, True Mystic Experiences (2001), Llewellyn Publications, St. Paul, Minnesota
Patti Starr, Ghost Hunting in Kentucky and Beyond (2002), McClanahan Publishing House, Kuttaway, Kentucky
Brad Steiger, The Awful Thing in the Attic (1995), Galde Press, St. Paul, Minnesota

Sherry Hansen Steiger and Brad Steiger, Hollywood and the Supernatural (1990), St. Martin's Press
George C. Steitz, Haunted Lighthouses and How to Find Them (2002), Pineapple Press, Sarasota, Florida
Frederick Stonehouse, Haunted Lakes (1997), Lake Superior Port Cities Inc., Duluth, Minnesota
Frederick Stonehouse, Haunted Lakes II (2000), Lake Superior Port Cities Inc., Duluth, Minnesota
Gary J. Svehla and Susan Svehla (eds), Cinematic Hauntings (1996), Midnight Marquee Press, Baltimore, Maryland
George Swetnam, Devils, Ghosts & Witches (1988), McDonald/Sward, Greensburg, Pennsylvania
L.B. Taylor, The Ghosts of Williamsburg (1983), 108 Elizabeth Meriwether, Williamsburg, Virginia
L.B. Taylor, The Ghosts of Richmond (1985), 108 Elizabeth Meriwether, Williamsburg, Virginia
L.B. Taylor, The Ghosts of Fredericksburg (1991), 108 Elizabeth Meriwether, Williamsburg, Virginia
L.B. Taylor, The Ghosts of Charlottesville and Lynchburg (1992), 108 Elizabeth Meriwether, Williamsburg, Virginia
L.B. Taylor, The Ghosts of Virginia (1993), 108 Elizabeth Meriwether, Williamsburg, Virginia
L.B. Taylor, The Ghosts of Virginia, Volume II (1994), 108 Elizabeth Meriwether, Williamsburg, Virginia
L.B. Taylor, Civil War Ghosts of Virginia (1995), 108 Elizabeth Meriwether, Williamsburg, Virginia
L.B. Taylor, Virginia's Ghosts: Haunted Historic House Tours (1995), Virginia Heritage Publications, Alexandria, Virginia
L.B. Taylor, The Ghosts of Virginia, Volume III (1996), 108 Elizabeth Meriwether, Williamsburg, Virginia
L.B. Taylor, The Ghosts of Virginia, Volume IV (1998), 108 Elizabeth Meriwether, Williamsburg, Virginia
L.B. Taylor, The Ghosts of Williamsburg, Volume II (1999), 108 Elizabeth Meriwether, Williamsburg, Virginia.
L.B. Taylor, The Ghosts of Virginia, Volume V (2000), 108 Elizabeth Meriwether, Williamsburg, Virginia
L.B. Taylor, The Ghosts of Virginia, Volume VI (2001), 108 Elizabeth Meriwether, Williamsburg, Virginia
L.B. Taylor, The Ghosts of Virginia, Volume VII (2002), 108 Elizabeth Meriwether, Williamsburg, Virginia
L.B. Taylor, The Ghosts of Virginia, Volume VIII (2003), 108 Elizabeth Meriwether, Williamsburg, Virginia
L.B. Taylor, A Treasury of True Ghostly Humor (2003), 108 Elizabeth Meriwether, Williamsburg, Virginia
Troy Taylor, Haunted Decatur (1995), Whitechapel Productions Press, Alton, Illinois
Troy Taylor, More Haunted Decatur (1996), Whitechapel Productions Press, Alton, Illinois
Troy Taylor, Ghosts of Milikin (1996), Whitechapel Productions Press, Alton, Illinois
Troy Taylor, Ghosts of Springfield (1997), Whitechapel Productions Press, Alton, Illinois
Troy Taylor, Dark Harvest: The Compleat Haunted Decatur (1997), Whitechapel Productions Press, Alton, Illinois
Troy Taylor, Where the Dead Walk (1997), Whitechapel Productions Press, Alton, Illinois
Troy Taylor, Ghosts of Little Egypt (1998), Whitechapel Productions Press, Alton, Illinois
Troy Taylor, Haunted Illinois (1999), Whitechapel Productions Press, Alton, Illinois
Troy Taylor, Haunted Alton (1999), Whitechapel Productions Press, Alton, Illinois
Troy Taylor, Season of the Witch (1999), Whitechapel Productions Press, Alton, Illinois
Troy Taylor, The Ghost Hunter's Guidebook (1999), Whitechapel Productions Press, Alton, Illinois
Troy Taylor, Spirits of the Civil War (1999), Whitechapel Productions Press, Alton, Illinois
Troy Taylor, Haunted Decatur: Revisited (2000), Whitechapel Productions Press, Alton, Illinois
Troy Taylor, Haunted New Orleans (2000), Whitechapel Productions Press, Alton, Illinois
Troy Taylor, Haunted Illinois: Revised (2001), Whitechapel Productions Press, Alton, Illinois
Troy Taylor, Beyond the Grave (2001), Whitechapel Productions Press, Alton, Illinois
Troy Taylor, No Rest For The Wicked (2001), Whitechapel Productions Press, Alton, Illinois
Troy Taylor, The Haunting of America (2001), Whitechapel Productions Press, Alton, Illinois
Troy Taylor, Flickering Images (2001), Whitechapel Productions Press, Alton, Illinois
Troy Taylor, Ghosts of Milikin (2001), Whitechapel Productions Press, Alton, Illinois
Troy Taylor, Haunted St. Louis (2002), Whitechapel Productions Press, Alton, Illinois
Troy Taylor, Season of the Witch: The History and Hauntings of the Bell Witch of Tennessee (2002), Whitechapel Productions Press, Alton, Illinois
Troy Taylor, Haunted St. Louis (2002), Whitechapel Productions Press, Alton, Illinois
Troy Taylor, Into the Shadows (2002), Whitechapel Productions Press, Alton, Illinois
Troy Taylor, Haunted Chicago (2003), Whitechapel Productions Press, Alton, Illinois
Troy Taylor, A Field Guide to Haunted Graveyards (2003), Whitechapel Productions Press, Alton, Illinois
Troy Taylor, Out Past the Campfire Light (2004), Whitechapel Productions Press, Alton, Illinois
Gina Teel, Ghost Stories of Minnesota (2002), Ghost House Publishing, Edmonton, Canada
Edrick Thay, Ghost Stories of Ohio (2001), Ghost House Publishing, Edmonton, Canada
Edrick Thay (2003), Haunted Houses, Ghost House Books, Edmonton, Canada
Edrick Thay (2003), Ghost Stories of the Old South, Ghost House Books, Edmonton, Canada
Cynthia Thuma and Catherine Lower, Creepy Colleges and Haunted Universities (2003), Schiffer Publishing, Atglen, Pennsylvaia
Keith Toney, Battlefield Ghosts (1997), Rockbridge Publishing Company, Berryville, Virginia
Beth Trapani, Ghost Stories of Pittsburgh and Allegheny County (1994), Exeter House Books, Reading, Pennsylvania
Sheila Turnage, Haunted Inns of the Southeast (2001), John F. Blair Publisher, Winston-Salem, North Carolina

Allan Turner and Richard Stewart, *Transparent Tales: An Attic Full of Texas Ghosts* (1998), Best of East Texas Publishers, Lufkin, Texas
USA Weekend, *I Never Believed In Ghosts Until...* (1992), Contemporary Books, Chicago
Christy L. Viviano, *Haunted Louisiana* (1992), Tree House Press, Metairie, Louisiana
Lloyd Vogt, *Historic Buildings of the French Quarter* (2002), Pelican Publishing Company, Gretna, Louisiana
Stephen P. Walker, *Lemp, The Haunting History* (1988), Lemp Presentation Society, Webster Groves, Missouri
Bert M. Wall, *The Devil's Backbone* (1996), Eakin Press, Austin, Texas
Frank Ward, *Close Behind Thee* (1998) Whitechapel Productions Press, Alton, Illinois
Ed and Lorraine Warren, and Robert David Chase (1991) *Ghost Hunters*. St. Martin's Paperbacks, New York
Ed and Lorraine Warren and Robert David Chase, *Graveyard* (1992), St. Martin's Paperbacks, New York
Joshua P. Warren, *Haunted Asheville* (1996), Shadowbox Publications, P.O. Box 16801, Asheville, North Carolina
Colin Waters, *Sexual Hauntings Through the Ages* (1993), Dorset Press, New York
Daryl Watson, *Ghosts of Gallena* (1995), Galena/Jo Daviess County Historical Society, Galena, Illinois
Richard Webb, *Great Ghosts of the West* (1071), Nash, Los Angeles
Alyce T. Weinberg, *Spirits of Frederick* (1992), P.O. Box 175, Braddock Heights, Maryland
Ron Wendt, *Haunted Alaska: Ghost Stories from the far North* (2002) Epicenter Press
Charles Joseph Whedbee, *The Flaming Ship of Ocracoke & Other Tales of the Outer Banks* (2000) John F. Blair, Winston-Salem, North Carolina.
Charles Joseph Whedbee, *Pirates, Ghosts, and Coastal; Lore: The Best of Judge Whedbee* (2004) John F. Blair, Winston-Salem, North Carolina.
Michelle Whitedove, *Ghost Stalker: A Psychic Medium Visits America's Most Haunted Sites* (2003), Whitedove Press, Fort Lauderdale, Florida
Mitchel Whitington, *Ghosts of North Texas* (2003), Republic of Texas Press, Plano, Texas
Clayton and Kathleen Whitley, *Guide to Flemington New Jersey* (1987), Clayton and Whitley Press, New Jersey
Brad Williams and Choral Pepper, *The Mysterious West* (1967), World Publishing, New York
Brad Williams and Choral Pepper, *Lost Legends of the West* (1970), Holt, Rinehart & Winston. N.Y
Docia Schultz Williams and Reneta Byrne, *Spirits of San Antonio and South Texas* (1993) Republic of Texas Press
Docia Williams, *Ghosts Along the Texas Coast* (1995), Republic of Texas Press, Plano, Texas
Docia Schultz Williams, *Phantoms of the Plains* (1996), Republic of Texas Press, Plano, Texas
Docia Schultz Williams, *When Darkness Falls*, (1997), Republic of Texas Press, Plano, Texas
Docia Schultz Williams, *Best Tales of Texas Ghosts* (1998), Republic of Texas Press, Plano, Texas
Docia Schultz Williams, *The History and Mystery of the Menger Hotel* (2000), Republic of Texas Press, Plano, Texas
Stephanie Burt Williams, *Ghost Stories of Charlotte and Mecklenburg County: Remnants of the Past in a New South* (2003), Bandit Books, Winston-Salem, North Carolina
Wanda Lou Willis, *Haunted Hoosier Trails: A Guide to Indiana's Famous Folklore Spooky Sites*.Guild Press, Emmis Publishing,Zionsville, Indiana
Patty Wilson, *Haunted Pennsylvania* (1998), Belfry Books, Laceyville, Pennsylvania
Patty Wilson, *The Pennsylvania Ghost Guide, Vol. I* (2000), Piney Creek Press, Roaring Spring, Pennsylvania
Patty Wilson, *The Pennsylvania Ghost Guide, Vol. II* (2001), Piney Creek Press, Roaring Spring, Pennsylvania
Patty Wilson, *Where Dead men Walk, Vol. 1* (2001), Piney Creek Press, Roaring Spring, Pennsylvania
Patty Wilson and Scott Crownover, *Boos and Brews* (2002), Piney Creek Press, Roaring Spring, Pennsylvania
Kathryn Tucker Windham and Margaret Gillis Figh, *13 Alabama Ghosts and Jeffrey* (1969), The University of Alabama Press, Tuscaloosa
Kathryn Tucker Windham, *Jeffrey Introduces 13 More Southern Ghosts* (1971), The University of Alabama Press, Tuscaloosa
Kathryn Tucker Windham, *13 Georgia Ghosts and Jeffrey* (1973), The University of Alabama Press, Tuscaloosa
Kathryn Tucker Windham, *13 Mississippi Ghosts and Jeffrey* (1974), The University of Alabama Press, Tuscaloosa
Kathryn Tucker Windham, *13 Tennessee Ghosts and Jeffrey* (1977), The University of Alabama Press, Tuscaloosa
Kathryn Tucker Windham, *Jeffrey's Latest 13: More Alabama Ghosts* (1982), The University of Alabama Press, Tuscaloosa
Richard Winer, and Nancy Osborn, *Haunted Houses* (1979), Bantam Books, New York.
Robert J. Wlodarski, Anne N. Wlodarski, and Richard Senate, *A Guide to the Haunted Queen Mary* (1995), G-Host Publishing, West Hills, California
Robert Wlodarski and Anne Wlodarski, *Haunted Catalina* (1996), G-HOST Publishing, West Hills, California
Robert Wlodarski and Anne Wlodarski, *The Haunted Whaley House* (1997), G-HOST Publishing, West Hills, California
Robert Wlodarski, Anne Wlodarski and Michael Kouri, *Haunted Alcatraz* (1998), G-HOST Publishing, West Hills, California

Robert Wlodarski and Anne Wlodarski, *The Haunted Alamo* (1996), G-HOST Publishing, West Hills, California
Robert Wlodarski and Anne Wlodarski, *Spirits of the Alamo* (1999), Republic of Texas Press, Plano, Texas
Robert Wlodarski and Anne Wlodarski, *Southern Fried Spirits* (2000), Republic of Texas Press, Plano, Texas
Robert Wlodarski and Anne Wlodarski, *The Haunted Queen Mary, Long Beach, California* (2000), G-HOST Publishing, West Hills, California
Robert Wlodarski and Anne Wlodarski, *A Texas Guide to Haunted Restaurants, Taverns and Inns* (2001), Republic of Texas Press, Plano, Texas
Robert Wlodarski and Anne Wlodarski, *Dinner and Spirits* (2001), iUniverse.com, New York
Robert Wlodarski and Anne Wlodarski, *Spirits of the Leonis Adobe: History and Hauntings in Calabasas, California* (2002), G-HOST Publishing, West Hills, California
Robert Wlodarski and Anne Wlodarski, *California Hauntspitality* (2002), Whitechapel Productions Press, Alton, Illinois
Robert Wlodarski and Anne Wlodarski, *Louisiana Hauntspitality* (2004), Whitechapel Productions Press, Alton, Illinois
Robert Wlodarski and Anne Wlodarski, *The Haunted Whaley House II* (2004), G-HOST Publishing, West Hills, California
Ted Wood, *Ghosts of the Southwest* (1997), Walker and Company, New York
Ted Wood, *Ghosts of the West Coast* (1999), Walker and Company, New York
Chris Woodyard, *Haunted Ohio* (1991), Kestral Publications, Beavercreek, Ohio
Chris Woodyard, *Haunted Ohio II* (1992), Kestral Publications, Beavercreek, Ohio
Chris Woodyard, *Haunted Ohio III* (1994), Kestral Publications, Beavercreek, Ohio
Chris Woodyard, *Haunted Ohio IV* (1997), Kestral Publications, Beavercreek, Ohio
Chris Woodyard, *A Ghost Hunter's Guide to Haunted Ohio* (2000), Kestral Publications, Beavercreek, Ohio
Chris Woodyard, *Haunted Ohio V* (2003), Kestral Publications, Beavercreek, Ohio
Richard A. Young and Judy D. Young, *Ghost Stories From The American Southwest* (1991), August House Publishers, Little Rock, Arkansas
Richard A. Young and Judy D. Young, *Ozark Ghost Stories* (1995), August House Publishers, Little Rock, Arkansas
Darren Zenko, *Ghost Stories of Pets and Animals* (2004), Ghost House Books, Edmonton, Canada.
Terrance Zepke, *Ghosts of the Carolina Coasts* (1999), Pineapple Press, Sarasota, Florida
Terrance Zepke, *Best Ghost Tales of North Carolina* (2001), Pineapple Press, Sarasota, Florida
Terrance Zepke, *Best Ghost Tales of South Carolina* (2004), Pineapple Press, Sarasota, Florida
Zimmermann, Linda, *Ghosts of Rockland County* (1998), Spirited Books, Blooming Grove, New York
Zimmermann, Linda, *Haunted Hudson Valley* (1999), Spirited Books, Blooming Grove, New York
Zimmermann, Linda, *More Haunted Hudson Valley* (2001), Spirited Books, Blooming Grove, New York
Zimmermann, Linda, *Haunted Hudson Valley III* (2003), Spirited Books, Blooming Grove, New York
Zimmermann, Linda, *Ghost Investigator, Volume 1: Hauntings of the Hudson Valley* (2002), Spirited Books, Blooming Grove, New York
Zimmermann, Linda, *Ghost Investigator, Volume 2: From Gettysburg, PA to Lizze Borden* (2002), Spirited Books, Blooming Grove, New York
Zimmermann, Linda, *Ghost Investigator, Volume 3* (2003), Spirited Books, Blooming Grove, New York

What to do if you see a Ghost

1. Don't panic! Just try to relax, and then sit back and enjoy the phenomenon. Concentrate and try to notice every detail you can.
2. As soon as you can after the event concludes, write down exactly what you saw in as much detail as possible. Try to remember if there were any particular smells (perfume, cigar smoke, foul odors), sensations such as cold spots, gusts of air, or feelings of nausea; music playing or other audible sounds, voices or conversations in the background, or feelings of being watched or touched, etc.
3. Even if you are not the greatest artist, try to sketch what you saw: What the image was wearing, include the style of clothing, shoes, glasses, hats, etc., anything which may give an indication of a particular time period or era.
4. Draw a diagram or map of where the apparition was sighted, and your location when the event took place. Note the wallpaper (if any), furnishings in the room, types of windows (sash, hinged, pivoted, sliding), flooring (adobe, hardwood, carpeting), or other features in relation to the sighting.
5. Note what time of the day the event took place as well as weather conditions and temperature, if possible. Also, see if you can locate any nearby vents, or openings which might help explain away colds spots or drafts.
6. Record general information regarding how the event made you feel (happy, sad, depressed, frightened, exhilarated.
7. Note any unusual circumstances surrounding the event including; storms, high winds, power outages, other people working in the area, construction activities nearby, remodeling being performed, etc.).
8. Note other people present; include any children or animals who might have witnessed the event, or who may have been affected.
9. Attempt to investigate and research the experience further including who the ghost might have been, or a tragedy which may explain the haunting.
10. Attempt to rule out any explainable or natural causes for the occurrence, or associated noises, or smells. Check for earthquakes, sonic booms, construction, cooking nearby, animals or pests in the house—rule out the obvious.
11. If you are able to summon the courage, talk to the spirit in a sincere manner, and tell it to pass on to the next realm by looking for, and following the white light—prayers to release a trapped spirit oftentimes yield positive results.

The Ghost Hunters' Kit

Permission to use the following information was granted by Richard Senate. In the investigations of haunted sites, Senate has put together a collection of tools he has have found useful.

1. 35mm camera loaded with XXX black and white film. A red gel should be placed over the flash unit. This causes the ASA to push into the infrared Spectrum [do not know why it works but using this configuration I have managed to take photographs of ghosts]. A stereo camera is also useful. Take along at least two cameras—one loaded with high-speed film for low light and the other with XXX Film.

2. Tape Recorder with an external microphone. Use music quality tape and Always use brand new tape! Never use the Chromium Oxide tape as sometimes a voice might double record. Use in walk-though of haunted sites. When you are in a haunted place, you may hear nothing! It is only when the tape is played back to spirit voices come out. They have a harsh, whispered quality and they only say one or two words, less than a sentence. This is called EVP for Electronic Voice Phenomena. Take along two tape recorders. One just as a back up with regular tape and a built in microphone.

3. A good flashlight—but even the best can fail when you enter a haunted site—it seems that ghosts can manipulate electronic units. Sometimes a good kerosene lantern is better or a good old candle and match.

4. Notebook of paper and a pen is one of the best tools to save data. Write down all that you see and feel and record the times when it happened —Keep a journal of your overnight ghost stakeout. Paper is also useful for drawing floor plans of the haunted site and sketching a likeness of any ghosts you happen to see.

5. A compass. This small thing can be very helpful in finding your way around county back roads and in mapping out a site. In addition, I have found that a compass needle may act strangely in haunted places.

6. A good EM Detector (Or Gauss Meter) is very good tool. Ghosts are found in electro- magnetic fields. We still do not know why, but there is some interesting new research being done on these phenomena.

7. Thermometers are always of help in any ghost hunt. Electronic ones are excellent but ghosts can manipulate them. Any change in the

surrounding environment can indicate the presence of a phantom. For countless centuries, people have felt an icy cold in haunted places. Some cold spots have a six-degree difference in temperature and in some of the literature, twenty degrees are recorded in haunted rooms (I haven't encountered that much of a temperature difference yet!).

8. Silver Cross and a small bottle of holy water. (One can never be too careful you know-like chicken soup it can't hurt). Over the years silver has been liked to psychic events and I have noticed that women who wear a lot of silver jewelry seem to have more ghostly sightings— Why?I don't know.

9. Dowsing Rods have been used for centuries to find water. However, strange as it sounds they can be used to find areas of psychic disturbances. They seem to react in places of murder and death places where ghosts and poltergeists infest. Almost anyone can use dowsing rods and find lost items, and places where ghosts are found—but be sure you are not just finding buried water pipes! A little practice and you will discover how useful dowsing rods can be! If you wish to understand more of how ghost hunters seek answers to the riddle of a haunted house read Senate's book *The Haunted Southland*.

How to Stalk Ghosts

Permission to use "How to Stalk Ghosts" was provided courtesy of The Ghost Stalkers, www.ghoststalkers.com - phone 817-731-HAUNT - E-mail: ghosttx@ghoststalkers.com

Equipment for Investigation
Bag, Case or Box (with compartments for each piece of equipment)
Notebooks/Sheets of plain paper/Graph paper
Pens and pencils
Rough plans or sketches of location
Colored pencils (for identifying special areas)
White & colored chalk (marking walls & furniture, easily removable)
Reels of black thread & black cotton
Transparent adhesive tape (various widths)
Thin & thick nylon twine
Various transparent envelopes (baggies)
Various transparent containers (for questionable evidence)
Thermometers (used for registering sudden fluctuations in temperature)
Maximum and minimum thermometers
Tape recorders (voice activated)
Apparatus for measuring atmospheric pressure
Metal detectors
Walkie talkie sets
Video cameras
A small tin of sand and a small hole at the bottom (leaves a trail of fine silver sand if moved)
First aid kit
Cellular phone
Flour on newspaper to indicate footsteps
Small paint brush (finger prints)
Compass
Tripod
35mm camera
Instamatic Polaroid
Spare b/w film
Spare batteries
Flash
Infra-red film
Steel or tape measuring tape
Ruler (large)
Magnifying glass
Strain gauge (measures force it takes to open doors, drawers)
Each person carry a watch (preferably with luminous dials - synchronize watches at beginning of investigation)
Stopwatch
Few ties from luggage labels (enable you to seal most room passages, doorways, to know when they are used without your knowledge)
Several flashlights (spare batteries & bulbs)
Fountain pen-type flashlight (other various sizes)
A couple of boxes of matches
One or two small mirrors
A small bell
A Bible
A cross

A small toy
Soft shoes
Extra clothing

Learn of Historic Information
History of the locale
Duration of the presence
Season the event it took place
Time of day
Position of witnesses
Historical characters of note who occupied the dwelling
Get an impression the area has on others
Request permission of owner or director
Inform local police what is taking place
Plan program of events.

Repeated Atmospheric Ghosts
Pay careful attention to: Time; Date; Atmospheric conditions; Presence of witnesses; Take photographs whether you see anything at that time or not; Sound recording equipment should be running

Best way to stalk ghosts/tips to assist in your investigations
Find out as much about the location that is reportedly haunted as you can by checking some of the following data sources:
- The Tax Assessors Office provides information on the former residents
- Check local newspapers for documentation of events, deaths, suicides, etc.
- Check with your local library reference librarian for histories, indexes, maps, photos, letters, or other information about a specific location
- Have the title on the property researched for names of prior owners
- Check police files if murder is suspected
- Check obituaries if you have a name
- Check with the coroners office about deaths
- Early Township/Range Plat Survey maps will show very early structures at a particular location and may even provide a name of an old homesteader
- Sanborn Fire Insurance maps provide structural information from later 1800s on.
- USGS topographic maps from 1890 to present show the presence of buildings
- Dimensions of the structure
- Determine the age of the location
- Bring music from suspected time period of spirit to help sooth or bring out the ghost
- Bring a sleeping bag if you want, but don't go to sleep. Save that for home, you're on an investigation, so keep your eyes and ears open.
- Investigate in pairs. Accounts of sightings are more credible when there's a second or third eyewitness.
- Plan to utilize video and audio recording equipment.
- Bring enough food for the night, however no alcoholic beverages. Much like when you're gambling, it impairs your senses and judgement.
- In the event, something out of the ordinary happens, record on a notepad the time, date, location of occurrence, exact movement and sounds and your personal feelings at that time. Have each researcher enter this in their journals before anything is discussed. Then talk about the matter afterwards and compare notes and descriptions.
- Adults should be cautious of any children that are joining your investigation. An appearance of an apparition has been known to affect that person for the rest of his life. It's best to be with a group that is open-minded, yet slightly skeptical. You don't want anyone to jump up every time a floor creaks, claiming to hear a ghost.
- Be cautious anytime a psychic or medium joins your investigation. Be prepared to be taken down a wild goose chase that is without any factual or documented evidence. As a test sometime, when you find a reportedly haunted location, bring three psychics in at different times to give their perception or interpretation of the location. What you'll have in the end is three different stories of the haunted history of the home.

Photograph Release Form

If you've experienced anything out of the ordinary, something unexplainable, or an event that might be considered paranormal while visiting a bar or tavern, we would love to hear from you by enclosing this form as well as the following, Documenting Your Event form for possible inclusion in revised additions of this book. We would appreciate only first-hand experiences, and if you have them, and photographs taken of the event.

Again, if you would like your story told, please fill out the enclosed release form, and documenting your event form, and send it to the address below. If your story or photograph is used, we wish to provide proper you with the proper credit. If you wish to remain anonymous, please fill out the forms with the correct information, then attach a brief note stating that you wish to remain anonymous.

Send Form to:

G-Host Publishing
Rob and Anne Wlodarski
8701 Lava Place • West Hills, California 91304-2126
Phone/Fax: 818-340-6676 • E-mail: robanne@ix.netcom.com

I hereby grant to G-HOST Publishing, permission to reproduce the attached material and/or photographs I have supplied for inclusion in revised editions of the Haunted Whaley House, or other subsequent publications dealing with ghosts and the paranormal.

I further consent to the publication and copyrighting of this book to be published in any manner G-HOST Publications may deem fit.

Proper acknowledgment of my photograph(s) material(s) will be provided by G-HOST Publishing within the context of the publication at the publisher's discretion.

Name: _____

Address: _____

Phone number: _____

Date of submission: _____

Signature: _____

Documenting Your Whaley House Encounter

Name _____

Address _____

City _____ State _____ Zip _____

Phone: _____ Fax: _____ E-mail: _____

Birth Date: _____ Occupation _____

Married: _____ Single: _____ No. of Children: _____

Number of people residing at the place of the event: _____

Number of people witnessing the event: _____

Name of the person who witnessed the event #1: _____
Relationship: _____ Age: _____

Name of the person who witnessed the event #2: _____
Relationship: _____ Age: _____

Name of the person who witnessed the event #3: _____
Relationship: _____ Age: _____

Other witnesses by name and age: _____
_____
_____
_____

Were there any pets present? (If yes, explain): _____
_____

Date(s) the event(s) took place: _____
_____

Approximate time(s) the event(s) occurred: _____
_____

What were the weather conditions at the time the event occurred: _____
_____
_____

Briefly describe the event: _____
_____
_____

(Continue on the back)

Documenting your Whaley House Encounter (continued)

Describe how you felt at the time of the event (I was frightened, amazed?)
_____
_____

If you can, draw what you saw using the space provided below:

What rooms did the event occur in: _____
_____

Describe the furnishings in the room(s) where the event(s) occurred: ____
_____

Describe the approximate duration of the event(s): _____
_____

Have events occurred before that you know of? (If yes, please elaborate):
_____

Have the event(s) increased in frequency (If yes, briefly explain): _____
_____
_____

Do you know the history of the place (If yes, please elaborate): _____
_____

Do you know the name(s) of the prior owners (If so, please provide):_____
_____

Please return this questionnaire to:
G-Host Publishing
8701 Lava Place • West Hills, California 91304-2126
Phone/Fax: 818-340-6676 • E-mail: robanne@ix.netcom.com

(Thank you for your time and patience in completing this form)

Paranormal Research Equipment

This basic equipment is available through www.prairieghosts.com/detector.html or by contacting Whitechapel Productions Press - American Ghost Society, 515 East Third Street - Alton, Illinois 62002 - Phone: 618-465-1086, 1-888-GHOSTLY or www.prairieghosts.com

Digital Thermal Scanner
This piece of equipment is also referred to as an Infrared Non-Contact Thermometer. This device can track down a ghostly, or paranormal, presence by taking instant readings from the air and detecting any changes in temperature that might be sudden or extreme. The device detects "cold spots" (unexplained temperature variances) that often signal that a ghost is present. The ghost uses the energy in that spot to manifest itself and in return, produces a cold mass. The ghost may be invisible to the naked eye but still detectable by these devices.

Remote IR Thermo-Probemeter
This thermal scanner is pocket-sized, fits easily into your hand and measures temperatures down to 0 degrees with amazing accuracy. It comes equipped with a laser sight and a carrying case. Like the other meters mentioned, it takes instant readings by simply pushing the trigger and has a back-lighted display for viewing in dark locations.

Room Guardian IR Motion Detector
This dual technology device can pick up activity and intruders in a controlled area! The Room Guardian uses 360 degrees passive infrared motion detection and is completely self-contained and portable. It operates on a 9-volt battery or AC adapter, and can be mounted or placed in any location. The unit can also be armed and disarmed from up to 30 feet away with the handheld remote. PIR technology uses infrared radiation to detect temperature changes and it also uses an Infrasonic detector to measure shock waves and physical movement. Sensitivity on the unit can be easily adjusted. Produces a loud (100 db) alarm for 30 seconds when activity is detected.

EMF Field Tester 200A
An easy to handle meter that is very simple to use with an on-off switch and a digital read-out screen that gives you a constant reading of any activity that you encounter. This is also an extremely reliable meter for measuring changes, readings and fluctuations in the EMF field of a location. We recommend it to anyone who prefers a digital reading rather than an analog scale.

TRI-Field Meter
This device combines magnetic and electric readings in one package for fast and accurate measurements. It has been adapted for paranormal research for several years and can be used by hand in taking readings of locations. In addition, this newly upgraded device is more sensitive than ever before. It features a continuous analog reading, registers a much higher sensitivity than ordinary meters, and is much easier to use than other Tri-Field Meters.

TRI-Field Extended Range Meter
This is the modified version of the standard Tri-Field meter with enhanced sensitivity that can pick up lower range electric and magnetic fields including slow-moving static fields, which may be essential to paranormal investigating. Also features a continuous analog reading and is very portable, although not as highly recommended as the Standard and Natural EM Models.

TRI-Field Natural EM Meter
One of the most sensitive and complex devices on the market. It is not recommended for beginners and is so sensitive that it can even pick up the fields of living persons. It was originally designed to read the activity of geo-magnetic storms so it can be delicate to carry around in an investigation. The best use for it is to place it in a stationary location and allow it to pick up movement in the extended range around it. It can also be used as a hand-held device but must be used carefully. Features a continuous analog reading and a SUM setting that allows it to pick up electric and magnetic fields at the same time. Signals any changes in field with an audio alarm.

Multidetector
Using the German-engineered ergonomic design and 11 LED light bar scale (3 green, 4 yellow, 4 red), this multidetector can pick up a number of different fields all at the same time, including magnetic and electric (with extremely high sensitivity) and with a high and accurate range. It also features integrated, switchable frequency filter to allow monitoring of high- and low frequency fields (VLF and ELF) separately. This device can be used in dark areas, so you'll never miss a reading.

Dr. Gauss EMF Meter
This is an excellent model for the beginner. It operates with an easy-to-read, analog scale with a range of 0-10 milligauss. This convenient device features a colored scale so that you will be alerted as to what readings to look for. In most cases, the yellow portion of the scale points to readings, which may be supernatural in origin. The device is activated by punching the panel on the side of the meter.

Three-Axis Digital Gaussmeter
True 3-axis sensors insure that measurements remain accurate regardless of the orientation of the instrument, making this the fastest digital Gaussmeter to use, by far! Lightweight and self-contained, this unit is rapid changes in paranormal investigations and detects magnetic fields emissions and fluctuations with accuracy. This meter is auto-ranging and includes a deluxe carrying case and 9 volt alkaline battery.

EMF Headset
Simple single axis magnetic pick-up coils with built-in audio amplifiers translate the frequency of the magnetic field to the same pitch of audio tone. And the sensitivity is such that the sound is louder in the ear nearest the field giving a realistic sensation of hearing the field, making it extremely useful for locating sources of the disturbance. A pair of devices, each with a AA battery is included.

Instrument Case
Durable case for storing your EMF detection (or other) instruments! Hard black plastic case has real hinges that won't break after flexing. Snap closures. Ample size: Inside dimensions: 11-5/8" x 8-3/4" x 2-3/4" H, outside dimensions: 12-1/2" x 11-3/4" x 3". Has removable partitioned insert with its own lid for small parts. The case will fit a Trifield Meter, Geomagnetometer and almost all other EMF meters.

Hygro-Thermometer Clock
Check out humidity levels in your investigation sites with this inclusive device to check the ambient temperature and humidity levels in any location. The meter combines all three into digital scales and even has a memory reset button that stores the two different readings.

Ion Detector
This hand-held ion detector possesses excellent sensitivity, is fully electrostatically shielded and can take accurate readings even under adverse conditions. This device can be adjusted to measure positive, or in paranormal investigation cases, negative ions separately. Much like with an electro-magnetic field detector, the ions in the air will measure a high disturbance when spirit energy is present. This device is great for investigations also because it is sensitive to natural effects like radiation, electrical storms and radon, thus, is not easily disturbed by power outlets.

Monitor 4: Geiger Counter
This device measures Alpha, Beta, Gamma and X-ray radiation and searches for fluctuations in radiation which will point to a disturbance in spirit energy. Great for investigations with an easy to read analog meter, red light counter, audible indicator and all in a hand-held unit It can also

be used to check background levels of radiation in a location and uses a Geiger Mueller tube with a thin mica window.

Chapman Electrostatic Field Meter
This handheld meter comes with a certification of calibration and is extremely sensitive with ±5 volt accuracy. Automatic zero, with 2 scales and 2 ranges. Metal housing allows you to use this meter safely and makes it more durable for long-lasting use. Excellent analog readout for up close measurements of static (DC) electric charges.

Compass
It is believed that carrying one of these devices into a haunted location will direct you to the ghost or energy field and then spin while the field is present.

Dowsing Rods
Dowsing rods are usually constructed of brass with copper or plastic handles, and are bent into an L-shape. By holding the short ends of the rods loosely in each hand, they can point or sway in the direction of an energy field. When the spirit energy is discovered, they cross. The focus of the person holding the rods is extremely important. They have also been used to answer specific questions about the forces present in a haunted location (contact www.dowsers.org or call 802-684-3417).

Digital Cameras (proper use)
According to author and paranormal investigator, Troy Taylor, digital cameras are excellent for documenting a location and also as a secondary, back-up camera, but they cannot produce irrefutable proof of the paranormal. The incorrect use of the camera had led to some disastrous results for the credibility of paranormal investigations. According to the tech support people, under low-light conditions, resulting images were plagued with spots that appeared white or light colored and where the digital pixels had not all filled in. In this manner, the cameras were creating "orbs", and they had no paranormal source at all. Other problems include the facts that: Emulsion on traditional film is based on infrared light values and the temperature associated with that light value. A digital camera cannot determine these values, it simply creates an image based upon the tones it receives from the reflection of light off of the subject matter; and, to be able to analyze a photo and to be able to determine the photo's authenticity, two things are needed, a print of the photo and its negative. A digital photo can provide neither of these essential elements; therefore, tt is impossible to prove they are authentic! Digital cameras have their place and a number of benefits, but probably don't benefit the study of the paranormal.

Note

Note

Note

Note

Note

Note

The Haunted Whaley House II Order Form

Please send me_____copies of The Haunted Whaley House. The purchase price is $14.95 (Do not send cash). To order by mail, please add the following:

- For postage and handling in the United States, please add $3.95 for the first book and $1.95 for every book thereafter (allow 3 weeks for delivery before panicking). All books are shipped U.S. First class rate unless other arrangements are made in advance. Books are usually shipped within 48 hours unless circumstances beyond our control occur).
- California residents add $1.23/book to cover sales tax.
- Canadian customers add $5.00 for shipping and handling for the first book and $2.95 for every book thereafter.
- International customers add $10.00 for shipping and handling (U.S. Funds only) and $5.00 for each book thereafter. Contact publisher for discounts on multiple orders over 10.
- No charge cards orders accepted.
- PayPal is accepted

U.S. Orders: $14.95 x no. of copies =$_____
Shipping (U.S.): $3.95 first copy ($1.75 thereafter) =$_____
California sales tax $1.23 x no. of books =$_____
Shipping (Canada): $5.00 for first copy ($2.95 thereafter) =$_____
Shipping (International): $10.00 x no. of copies =$_____
Total Enclosed: =$_____

You may also purchase the book through G-Host Publishing, through Amazon.com, Barnes & Nobles, or Whitechapel Productions Press - 515 East Third Street, Alton, Illinois 62002, Phone: 618-465-1086 /Fax: 618-465-1085, Toll Free: 1-888-GHOSTLY, E-mail: ttaylor@prairieghosts.com, Website: www.prairieghosts.com).

Order other books through G-Host Publishing: Haunted Catalina - $12.95 p us 1.07 cents for sales tax (in California only) and $3.95 shipping & handling ($1.95 for every book thereafter) if ordering in the United States: Canadian orders add $5.00 for shipping and handling ($2.95 for every book thereafter): international orders send $10.00 per book: The Haunted Queen Mary - $13.95 plus $1.15 cents sales tax (in California only) and $3.95 shipping & handling ($1.95 for every book thereafter) if ordering in the United States: Canadian orders add $5.00 for shipping and handling ($2.95 for every book thereafter): international orders send $10.00 per book: Haunted Alcatraz - $13.95 plus $1.15 cents sales tax (in California only) and $3.95 shipping & handling ($1.95 for every book thereafter) if ordering in the United States: Canadian orders add $5.00 for shipping and handling ($2.95 for every book thereafter): international orders send $10.00 per book; Spirits of the Leonis Adobe - $13.95 plus $1.15 cents sales tax (in California only) and $3.95 shipping & handling ($1.95 for every book thereafter) if ordering in the United States: Canadian orders add $5.00 for shipping and handling ($2.95 for every book thereafter): international orders send $10.00 per book; California Hauntspitality - $16.95 and $4.25 shipping & handling ($3.25 for every book thereafter) if ordering in the United States: Canadian orders add $7.50 for shipping and handling ($3.95 for every book thereafter): international orders send $10.00 per book; and, Southern Fried Spirits, or A Texas Guide to Haunted Restaurants, Taverns and Inns - @ $16.95 each and $4.25 shipping & handling ($3.50 for every book thereafter) if ordering in the United States: Canadian orders add $7.50 for shipping and handling ($3.95 for every book thereafter): international orders send $10.00 per book

---

Send Check or Money Order (U.S. Funds) To: **G-HOST Publishing**
8701 Lava Place, West Hills, California 91304-2126
Fax: 818-340-6676

Mail my book(s) to: Name: _____
Address: _____
City_____ State: _____ Zip Code: _____
Phone Number: _____ E-mail: _____